THE COLLECTED POEMS O

THE COLLECTED POEMS OF
Vernon Watkins

GOLGONOOZA PRESS

First published 1986
reprinted with corrections 2000
by Golgonooza Press
3 Cambridge Drive
Ipswich, Suffolk IP2 9EP

British Library Cataloguing in Publication Data
A catalogue record for this book is available
from the British Library

ISBN 0 903880 73 3

Printed by
Woolnough Bookbinding
Wellingborough

Foreword

The *Collected Poems of Vernon Watkins* brings together for the first time all the original poems which have been published in separate collections. The first seven books are those which Vernon Watkins himself prepared for publication with Faber and Faber. They are: *Ballad of the Mari Lwyd* (1941, second edition 1947); *The Lamp and the Veil* (1945); *The Lady with the Unicorn* (1948); *The Death Bell* (1954); *Cypress and Acacia* (1959); *Affinities* (1962); *Fidelities* (1968); (*Fidelities* was prepared for publication by the author, but published posthumously). A few misprints have been corrected editorially on manuscript authority, and the text of 'Yeats in Dublin', in *The Lamp and the Veil*, is given in a version substantially revised by Vernon Watkins in the year of his death, and published in *The Dublin Magazine* (1967); the second edition of *Ballad of the Mari Lwyd* has been used; otherwise the texts are presented as they first appeared in their original collections. The over-riding consideration in choosing this arrangement is that it preserves the integrity of each book as the author conceived it: Vernon Watkins based each book on one theme.

It was the author's rigorous exclusion of many fine poems from collections whose theme they did not fit that made desirable the posthumous publication of three further collections of his work: *Uncollected Poems* (Enitharmon Press, 1969); *The Ballad of the Outer Dark* (Enitharmon Press, 1979); and *The Breaking of the Wave* (Golgonooza Press, 1979). These three books are presented here in the same way as the Faber collections. *Uncollected Poems* was chosen and arranged by Kathleen Raine, *The Ballad of the Outer Dark* and *The Breaking of the Wave* by Gwen Watkins.

Ruth Pryor
30 June 1985

Contents

BALLAD OF THE MARI LWYD
and other poems (2nd edition 1947)

THE LAMP AND THE VEIL (1945)

THE LADY WITH THE UNICORN (1948)

THE DEATH BELL poems & ballads (1954)

POEMS

BALLADS

CYPRESS AND ACACIA (1959)

AFFINITIES (1962)

FIDELITIES (1968)

UNCOLLECTED POEMS (1969)

THE BALLAD OF THE OUTER DARK
and other poems (1979)

THE BREAKING OF THE WAVE (1979)

Ballad of the Mari Lwyd

and other poems

1947

The Collier

When I was born on Amman hill
A dark bird crossed the sun.
Sharp on the floor the shadow fell;
I was the youngest son.

And when I went to the County School
I worked in a shaft of light.
In the wood of the desk I cut my name:
Dai for Dynamite.

The tall black hills my brothers stood;
Their lessons all were done.
From the door of the school when I ran out
They frowned to watch me run.

The slow grey bells they rung a chime
Surly with grief or age.
Clever or clumsy, lad or lout,
All would look for a wage.

I learnt the valley flowers' names
And the rough bark knew my knees.
I brought home trout from the river
And spotted eggs from the trees.

A coloured coat I was given to wear
Where the lights of the rough land shone.
Still jealous of my favour
The tall black hills looked on.

They dipped my coat in the blood of a kid
And they cast me down a pit,
And although I crossed with strangers
There was no way up from it.

Soon as I went from the County School
I worked in a shaft. Said Jim,
'You will get your chain of gold, my lad,
But not for a likely time.'

And one said, 'Jack was not raised up
When the wind blew out the light
Though he interpreted their dreams
And guessed their fears by night.'

And Tom, he shivered his leper's lamp
For the stain that round him grew;
And I heard mouths pray in the after-damp
When the picks would not break through.

They changed words there in darkness
And still through my head they run,
And white on my limbs is the linen sheet
And gold on my neck the sun.

Sonnet

PIT-BOY

When sleep's propped scenery falls about the house
And dancing women vanish, quick to unmask,
The brick world wakes up, willing to espouse
The child whose parents left the empty flask.

When sleep's propped scenery falls, alarums rouse
Children of light, each to his dreaded task.
Around Laocoon and his children's brows
Strangling their violence with venom, three serpents bask.

Harnessed to mines, who shall inherit wealth?
To whom, here praying, shall pasteurized milk bring health?
What horror of dawn shall hide our born disgrace?

Torn, with torn satchel, reared in grit and filth,
His misery shows a town taken by stealth,
And all the accusing heavens in that Welsh face.

Elegy on the Heroine of Childhood

in memory of Pearl White

'. . . We died in you, and offered
Sweets to the Gods . . .'

Who flung this world? What gangs proclaimed a truce,
Spinning the streets from bootlaces come loose?
What iron hoop in darkness slid
Chased by electric heels which hid

Cold faces behind pamphlets of the time?
Why was I left? What stairs had I to climb?

Four words catch hold. Dead exile, you would excite
In the red darkness, through the filtered light,
Our round, terrified eyes, when some
Demon of the rocks would come
And lock you in his house of moving walls:
You taught us first how loudly a pin falls.

From penny rows, when we began to spell,
We watched you, at the time when Arras fell,
Saw you, as in a death-ray seen,
Ride the real fear on a propped screen,
Where, through revolting brass, and darkness' bands,
Gaping, we groped with unawakened hands.

A sea-swung murmur, and a shout. Like shags
Under carved gods, with sweets in cone-shaped bags,
Tucked in to-morrow's unpaid fears,
Rucked there before the unguarded years,
We watched you, doomed, drowned, daggered, hurled from sight,
Fade from your clipped death in the tottering light.

Frantic, a blunted pattern showed you freed.
Week back to week I tread with nightmare speed,
Find the small entrance to large days,
Charging the chocolates from the trays,
Where, trailing or climbing the railing, we mobbed the dark
Of Pandemonium near Cwmdonkin Park.

Children return to mourn you. I retrace
Their steps to childhood's jealousies, a place
Of urchin hatred, shaken fists;
I drink the poison of the mists
To see you, a clear ghost before true day,
A girl, through wrestling clothes, caps flung in play.

From school's spiked railings, glass-topped, cat-walked walls,
From albums strewn, the streets' strange funerals,
We run to join the queue's coiled peel
Tapering, storming the Bastille,
Tumbling, with collars torn and scattered ties,
To thumbscrewed terror and the sea of eyes.

Night falls. The railing on which fast we pressed
Bears you, thumb-printed, to a death unguessed,

Before the time when you should rise
Venus to adolescent eyes,
A mermaid drying from your acid bath
Catching our lechery on a flying path.

Who has not seen the falling of a star?
Black liquorice made you bright before the War.
You glittered where the tongue was curled
Around the sweet fear of this world.
Doom's serial writing sprang upon the wall
Blind with a rush of light. We saw you fall.

How near, how far, how very faintly comes
Your tempest through a tambourine of crumbs,
Whose eye by darkness sanctified,
Is brilliant with my boyhood's slide.
How silently at last the reel runs back
Through your three hundred deaths, now Death wears black.

Prime Colours

How can I praise what is not painted with
The first five colours? That winged horse of myth
Seems now a circus horse, paid to be clever:
The ride from Bethphage will last for ever.

One man may count, with imitative hooves,
The huge, high landcape that another loves,
Empound the apocalypse, till truth is pent
To satisfy the turnstiles of a tent.

Vast libraries vault their dead, but I can trust
White dust to resurrect the moving dust,
White dust of donkeys shedding dusty loads
Where swallows' wings paint Zechariah's words.

Swift, chattering swallows, flying in cloisters cool,
See through their darting eyes the imprisoned school,
Cramped, figured scribes, distorted by possession:
The upright man is always out of fashion.

Swallows come back to their first house of mud
Knowing no wider rainbow can be made;
And that first nest eclipsing heaven, that roof,
May find its image in an ass's hoof.

For when the garments and tree-branches strawed
The way, a child into the mountain strayed
And on the mountain-path, in heaven's eclipse,
He found a swallow's wings, an ass's steps.

And time stopped still, stopped when an ass went down
Slowly from Bethphage to that still town.
That ass, that swallow, through the window's gap
Meet in his eyes who wears the mockers' cap.

Born of that mud, innocent light he sees,
The cornerstone in crumbling masonries.
His washed eyes, marvelling, resurrect the mountain
Where love's five colours leap into light's fountain.

Griefs of the Sea

It is fitting to mourn dead sailors,
To crown the sea with some wild wreath of foam
On some steep promontory, some cornercliff of Wales
Though the deaf wave hear nothing.

It is fitting to fling off clothing,
To enter the sea with plunge of seawreaths white
Broken by limbs that love the waters, fear the stars,
Though the blind wave grope under eyes that see, limbs that
wonder,
Though the blind wave grope forward to the sand
With a greedy, silvered hand.

It is a horrible sound, the low wind's whistle
Across the seaweeds on the beach at night.
From stone to stone through hissing caves it passes
Up the curved cliff and shakes the prickly thistle
And spreads its hatred through the grasses.

In spite of that wicked sound
Of the wind that follows us like a scenting hound,
It is fitting on the curved cliff to remember the drowned,
To imagine them clearly for whom the sea no longer cares,
To deny the language of the thistle, to meet their foot-firm
tread
Across the dark-sown tares
Who were skilful and erect, magnificent types of godhead,

To resist the dogging wind, to accuse the sea-god;
Yet in that gesture of anger we must admit
We were quarrelling with a phantom unawares.

For the sea turns whose every drop is counted
And the sand turns whose every grain a holy hour-glass holds
And the weeds turn beneath the sea, the sifted life slips free,
And the wave turns surrendering from its folds
All things that are not sea, and thrown off is the spirit
By the sea, the riderless horse which they once mounted.

Old Triton Time

Old Triton Time responds to every mood:
He's the newborn who's older than the flood.
He babbles water from a dull stone tongue.
He's old and cold, and yet the water's young.
To gain him is to lose him. I have seen
Loss bind him up with lichens: he grew green.
But if my fingers touch the water cold,
He suddenly seems young, the water old.

From My Loitering

From my loitering as a child
In paving-square and field
And from my stone-still tongue
Time is unsealed.

Thc ages are unstrung
By water from a Triton flung
And the world finds its heart
Which was not always young.

I cannot tell what art
Set the grave spring to start
In whose old pipe and stop
Time plays no part.

But where green eyes look up,
Eyes that are blind with sun,

Uncertain fingers grope
Around the vine-leaved cup.

There little children run
And climb the singing stone
And their sweet dialect
Is learnt by none.

Shadows and leaves infect
The brooding intellect
Beneath whose tongueless wave
Those lives are wrecked.

But they low music have
Winding and gold and grave.
Time's measure they can set
By light, by love.

And in the sun-thrown jet:
'Sweet moment, sweet!' and 'sweeter yet!'
Cry, make the foiled eyes clear,
The parched lips wet.

Empty Hands

O spendthrift lover, see that miser there
Putting a dunce's cap upon a mound
Because, although it holds your golden hair,
It keeps no kind of coinage underground.

Now make a cage for him, and dream his hour
Is manacled and stopped with sterile sands,
But he's a stream, a mountain and a tower,
And he, too, knows delight has empty hands.

Indolence

Count up those books whose pages you have read
Moulded by water. Wasps this paper made.
Come. You have taken tribute from the dead.
Your tribute to the quick must now be paid.

What lovelier tribute than to rest your head
Beneath this birchtree which is bound to fade?
And watch the branches quivering by a thread
Beyond interpretation of the shade.

The Turning of the Leaves

Not yet! Do not yet touch,
Break not this branch of silver-birch,
Nor ask the stealthy river why it laves
Black roots that feed the leaves.

Ask first the flickering wren.
He will move further. Ask the rain.
No drop, though round, through that white miracle
Will sink, to be your oracle.

Not yet! Do not yet bend
Close to that root so tightly bound
Loosened by creeping waters as they run
Along the fork's rough groin.

Ask not the water yet
Why the root's tapering tendrils eat
Parched earth away that they may be
Nearer the source those fibres must obey.

Behind the bark your hands will find
No Sycorax or flying Daphne faned
And the brown ignorant water bindweed breeds
Not caring there what brows it braids.

Light in the branches weaves.
Hard is the waiting moment while it waves,
This tree whose trunk curves upward from the stream
Where faltering ripples strum.

See how it hangs in air.
The leaves are turning now. We cannot hear
The death and birth of life. But that disguise,
Look up now, softly: break it with your eyes.

The Sunbather

Inert he lies on the saltgold sand
And sees through his lids the scarlet sky.
The sea will run back if he breathes a sigh.
He can hide the sun with a roselit hand.

Loitering, he crossed the shingle-shore
Where his eyes looked back at the glint of shells.
With a quoit of stone he startled the bells
That sleep in the rocks' vibrating core.

Thought-blind to the chosen place he passed.
The seagulls rose, and circled, and dropped;
And there, throwing down his coat, he stopped.
He, touching the mould of the world, lies fast.

The noon-sun dodges around his knee.
The sand at his head now trembles pale.
The wind at his temples carries a tale
And before him flies the bewildered sea.

The sun, the sea and the wind are three
But he narrows them down with a dreaming eye.
With his hands at rest and his drawn-up thigh
He can imagine the sacred tree.

For a point of light has seeded all
And the beautiful seed has come to rest
For a sunblown moment in his breast,
A tree where the leaves will never fall.

'Come back. You were with us ages ago.
We have thrown your bones to the carrion gull.
To the dripping cave we have sold your skull,
And the delicate flower which was born to blow

Is lost in the flow of the marble sea.
We have made seaweeds out of your locks,
And your star-white bones in the vaulted rocks
Lie broken and cold, like shells in the scree.'

So Shades converse, and the world's dumb thud
Muffles their argument, Man, more strong,
Gives, to console their frightened song,
The beat that consoles them most, his blood.

Sycamore

O, I am green and fair:
Is there a fairer tree?
Who is it underneath
Sleeps the sleep of death?
There is no answer there.
There is no answer there.

Centuries made me firm.
Far I have spread my roots.
I grip the flying stream.
Aching, I drop my fruits.
Who is it sleeps below?
Who is it sleeps below?

My wood made long ago
Lutes of true, hollow sound.
Lovers still carve them out
Above this burial mound.
Who is it sleeps below?
Who is it sleeps below?

Who sleeps? The young streams feed
My boughs. The blind keys spin.
Hark, he is dead indeed.
Never shall fall again
My natural, winged seed
On this small-statured man.

The Room of Pity

to Dylan Thomas

The room of pity, marked with murder's cross,
Danced in the worlds of reawakened tears
Sprung from grief's heart, emblems of utter loss.

Love climbed there sobbing, but this Nazarene
Leaned on the beams which raftered hopes and fears:
This was love's source, and this, grief's evergreen.

Life withered back to water from a rock.
Steps in the court still wrung that stone for blood:
A knot of murmuring voices, then the knock.

God's heart beat seconds where there was no clock,
Nor felt those hands which nailed him to the rood,
Nor heard the denial cried by Peter's cock.

But Mary, Mary Magdalen, and they
Whom Sorrow chose, who never shall be old,
Marvelled the world could shake so, and still stay;

Till the last cry rent wide the temple struck
And showed blind ignorance running to a mould,
The soldiers' god, the wolf that gave them suck.

Yeats' Tower

Surely the finger of God that governs the stars
And feels the flashed mystery of the moving world
Stirring the water to leaves in fold on fold,
Now touches this, this long grass in the field:
O under grass, O under grass, the secret.

Surely the seed that stirs beneath this touch
Hears in its ear the wand within the wind,
The miraculous fire from which all years have waned.
This, if it moves, must heal the martyr's wound:
O under grass, O under grass, the secret.

Surely from this the snow-white blood is blown;
Gold marguerite's doom that never comes, comes soon.
Dead saints, white clouds, they stop not near the shrine
But cross the skeleton harp, the unplucked bone:
O under grass, O under grass, the secret.

Ivy entwined about the walls of pride
Clings, where the tales of time in centuried scrawl
Compass the delicate mind, the hand of skill
Touching this fire which never formed a school:
O under grass, O under grass, the secret.

The wired walls hold a castle of desertion.
Already round the gate the nettle springs.
Old, wily murmurs have usurped those songs.
Sheer over this the kestrel ruin hangs:
O under grass, O under grass, the secret.

Children pass by for whom a bell has chimed.
Hunters pass by: for these a bell has tolled.
Horns echo backward, but the tower deep-welled
Hangs in the stream with all its woven scroll:
O under grass, O under grass, the secret.

After Sunset

Deep darkness—O delight!
The new-seen stars!
Ideas at twilight:
'In Vishnu-land what Avatars?'

Out to swift spaces come!
Lift up your eyelids.
Leave the broken column,
The crumbled Parthenon, the pyramids.

Leave the cave drawing,
The grey, the granite rose,
The Arabian phœnix-wing;
Tombs of the Pharaohs.

Leave, where bats dwell
And the dark bird of night,
The Grecian temple.
Look up to stars milkwhite.

Forget—sky-foundered, dumb—
The figured frieze,
Marble from Sunium
And the three Destinies.

We pushed keels from dark shores,
Storm-red the sky.
Harpies calling the sailors
Strewed on the winds their cry.

Dark sailors, men
Bent on the powerful oar
Dreading the Siren,
Equipped with ropes, earwax, anchor.

Lost in a shell of the sea
Sea-myths. Isles of acorns.

The wine of Circe.
The red-mouthed Tritons' horns.

Heard from the lip of the shell
Cruelty, savagery,
And shipwreck terrible,
The returning story.

In the air the legend,
Over the sea the myth,
The setting-forth, the end,
The travail, the zenith.

Phoenicians bring
News from beyond the spray:
Pattern of darkness moving,
It takes the breath away.

The midsea stirring;
The immane sky a mask;
Watching the lucky wing
From wines, wares, damask.

Birds of augury
Faint in the mist.
The seawaves two and three
Where night is darkest.

And who knows yet
Over the prow far-pushed
Crescent through violet
What fates are ambushed?

The myth changes. New forms
Trouble the waters' face.
Sky-skeins of the Norns
Cross and recross the surface.

The low winds sing
And the wings sway.
Pattern of darkness moving,
It takes the breath away.

Where great sails fling
Black hawk-wings to the crest
Lust of the Viking
Swoops with a bird's unrest.

Chained to the bench
Slaves in the galley row
Feeling sea's death-wrench
Up dawn's white furrow.

The seawaves swift and slow.
The churn of brightness.
The returning swallow.
The search for land. The guess.

Stars new—all myths abandoned—
True points in heaven.
The constellations conned
By a new age, new men.

Night's hush by needle parted.
Myth's marionettes
Cutting the strings of dread
Map the winds' trumpets.

Their sails in shore
To sharp points furled,
Explorers at anchor.
Curved sea-line, the suspended world.

The water's fickle smile.
The carven Sibyl.
The myth in exile
Killed by the starry wheel.

Blue-cold the dolphin
Under the wave reclines
Though firm these win
The fair world's outlines.

And still Odysseus
Cresting those hate-white seas;
Wind-carried words profuse,
Sibylline imageries.

Meanwhile what timbers swished
By hostile swell.
What good hands perished
Far from fear's oracle.

Dusk. Grief of the Gods!
Titans the mind imagined

In awful synods.
Gold lightning in the wind.

Supernatural wrath.
The far-blown clarion.
Accurst Harisuth.
The downfall of Hyperion.

And far beyond
The saga-laden sea,
Visionless diamond,
The sandgrains of infancy.

There is laid no track
For the nomad here.
All things haunt back
To a more ancient order.

Then flows the demi-urge
Out of his hungry side
Restless as sea-surge,
Cries out across the tide:

O life, my mistress,
This moment reclaims you
From the proud figured dress
Of time's imagery.

The Fountain

Centuries, years, barbarian, scorned by schools,
Mellowing while minute-glasses caught their sands,
From sextant, compass far, from creeds and rules,
Water, like tears, has fallen through these hands.

Beyond the merry world of rocking tables
What wonder winking from the golden cup
Lit on a leaning star the fire of fables?
What swallows crossed when pupils' eyes looked up?

Lichens may thrive where once my sculptor's eyes
Weaned the sweet changeling from the nerveless stone.
No skill from books will read my mermaid's eyes.
Fingers that seek my touch must find their own.

Driven by the screed, worn still, like wave-torn pebbles,
Men may look years on me and still see nought.
Beyond the scriveners' world of working tables
I, going empty, mock the gifts they brought.

Say nothing; or say this: No time ago
Ran past me, singing of the land and sea,
One who was brilliant as the broken snow,
And springing sunward, left her ghost in me.

The Age-Changers

Swear by no god. Call not
Youth hot, age cold. Be as the Cariatids
Alert. The sea is theirs; and through their lids
Light breaks. Their fingers feel the tides.

Sink in the well of dust.
Ah think: the skeletons of leaves have rest.
A mad sea rages through the bud encased.
The blind winds whirl; that whirlpool trust.

Do not look back. The track
Of vertical terror's questing shadow runs
Figure to figure, vainly seeking one
Dropped here in marble from the sun.

Notes through the pipe run back.
A knot of rivers; wound within that knot
Mute wonder through the sweet, blind eyes looks out,
Starts the sun's memories life forgot.

Diamonds, thundering diamonds
Drop on the speechless lip. The wands of winds
Steady the cataract's pulse. Your hands
Touch under still stone whirling sands.

Time, by those dolphin's eyes, those hands,
Held ever still, the fountain grains deny,
Holding the fan-tailed rivers as they fly,
Shrinks to one drop, one dolphin's eye.

Distance outrun by toil!
Coiled from oracular, silence-bearing sides,
Babbles the fountain. Light through downcast lids
Is rising, where one drop of light decides.

Two Decisions

I must go back to Winter,
The dark, confiding tree,
The sunflower's eaten centre
That waved so tenderly;
Go back, break fellowship
With bud and leaf,
Break the loud branch and strip
The stillborn grief.
I must restore the thorn,
The naked sentinel,
Call lash of hail, wind-scorn
To laughter's lintel;
End argument in a way
Sudden and swift,
Leave stillness, go away
Beyond this leaf-drift,
Leave the ten-windowed house
And merely remark,
The ivy grew too close:
That house was dark.

Then I look out:
Rut, road and hill I see.
Tracks turn about.
Winter must come to me.
I shall not go,
I shall wait here
Until the snow
Bury the old year,
Until the swallows are gone
And the lintels wet
Tell that the rain that has blown
Is blowing yet.
Let me be nowhere
A melodramatic guest
Since here as anywhere
The light is best.
Though distant things entreat
The afraid, the fanciful,
The near is faithful:
Do not deny it.

Portrait of a Friend

He has sent me this
Late and early page
Caught in the emphasis
Of last night's cartonnage,
Crumpled in the post,
Bringing to lamplight
Breath's abatement,
Over- and under-statement,
Mute as a mummy's pamphlet
Long cherished by a ghost.

Who for annunication has
The white wings of the sheldrake,
Labouring water's praise,
The blind shriek of the mandrake,
Broken shells for story,
Torn earth for love's near head
Raised from time's estuary,
Fed by the raven's bread;
A trespasser in tombs,
He bids the grey dust fall,
Groans in the shaping limbs:
'All stars are in my shawl.'
Who feels the deathbound sighs,
Mocks the Winged Horse's fake,
Toiling, as with closed eyes,
Love's language to remake,
To draw from their dumb wall
The saints to a worldly brothel
That a sinner's tongue may toll
And call the place Bethel.

Trusting a creaking house,
His roof is ruinous,
So mortal. A real wind
Beats on this house of sand
Two tides like ages buffet.
The superhuman, crowned
Saints must enter this drowned
Tide-race of the mind
To guess or understand
The face of this cracked prophet,

Which from its patient pall
I slowly take,
Drop the envelope,
Compel his disturbing shape,
And write these words on a wall
Maybe for a third man's sake.

A Prayer against Time

God, let me not know grief
Where time is uppermost,
Not though it handle me
More wretchedly than all;
That were to give a thief
Tears that I owe to Thee.
Take all I shall have lost:
Where the curls fall, they fall.

Delicate thoughts I love,
Thoughts of great secrecy;
Sweet vigour now I have
For the ingenious leaf.
Thought into shape I shove.
Seeds in the silent grave
Contain the breathing tree;
Keep fast this dumb belief:

We approach youth in death,
The ecstatic dance in age.
Youth is itself infirm
Until those sightless eyes
Rarify youth and breath;
Then the miraculous form
Casts out a dying sage:
Always another dies.

I have been luckier than
All others in one thing,
Devoted secret time
To one love, one alone;
Found then that dying man
Exulting in new rhyme:
The river standing,
All but miracle gone.

The Dead Words

So flies love's meteor to her shroud of winds.
The crisp words couch in their last battling-place
Where widowed silence, threaded like black lace,
Held a dumb minute, stabs the dark like pins.
It is so breathless. There the flower begins
To seed, we know not how. There blows the race
Of spirits, and they watch the stiff leaves brace
With last look backward to the town of sins.
There clenches the close fist through wreath and wraith
The sooted page where wrought like golden wire
The sly words glitter with an angel's breath;
Love's moistening seal is mastered there entire,
And the wind proves, where they are dressed for death,
Cinders are priestlike in their tale of fire.

The Keen Shy Flame

The keen shy flame holding this poem's ash,
Texture and syllable,
Bears on its point the precious crucible
Transforming utterance to a breath more rash.

Silence is there within the flying bowl
Bright as a waving poppy.
Still from the ignorant pattern falls the copy.
That pivot has all time in its control.

Once through the mummy-cloth it wound its way;
Through music, myrrh and gold
And sacred parchment's wrinkled sounds of mould
Its violet fingers clasped the sleeping clay.

It could not wake the dead lips white and dry
Nor give time's pictures back,
Nor yet release the mute hands gloved in black,
So great a thrall had conquered their last cry.

This in the censer swinging gave forth smoke
And ground the pilgrims' fire;
Silently weeping near the saints' dumb choir
This in the taper gave dark grief a cloak.

Fire-fingers crawling through this last white page
Have played such harps of bone.
Through that black graveyard what faint feet are gone
Where soul puts off the cerements of age.

The Mummy

His eyes are closed. They are closed. His eyes are closed.
His hands are clenched. They are clenched. His hands are
clenched.
The messenger comes. The letters are disciplined; they are disposed.
The black light quivers. Earth on Earth is avenged.

What has left music fast in the sockets of bone?
Had all been pattern, images sight had seen,
Blood would lie quiet, but something strokes the light, and a groan
Of great-rooted calm repels those images: nothing they mean.

Nothing here lives but the music in the eyes.
Hunting-scene, warriors, chariot, palm and wing
Bid the blood rest, thought perch where the time-bird sings or flies,
Year chasing year, following and following.

But tears wash these bones where parchments whisper to sand.
Here a laid vase offers the flying stream.
Sand darkening wakes a harp-string hidden, plucked by a blind hand,
Crying this theme to the world, this world-surrounding theme:

Valiant, alive, his voice pursued the lands,
Ruled the white sea, held mountains in his keep.
Leave him with delicate instruments formed for delicate hands;
In this locked room of treasures let him who chose them sleep.

I lean down, crying: 'Touch me, lay hold on my Spring,
Reach up, for I have loosened, tearing your skies,
Fountains of light, ages of listening!'
But the bound hands are folded, the fold its word denies.

What shudder of music unfulfilled vibrates?
What draws to a dust-grain's fall most distant stars?
In the last taper's light what shadow meditates?
What single, athletic shape never cast on wall or vase?

What shudder of birth and death? What shakes me most?
Job his Maker answering, the Stricken exclaiming 'Rejoice!'
Gripping late in the shifting moment giant Earth, making Earth a
    ghost,
Who heard a great friend's death without a change of voice.

Mana

When smoke's white blooms have seeded from the bones,
When creeds of flame have crossed the sacrificial breast,
The twitching ashes wait
For those light syllables less than undertones
Murderous, immediate,
Caressing nearer than love's hand caressed,
At whose command Death runs, at whose behest
Sleep claps two stones.

Here sacred walls surround their withered guest.
Vain are tall vases and the velvet offerings;
Virtues are vain
For this whose vigil cowers, whose voice at rest
Speaks to the Slain
With Pentecostal tongues, the lightning's wings.
Perched where this lies a bird of water sings
Watching the West.

Strewn dust, left still for love's warm scatterings,
Black in the fiery centre of grief's aureoled thought,
Our palm must scatter these
Forgiven particles, like seeds in wings,
To the five seas.
Day's burial and the nails of Night have brought
This silence, and an image burnt to nought
Through light's gold rings.

Paint on this breath a flying chariot.
Carve the known relic near the unapproachable coast.
Stoop, and engrave
One afraid ship above the whirlpool's knot,
And let the wave
Leap to that life, until the deluge host
Heaven-high and falling, gather sail and ghost
Where winds are not.

What may love's language near the dead tongue trust?
Fire steals the cherished parchment crumbling to astound
The staring dark
Stunned by true dust as by a trumpet blast
Whose point, whose spark,
Guiding God's circle where all stars are found,
Sinks to this changeling's pall, this mummer's mound,
With all the Past.

Tree of all leaves, skin of all creatures, ground
Where eyes still seek an image in the Godhead made,
Our hands have tied
What death must now undo without a sound;
But you, the bride
Of morning, shining through the yew-tree's shade,
Hold with unique unrest, so naked laid,
Our eyes spellbound.

Earth-Dress

What shining raiments rise
Tempting the naked one
Whom the unjust skies
And the proud, bounteous sun
Use for their lasting shame;
Whose naked sufferings write
A true redeemer's name
Who gave them their first light,
And who, to succour us,
Projects the fourfold man
Proudly anonymous,
Knowing all pride is vain.

Not impossibly may,
And when least thought upon,
A thoughtless moment stay
When all time's years are gone;
So deep a pledge
One diamond cuts in glass,
From this close window-ledge
All books may pass,
Yet may some casual thing

Unnoticed by us
Hatch late an early wing
Chance-lit, tremulous.

Caught in the whirling spin
Of winds and days,
The snake changes its skin
And the mind its ways,
But the spirit is loyal
To what, before time stood,
Was single and royal,
Alone in multitude,
Thought and unthought.
Everything made must be
More exquisitely wrought
Than human eyes can see.

I would awaken eyes
Time has made unaware
Of wonders of world size;
But when hawk-hovering air
On the unsheltered road
Scours for divinity
The beggar and the god,
Men clutch mortality,
Cling the ruinous,
Perishing fabric of things,
To build the grave's dark house,
Terrified by those wings.

They thatch with fears and calms
Their shadowy home.
When roofless men ask alms
Of the star-shivering dome,
Winter meets them then,
Driving frost in the blood
Of passionate, naked men.
Then most they need men's good
Quarrels, rough words, kind touch,
Habitual words to say
That clothe the god and the wretch
With the close-knit joy of day.

Not impossibly may,
When bloodless icicles

In fossil-caves of clay
Freeze rough, kind hands that bless,
A single breath create
Out of the ruined bones
And trophies of hard Fate,
The fireless, sacred stones,
A flame so purified
That it may resurrect
From the estranging tide
All lives the Lifeless wrecked.

I know, the weariest friend
May be transfigured, may
Gloriously ascend
To the summit of glad day,
And the labyrinth he has gone
Promising no end
But death, that obvious one,
Whose sorrows none may mend
But gravestone and grave-sod,
May suddenly reveal
In the beggar and the god
The dragging, winged heel.

Age, Winter, solitude
Hover, and hem him in.
But the eagle is renewed
Like gold when it grows thin.
Where clothing is cast away
The diver drops to swim
And naked in the spray
All light is worn by him.
Exulting in his youth
He tenderly sings
Though the ravages of truth
Tear him, with claws and wings.

Strike him; his strength is rougher.
Bow him; but braced, he will
Defy thought, dare to suffer
Till he has thrown his hill,
Mole-like and eagle-like
Turning the scales of the wind,
Turning the clouds that strike

A Titan that has sinned.
Night, hell and hail are nothing
To his great heart, Earth-born,
Knowing its natural clothing
Of elemental scorn.

Thames Forest

Years are divine rings: moments are immortal.
The months are saplings, centuries are oakenshaws.
Lightfoot the soul goes. Impressive is the shadow
Cast by those time-groves.

Darkness of the sycamore flies across the river.
From a pattern of foliage see the spirit struggling
Through meshes like memories, woven of their terror,
Wondering, emerging.

Thought, like a thread, still glitters on his fingers.
Still from the dark earth, mythical and gleaming,
Draws he the life-skein, flying ever forward,
Wound by a dead hand.

Light on the wet ground, lighter on the leafmould
Dances that energy, rising to the sunbeam.
Black flies the shadow, asking of the dead leaf
Garment for burial.

Stilled on the charmed world, upward the life looks,
Stunned by that oracle speaking from the tree's root:
'One that is strange-born, one that dies to-morrow
Dances to-day here.'

Dumb roots are whispering; light breaks in darkness;
Frail fibres grasp there, clinging to the close clod.
Under the warm green vellum of the meadow
Trance-wise the seeds break.

Light is a great pool. Look, the clouds are flying.
Of all forms living, man alone deliberate
Scrawls on a leaf the impression of his going.
These leaves are numbered.

Fate unforeseen, deformer of the branches,
Will grapple the great tree, lay it in the low field.

Out of such torment, fingers draw the Spring's
Evocative ritual.

Easily time, and quickly, can forsake him,
Leave, in a moment, intricate the shuttles
Idle, the still thread, while the mighty loom works
Suns ever turning.

Spring Song

Now the green leaves are singing,
Now the white snows are gone.
Sparkling, the water leaps
Over the stones, runs on:
Darkness holds my steps.

Straight to the upland furrow
The labourer keeps the plough.
The sharp knives turn the mould.
Where earth lies naked now
Clay can divine no sorrow
The winds have not made cold.

Across our silver morning
The swallows are returning;
The blue light of the sea
Already in the sky
Is knife-edged with their wings.

And have they crossed
The Capricorn of air?
Broken the seeming-lost
Autumn of despair,
Found no new light deceiving,
Yet found the first light wise?

I saw them leaving,
Heard their chattering cries;
I fast and thirst,
Unsatisfied, believing
My Spring was first,

That filled my eyes,
Made my cheeks wet,

When first I broke disguise,
Walking with one who gave
Words from the grave,
A song no birds repeat.

Autumn Song

Sycamores must fade,
Yellow acorns be lost,
Before this ghost be laid
In earth, in frost.

Then will this Jack of green
With mouth of leaves, this mummer
Be no more seen,
Sunk with the Summer.

Though now the stops he shuts
With minstrelsy
Slant eyes of buried nuts
Can hardly see,

Then shall his hands be taught.
Hush, he'll forget
How the blue sloes were caught
In grasses wet.

And here, where meet
The lines of heart and head,
Where softest words are sweet,
Words for the dead,

His cap of light, his bells
Shall faded play
Among the broken shells
In disarray.

The Shooting of Werfel

'Werfel has been shot in Paris.'—*(Newspaper Report)*

Werfel dead? Hark. The forest is empty.
The myth of light, the lithe, fortuitous shadow

Is changed to dust, to a whirl of rustling leaves.
Winter hovers above the shivering seed.

His early words creep back through the crisp, dead leaves;
'As great you are as death looks little before you';
'What sweeter joy on Earth than be wounded and say nothing!'
—Werfel, who sought in each the return of the Saviour.

Dead. Dead. A voice from the skull's great cavern
Breathes, 'I forgive you. Forget me. This is Werfel.'
Will the woman carrying the bag pause, will the child turn from his game?
Yet his stopped heart is here, a magnet for silence.

Werfel in exile under the huge, inhuman wheels, caressing the curled
Frail leaf, so different from Rilke's that is like the skin of a pear,
Listening to the trunks of trees in the forest of evocation,
Werfel who knew the colour of the leaves, their falling.

How all his words followed an unknown needle!
He was drawn to the unborn from tyranny, persecution,
Driven from Prague, Vienna,
At last to Paris, the place of Heine's exile.

Found there in Paris, in a corner, alone with all ages,
Child of infinite space with the ages in his hand:
They will kill you, child, with a rifle-butt.
Arise. Shine. They will shoot you through the eyes.

O God, the atom has split in Werfel's brain!
The room is rigid with the death of his brain.
O small, diminished wall of their jealous fury
Propping the chaste stars of his huge horizons!

Ah calculating bullets against the artist
Driven from the shoulder, piercing blind windows
Draped from night's terror of whirling, flaming wheels,
They have struck: the lamp is a skull.

Killed. Now clash the unbelievable cymbals.
O two worlds! O clash of two worlds!
They have bandaged their own eyes. Rigid with ecstasy
They leave him, bleeding to death on the god-stained ground.

Their minds had returned to iron forms, but he had put forth
Antlers, like those invisible ones of Moses,
His lofty forehead, his eyes
Beautiful as a stag's that see no dogs for the god.

'That once this life was mine! That once this life was mine!
That once those pines stood up in my blood's meadows!
That once this life was mine!' Forget him, deformed shadows,
Reel back from him. The dust is drinking wine.

Stone Footing

Stopping my ears to Venus and her doves,
I steal stone footing, find death's carved decree;
I choose this path, the rock which no man loves
Familiar to birds, cast by a barren sea.
Cold on this ridge among the breeding winds,
Starved in the famine forced by Adam's rib,
Here I hold breath, knowing the door of my friends
Is rock, and I am exiled from their tribe.
I put my ear to the ground, I plant my foot
Against grey rock, but wind and seawave smother
The stone's coiled fossil-saga; this navel-knot
Fastens my moving to the great rock-mother.
I would unchain them; but there flies that other
Bearing the sea, and kills me with her shot.

Atlas on Grass

Atlas on grass, I hold the moving year.
I pull the compass to a point unguessed.
Vast midnight flies to morning in the breast,
All moves to movement, moves and makes a sphere.
Rough Winter loosens leaves long-veined with fear,
Then the seed moves to its unsleeping rest.
Faith springs where beads of longing lie confessed.
Time lost is found; the salmon leaps the weir.
Death stops the mouths of graves, is coverer
Shrouding and hiding what the pulse reveals,
But he, too, moves to his Deliverer;
Judgment will never stop the dancer's heels.
What's gone forever is forever here,
And men are raised by what a myth conceals.

Sonnet

INFANT NOAH

Calm the boy sleeps, though death is in the clouds.
Smiling he sleeps, and dreams of that tall ship
Moored near the dead stars and the moon in shrouds,
Built out of light, whose faith his hands equip.
It was imagined when remorse of making
Winged the bent, brooding brows of God in doubt.
All distances were narrowed to his waking:
'I built his city, then I cast him out.'
Time's great tide falls; under that tide the sands
Turn, and the world is shown there thousand-hilled
To the opening, ageless eyes. On eyelids, hands,
Falls a dove's shade, God's cloud, a velvet leaf.
And his shut eyes hold heaven in their dark sheaf,
In whom the rainbow's covenant is fulfilled.

A Lover's Words

Come down, dear love, be quick.
Now must our limbs' great follies
Fly through the zodiac
Where colts race with fillies.
Night, and the light-shafts fly.
Noon, and the stars are thick.
Naked through Earth and Sky
Come down, and hurl time back.

Tell the sun to rise.
Tell all the birds to sing.
Then cover the brightening skies
With a tented covering,
That under the sheet awake
The naked limbs flying
Bend, till the axle break,
All but their true lying.

Dive, sun, through my hand,
And pull the waters after;
Spin the whirling land

In a silkworm's darkness, softer
Than light, a luminous net,
That we, with meteors' arms
Far under the coverlet
May wind the winds and storms.

Beautiful head, lie still.
Light beats the pillows.
The cock crows, shrill:
That cry no lover follows.
Shining with glow-worms' light
We shape the world to our will,
Twined, hidden from sight
With blind-moles under the hill.

Three Epitaphs

1. The Miser

All things he spared, except his rod, and words;
The beggars knew his house, but not the birds;
For once his careless housemaid dropped a crumb,
False augury of barren years to come.

2. The Touch-Typist

Brought from time's glare and the electric bracket,
Her eyes close under yews and cypress-trees.
Bless, in these files where silence tells a packet,
Blind fingers, eyes which never saw the keys.

3. In Memory of Elizabeth Corbet Yeats

She drew his lightning to the needle's eye.
Now that the work is done, the last book bound,
The pains she took are quietly laid by,
The point in Earth's heart, lest a trumpet sound.

The Safe Soul

Shall soul wear thin with passion like a ring
Of beaten gold, or like an eagle's claw
Grow fine? Shall he become the winds' first king,
And tell the afraid rock-children what he saw?

Shall he discern the writing-room he left,
Wrought with strange books and stories edged with gold?
Shall he look down, a king above his cleft,
Hurled from pure heaven, and see the world unfold?

Shall he ascend in dews of morning's haze
Dispersed in atoms, starry-worlded airs,
Bright points on the capricious water-blaze,
Or under sea burn lamps of midnight fairs?

Shall soul, passed through so many golden rings
Nearer the heart's thread and the finger old,
Sleep, as an eagle sleeps on widespread wings,
When blind dawn deluges the world in gold?

Shall he, like Dante in his course of love,
Climb to the place where eagles cannot look,
Drink the clear stream, or with Cocytus move
Under the world, where lies the greatest book?

Shall he be pierced to death by cruel eyes,
Love's mistress with the vampire's ecstasy,
Fall to the malice of his enemies,
Or curse the cold moon by an exile's sea?

Shall soul teach stillness to become more still
As ancient pitchers do, that some dead hand
So shaped that none can fathom their dead will
Or penetrate the aura where they stand?

Shall soul fall softly like the one dead bloom
Too light for human ears, or like a wave
Thunder through rocks of adamantine doom
Binding love's two dreads to a single grave?

All demons scorn, but man was born to bear,
Where two great passions meet, the spark and shock.
Stone-like the eagle drops, his heart is there;
Stone-like he drops; he hears his great heart knock.

Stone-like the eagle drops, shakes off the air
Of murderous winds, of storms that tower and mock,
Safe. Though his plumage glitters for despair,
All that he loves lies naked in the rock.

The Eastern Window

How came that grief
At break of day when time's first characters
Made real the silks of camphored elegy?
When white hands laid an echo on our ears
Of ghostly burials in the years to be?
When, past the sighing shutters, first there filed
Those men of history with iron spades?
What thread was hid when fingers of a child
Pulled from white stars the curtains of the shades?

A night full-starred
Lent to the curtain-folds a scent of shrouds,
The constant heavens exciting mortal lips
To match Earth's memories to the moving clouds.
Then from the night the nursery in eclipse
Learnt superstition while the head was still;
Then ageless leaves first found their roots in graves
While a cold moon with stark, magnetic will
Sucked through the trees the blind, unerring waves.

God rose from this,
Shook once the hewn foundations of the world,
Earthquakes, volcanoes, and the bell-like sea;
His marl-made Adam into chaos hurled,
Left grief a mammoth on the spiny scree.
Through dawn's bright threads, the sundered veil, I see
Four legends meeting where the four lives cross.
O birth, that fourfold waking streamed to me
Fairer than Earth, and softer than green moss.

A rainbow's sheaf
Shone, then was gone, was lost, then shone again,
A rending brightness from the brandished arc
Where lashes fast evoked a goddess plain
Against that rock's inertia in the dark.

Love's foundered figurehead, her harp unstrung,
Dumb as Leviathan, fulfilled a frieze.
I saw, through shuddering colours, lit, made young,
Her living hand take up the ringing seas.

Waking from sleep,
As from a shell with all the lights of chance,
I sprang to find the dazzling water-fleece,
A film of sound carrying the water's dance
To the miraculous ear, the navel's peace
From nerveless rock wrenching the blood's bright way,
The luminous involutions of the fall
Commingling mortal with immortal day,
Tracked with beasts', birds', and fishes' ritual.

A mountain rose;
About its slopes were listening people spread.
They who looked up could see behind God's words
Distance transfigured while He broke the bread.
He cleansed the temple with a scourge of cords,
Stopped, while the woman touched His garment's hem,
Raised the dead, saved the adulterous, and revealed
Light to the blind. Being love, He died for them,
Whose resurrection by His blood was sealed.

From rock and wrong
First grief uncoils, ascending like a flower,
Climbs from dark music to the stonecropped land,
Climbs from killed music to the prisoner's tower
Scrawled with a diamond while the glass held sand.
I saw from dumb looms where the blind Shades keep
Their crooked shuttles whence all patterns run,
Cast like a vision from the coil of sleep,
Breath fly, and love's born hands surround the sun.

The Mother and Child

Let hands be about him white, O his mother's first,
Who caught him, fallen from light through nine months' haste
Of darkness, hid in the worshipping womb, the chaste
Thought of the creature with its certain thirst.
Looking up to her eyes declined that make her fair

He kicks and strikes for joy, reaching for those dumb springs.
He climbs her, sinks, and his mouth under darkness clings
To the night-surrounded milk in the fire of her hair.

She drops her arm, and feeling the fruit of his lips,
Tends him cunningly. O what secrets are set
In the tomb of each breath, where a world of light in eclipse
Of a darkly worshipping world exults in the joy she gave
Knowing that miracle, miracle to beget,
Springs like a star to her milk, is not for the grave.

Discoveries

The poles are flying where the two eyes set:
America has not found Columbus yet.

Ptolemy's planets, playing fast and loose,
Foretell the wisdom of Copernicus.

Dante calls Primum Mobile, the First Cause:
'Love that moves the world and the other stars.'

Great Galileo, twisted by the rack,
Groans the bright sun from heaven, then breathes it back.

Blake, on the world alighting, holds the skies,
And all the stars shine down through human eyes.

Donne sees those stars, yet will not let them lie:
'We're tapers, too, and at our own cost die.'

The shroud-lamp catches. Lips are smiling there.
'Les flammes—déjà?'—The world dies, or Voltaire.

Swift, a cold mourner at his burial-rite,
Burns to the world's heart like a meteorite.

Beethoven deaf, in deafness hearing all,
Unwinds all music from sound's funeral.

Three prophets fall, the litter of one night:
Blind Milton gazes in fixed deeps of light.

Beggar of those Minute Particulars,
Yeats lights again the turmoil of the stars.

Motionless motion! Come, Tiresias,
The eternal flies, what's passing cannot pass.

'Solace in flight,' old Heraclitus cries;
Light changing to Von Hügel's butterflies.

Rilke bears all, thinks like a tree, believes,
Sinks in the hand that bears the falling leaves.

The stars! The signs! Great Angelo hurls them back,
His whirling ceiling draws the zodiac.

The pulse of Keats testing the axiom;
The second music when the sound is dumb.

The Christian Paradox, bringing its great reward
By loss; the moment known to Kierkegaard.

NOTE ON THE MARI LWYD

Mari Lwyd – the Grey Mari, the Grey Mare – was, by tradition in Wales, carried from house to house on the last night of the year. It was a horse's skull. Sometimes it was supplanted by a copy, a white or grey horse's head modelled in wood, painted and hung with ribbons, but in all examples of the true tradition the skull itself was used. The skull had been chosen and buried when the horse died, and the burial-place marked, so that it could be exhumed for the ceremony. After it, the skull was kept, and used again on the next thirty-first of December, and so year after year.

The carriers were usually a party of singers, wits and impromptu poets, who, on the pretext of blessing, boasting of the sanctity of what they carried, tried to gain entrance to a house for the sake of obtaining food and drink. The method they used was to challenge those within to a rhyming contest. The inmates could keep them out so long as they were not in want of a rhyme, but when they failed to reply to the challenger the right of entry was gained. The singers would then bring their horse's head in, lay it on the table, and eat and drink with the losers of the contest.

This ancient custom, traceable perhaps to the White Horse of Asia, is still prevalent in many parts of Wales. The singers came every year to my father's house; and listening to them at midnight, I found myself imagining a skull, a horse's skull decked with ribbons, followed and surrounded by all kinds of drunken claims and holy deceptions.

I have attempted to bring together those who are separated. The last breath of the year is their threshold, the moment of supreme forgiveness, confusion and understanding, the profane and sacred moment impossible to realize while the clock-hands divide the Living from the Dead.

PRONUNCIATION NOTE

In case there should be confusion over the pronunciation of certain names in the Ballad, the following approximate pronunciations are given:

Mari Lwyd – – 'Marry Loo-id'
Gruffydd Bryn – – 'Griffith (*th* soft) Brin'
Machynlleth – – 'Machúnlleth' (*ch* guttural; *ll* and *th* aspirated)
Caerphilly – – *ll* as in English
Kidwelly – – *ll* as in English
Dolgelley – – *ll* aspirated, as in Machynlleth
Calgarw – – 'Calgarroo'

Ballad of the Mari Lwyd

PROLOGUE

Spoken by the Announcer of the Ballad

Mari Lwyd, Horse of Frost, Star-horse, and White Horse of the Sea, is carried to us.

The Dead return.

Those Exiles carry her, they who seem holy and have put on corruption, they who seem corrupt and have put on holiness.

They strain against the door.

They strain towards the fire which fosters and warms the Living.

The Living, who have cast them out, from their own fear, from their own fear of themselves, into the outer loneliness of death, rejected them, and cast them out for ever:

The Living cringe and warm themselves at the fire, shrinking from that loneliness, that singleness of heart.

The Living are defended by the rich warmth of the flames which keeps that loneliness out.

Terrified, they hear the Dead tapping at the panes; then they rise up, armed with the warmth of firelight, and the condition of scorn.

It is New Year's Night.

Midnight is burning like a taper. In an hour, in less than an hour, it will be blown out.

It is the moment of conscience.

The living moment.

The dead moment.

Listen.

Pitchblack Darkness—A Long Table laid with a White Cloth—A Door on Stage Right—A Broad Window next to it—The Two Loads of a Pendulum—When light comes it is so contrived as to throw their shadows to the extreme ends of the room—Between these ends stylistic figures whose movements exaggerate human movements—A Skull may be suggested at one shadow-limit of the Pendulum, and a Fillet at the other.

Midnight. Midnight. Midnight. Midnight.
Hark at the hands of the clock.
Now dead men rise in the frost of the stars
And fists on the coffins knock.
They dropped in their graves without one sound;
Then they were steady and stiff.

But now they tear through the frost of the ground
As heretic, drunkard and thief.

Why should you fear though they might pass
Ripping the stitch of grief,
The white sheet under the frosted glass,
Crisp and still as a leaf?
Or look through sockets that once were eyes
At the table and white cloth spread?
The terrible, picklock Charities
Raised the erected dead.

Under your walls they gnaw like mice;
Virtue is unmasked.
The hands of the clock betray your vice.
They give what none has asked.
For they have burrowed beneath the graves
And found what the good gave most:
Refuse cast by the righteous waves
In fossil, wraith and ghost.

Chalice and Wafer. Wine and Bread.
And the picklock, picklock, picklock tread.

Midnight. Midnight. Midnight. Midnight.
Hark at the hands of the clock.

Good men gone are evil become
And the men that you nailed down
Clamped in darkness, clamour for rum,
And ravish on beds of down
The vision your light denied them, laid
Above the neglected door;
And the chattering speech of skull and spade
Beckons the banished Poor.

Locked-out lepers with haloes come.
Put out the clock: the clock is dumb.

Midnight. Midnight. Midnight. Midnight.
Hark at the hands of the clock.

The breath of a numb thing, loud and faint:
Something found and lost.
The minute drops in the minute-glass;
Conscience counts the cost.
What mounted, murderous thing goes past

The room of Pentecost?
Sinner and saint, sinner and saint:
A horse's head in the frost.

Midnight. Midnight. Midnight. Midnight.
Hark at the hands of the clock.
What shudders free from the shroud so white
Stretched by the hands of the clock?
What is the sweat that springs in the hair?
Why do the knee-joints knock?
Bones of the night, in the naked air,
Knock, and you hear that knock.

Midnight. Midnight. Midnight. Midnight.
Hark at the hands of the clock.

A knock of the sands on the glass of the grave,
A knock on the sands of the shore,
A knock of the horse's head of the wave,
A beggar's knock on the door.
A knock of a moth on the pane of light,
In the beat of the blood a knock.
Midnight. Midnight. Midnight. Midnight.
Hark at the hands of the clock.

The sands in the glass, the shrinking sands,
And the picklock, picklock, picklock hands.

Midnight. Midnight. Midnight. Midnight.
Hark at the hands of the clock.

Light

FIGURES
Fasten the yard-gate, bolt the door,
And let the great fat drip.
The roar that we love is the frying-pan's roar
On the flames, like a floating ship.
The old Nick will keep the flies from our sheep,
The tick, the flea and the louse.
Open the flagons. Uncork the deep
Beer of this bolted house.

They stoop to the fire

ONE FIGURE
Unseen figures are aching now
(Hark at the pendulum's chain!)

Out of the night they have pulled the Plough,
Pulled the Dead Man's Wain.
Bones of the dead are clattering, clinking,
Pulling the Plough from the shore.
Dead men's fingers are feeling, knocking,
Knocking now on the door.

Midnight. Midnight. Midnight. Midnight.
Hark at the hands of the clock.

ANOTHER FIGURE

Crammed with food the table creaks.
The dogs grow fat on the crumbs.
God bless our board that springs no leaks,
And here no ruffian comes,
No beggars itching with jackdaws' eyes,
No fox on the trail of food,
No man with the plague from Hangman's Rise,
No jay from Dead Man's Wood.

Chalice and wafer that blessed the dead,
And the picklock, picklock, picklock tread.

Midnight. Midnight. Midnight. Midnight.
Hark at the hands of the clock.

THIRD FIGURE

Bones of the dead should come on their knees
Under a pilgrim's cloak,
But out in the dark what devils are these
That have smelt our kitchen-smoke?
Listen. Listen. Who comes near?
What man with a price on his head?
What load of dice, what leak in the beer
Has pulled your steps from the dead?

Midnight. Midnight. Midnight. Midnight.
Hark at the hands of the clock.

'Starving we come from Gruffydd Bryn
And a great meal we have lost.
We might have stayed by the fire of the inn
Sheltered from the frost.
And there a sweet girl stood and spread
The table with good things,
Felinfoel beer with a mountain's head,
And a pheasant with hungry wings.'

Midnight. Midnight. Midnight. Midnight.
Hark at the hands of the clock.

'There were jumping sausages, roasting pies,
And long loaves in the bin,
And a stump of Caerphilly to rest our eyes,
And a barrel rolling in.
But dry as the grave from Gruffydd Bryn
We are come without one rest;
And now you must let our Mari in:
She must inspire your feast.'

Midnight. Midnight. Midnight. Midnight.
Hark at the hands of the clock.

'For She knows all from the birth of the Flood
To this moment where we stand
In a terrible frost that binds the blood
In a cramp that claws the hand.
Give us rhyme for rhyme through the wood of the door
Then open the door if you fail.
Our wit is come from the seawave's roar,
The stars, and the stinging hail.'

Midnight. Midnight. Midnight. Midnight.
Hark at the hands of the clock.

Go back. We have heard of dead men's bones
That hunger out in the air.
Jealous they break through their burial-stones,
Their white hands joined in a prayer.
They rip the seams of their proper white clothes
And with red throats parched for gin,
With buckled knuckles and bottle-necked oaths
They hammer the door of an inn.

Sinner and saint, sinner and saint:
A horse's head in the frost.

'O pity us, brothers, through snow and rain
We are come from Harlech's waves.
Tall spears were laid on the mountain.
We hid in the warriors' caves.
We were afraid when the sun went down,
When the stars flashed we were afraid;
But the small lights showed us Machynlleth town,
And bent on our knees we prayed.'

Midnight. Midnight. Midnight. Midnight.
Hark at the hands of the clock.

Though you come from the grim wave's monklike hood
And Harlech's bitter coast,
White horses need white horses' food:
We cannot feed a ghost.
Cast your Lwyd to the white spray's crest
That pounds and rides the air.
Why should we break our lucky feast
For the braying of a mare?

Sinner and saint, sinner and saint:
A horse's head in the frost.

'In the black of En-gedi's cave we hid;
We hid in the Fall of the Bride.
And the stars flew back from the lifted lid;
We saw those horsemen ride.
We hid all night in the cowl of the wave;
Chariots and kings we saw
In Goliath darkness, bright and brave
Felled by an ass's jaw.'

Midnight. Midnight. Midnight. Midnight.
Hark at the hands of the clock.

'O white is the starlight, white on the gate
And white on the bar of the door.
Our breath is white in the frost, our fate
Falls in the dull wave's roar.
O rhyme with us now through the keyhole's slit
And open the door if you fail.
The sea-frost, brothers, has spurred our wit,
Ay, and the killing hail.'

Midnight. Midnight. Midnight. Midnight.
Hark at the hands of the clock.

What thirst consumed by the leaping flames,
What thirst has brought you back
From the starry writing of holy names
The spittle of Hell turns black.
Austere star-energies, naked, white,
Roused you, but still you play
With a bottle drowned in a drunkard's night,
Brought by the wicked spray.

Sinner and saint, sinner and saint:
A horse's head in the frost.

The slinking dead, the shrinking sands,
And the picklock, picklock, picklock hands.

Midnight. Midnight. Midnight. Midnight.
Hark at the hands of the clock.

Hark, they are going; the footsteps shrink,
And the sea renews her cry.
The big stars stare and the small stars wink;
The Plough goes glittering by.
It was a trick of the turning tide
That brought those voices near.
Dead men pummelled the panes outside:
We caught the breath of the year.

Midnight. Midnight. Midnight. Midnight.
Hark at the hands of the clock.

VOICE

Midnight. Midnight. Midnight. Midnight.
Hark at the hands of the clock.

Out in the night the nightmares ride;
And the nightmares' hooves draw near.
Dead men pummel the panes outside,
And the living quake with fear.
Quietness stretches the pendulum's chain
To the limit where terrors start,
Where the dead and the living find again
They beat with the selfsame heart.

In the coffin-glass and the window-pane
You beat with the selfsame heart.

Midnight. Midnight. Midnight. Midnight.
Hark at the hands of the clock.

Very faint

'We bring from white Hebron
And Ezekiel's Valley,
From the dead sea of Harlech
And mountain-girt Dolgelley,
All that singing way
From Cader to Kidwelly,

A stiff, a star-struck thing
Blown by the stinging spray
And the stinging light of the stars,
Our white, stiff thing,
Death and breath of the frost,
That has known the room of glass,
Dropped by the Milky Way
To the needle and thread of the pass.'

Hark, they are coming back, those fellows
Giving the stars another name,
Blowing them up with a pair of bellows
From a jumping, thumping, murderous flame;
Men of the night with a legion of wrongs,
Fists in the dark that shudder with shame,
Hated lechers with holy songs,
Bastard bodies that bear no name.

Loud and near
'We bring from Cader Idris
And those ancient valleys,
Mari of your sorrows,
Queen of the starry fillies.'

You'll not play skittles with us,
White Spirit. Spray of malice;
Froth from an old barrel:
Tell us if that be holy.

'Hers the white art that rouses
Light in the darkest palace,
Though black as a mole's burrow:
Truly we come to bless.'

You come from drunkards' houses
And bent, picklock alleys.
You come to thieve or borrow:
Your starved loins poke and press.

'Great light you shall gather,
For Mari here is holy;
She saw dark thorns harrow
Your God crowned with the holly.'

Have you watched snowflakes wither?
They fasten, then fade slowly,

Hither and thither blowing:
Your words are falling still.

'Deeper sadness knowing
Than death's great melancholy,
We journeyed from Calgarw,
From that skull-shaped hill.'

A white horse frozen blind,
Hurled from a seawave's hollow,
Fostered by spray and wind,
Profane and priestlike thing!

'She has those precious secrets
Known to the minstrel solely,
Experienced in the marrow,
Quick to tame beasts unruly.'

She should have been a whistle
For that tames our collie;
He darts on like an arrow,
Then he creeps up slowly.

'O, if she were a whistle
She would not call your collie,
But through this keyhole narrow
Try, your wits to rally.'

Go back to Cader Idris,
To your Dry Bones Valley.
Death shall pounce to-morrow,
And break upon your folly.

'Clustered thick are the stars,
And the fire-irons lying still;
Dust in the iron bars;
Frost on the window-sill.
The fire warms many hands,
But there where the shadows press
A single point of light
Can bring great loneliness.'

Midnight. Midnight. Midnight. Midnight.
Hark at the hands of the clock.

'In the black of the churchyard yew we lay
And the long roots taught us much.

We groped for the sober light of day,
Light that we dared not touch.
The sleet of the stars fell cold and thin
Till we turned, and it touched our crown;
Then we yearned for the heat in the marrow of sin,
For the fire of a drinkers' town.'

Sinner and saint, sinner and saint:
A horse's head in the frost.

'But brightest brimstone light on him
And burn his rafters black
That will not give when his fears are dim
The treasure found in the sack.
In the mouth of the sack, in the stifled breath,
In the sweat of the hands, in the noose,
In the black of the sack, in the night of death
Shines what you dare not lose.'

Midnight. Midnight. Midnight. Midnight.
Hark at the hands of the clock.

'Under the womb of teeming night
Our Mari tries your faith;
And She has Charity's crown of light:
Spectre she knows and wraith;
How sweet-tongued children are wickedly born
By a swivelling devil's thrust
Mounting the night with a murderous horn,
Riding the starry gust.'

Midnight. Midnight. Midnight. Midnight.
Hark at the hands of the clock.

'Under the edge of the spray of the stars,
In the hollow dark of a wave,
We heard the fire-irons stirring the bars,
Laying the ash of the grave.
We saw your faith in the pin of the tongs
Laying your fears at rest;
You buried our bones with your drinking-songs
And murdered what you love best.'

Midnight. Midnight. Midnight. Midnight.
Hark at the hands of the clock.

'But the pin goes in to the inmost dark
Where the dead and living meet,
And the clock is stopped by the shock of the spark
Or the stealthy patter of sleet.
Where disdain has cast to its utmost pitch
The strands of the finished thread,
The clock goes out, and the ashes twitch,
Roused by the breaking of bread.'

Sinner and saint, sinner and saint:
A horse's head in the frost.

Midnight. Midnight. Midnight. Midnight.
Hark at the hands of the clock.

Go back, with your drowned and drunken eyes
And your crooked mouths so small
And your Mari foaled of the starry skies:
Go back to the seawave's fall.
If we lift and slide the bolt in the door
What can our warm beer buy?
What can you give for the food we store
But a slice of starving sky?

Sinner and saint, sinner and saint:
A horse's head in the frost.

Midnight. Midnight. Midnight. Midnight.
Hark at the hands of the clock.

'O who has woven the skein of the hair,
And who has knotted the ropes of the fist,
And who has hollowed the bones of the eyes?
One of you answer: the hands have kissed.
I see in your eyes white terror,
I see in your locked hands hate.
Press, we are one step nearer
The live coals in the grate.'

Midnight. Midnight. Midnight. Midnight.
Hark at the hands of the clock.

The slinking dead, the shrinking sands,
And the picklock, picklock, picklock hands.

Hark, they are going; the footsteps shrink,
And the sea renews her cry.

The big stars stare and the small stars wink;
The Plough goes glittering by.
It was a trick of the turning tide
That brought those voices near.
Dead men pummelled the panes outside:
We caught the breath of the year.

VOICE

Dread and quiet, evil and good:
Frost in the night has mixed their blood.

Thieving and giving, good and evil:
The beggar's a saint, and the saint a devil.

Mari Lwyd, Lwyd Mari:
A sacred thing through the night they carry.

Betrayed are the living, betrayed the dead:
All are confused by a horse's head.

Midnight. Midnight. Midnight. Midnight.
Hark at the hands of the clock.
Lazarus comes in a shroud so white
Out of the hands of the clock.
While baskets are gathered of loaves of light,
Rape is picking the lock.
Hungering fingers, bones of the night,
Knock, knock, knock.

FIGURES

Bones of the dead with their crooked eyes
And their crooked mouths so small,
Night-nags foaled of the starry skies,
Threatening our feast, they call.
We face the terrible masquerade
Of robbers dressed like the dead.
The cold star-energies make us afraid,
Afraid of that picklock tread.

Midnight. Midnight. Midnight. Midnight.
Hark at the hands of the clock.

A starlit crucifix hits their knees
And a chain of bloodstained beads
Drops to the fork where the fingers seize
Their good and evil deeds.
Those blasphemous hands can change our mind

Or mood with a craftsman's skill;
Under their blessing they blast and blind,
Maim, ravish, and kill.

The slinking dead, the shrinking sands,
And the picklock, picklock, picklock hands.

Midnight. Midnight. Midnight. Midnight.
Hark at the hands of the clock.

Resurrection's wings and corruption's moth
Beat on the window-pane.
The tombs are ripped like a table-cloth,
And madmen teach the sane.
A voice redresses those ancient wrongs
With a wrong more deep than all.
Holy Charity's bastard songs
Burst from a seawave's fall.

Sinner and saint, sinner and saint:
A horse's head in the frost.

Midnight. Midnight. Midnight. Midnight.
Hark at the hands of the clock.

'Hell curse this house for a badger's holt
If we find no man devout.
God singe this doorway, hinge and bolt,
If you keep our evil out.
Long-limbed we hung in the taunting trees
And cried in our great thirst:
Give us a drink, light breaks our knees.
Give, or the house is cursed.'

Midnight. Midnight. Midnight. Midnight.
Hark at the hands of the clock.

Snatch off that mask from a drinker's mouth
All lit by phosphorus up.
Men of the night, I know your drouth;
Your mouths would blister the cup.
When the big stars stare and the small stars wink
You cry it's the break of day.
Out of our sight; you are blind with drink:
Ride your Mari away.

Midnight. Midnight. Midnight. Midnight.
Hark at the hands of the clock.

'Pity our penitent fingers now
Telling the beads of a chain.
Out of the night we have pulled the plough,
Pulled the Dead Man's Wain.
Out of the torment of huge night
Where the cruel stars are hung,
We have come with blessing to heal your sight
If first you will cool our tongue.'

Midnight. Midnight. Midnight. Midnight.
Hark at the hands of the clock.

Go back, with your drowned and drunken eyes
And your crooked mouths so small
And your Mari foaled of the starry skies:
Go back to the seawave's fall.
If we lift and slide the bolt in the door
What can our warm beer buy?
What can you give for the food we store
But a slice of starving sky?

Sinner and saint, sinner and saint:
A horse's head in the frost.

'Surely, surely you'll open the door
Now that you know our sins;
For all grows good that was foul before
Where the spark of heaven begins.
Where the spark that cleaves to the chimney's groove
Is blown to the freezing weather
It is men's good that breaks their love,
Their evil draws them together.'

Chalice and Wafer, Wine and Bread.
And the picklock, picklock, picklock tread.

'Know you are one with Cain the farm
And Dai of Dowlais pit;
You have thieved with Benjamin's robber's arm;
With Delilah you lay by night.
You cheated death with Barabbas the Cross
When the dice of Hell came down.
You prayed with Jo in the prisoner's fosse
And ran about Rahab's town.'

Midnight. Midnight. Midnight. Midnight.
Hark at the hands of the clock.

'O, had we never drunk a drop
You might receive us then,
Men of the snow-deep mountain-top
And soot-faced mining men.
Do you not hear like an anvil ring
The smith of the rock of coal
Who fell on his steel like that great king
And sundered body and soul?'

Midnight. Midnight. Midnight. Midnight.
Hark at the hands of the clock.

'O crouch and cringe by the bounding flame
And close your eyelids fast.
Out of the breath of the year we came.
The breath of the year has passed.
The wits of a skull are far too great
Being out of the hands of the clock.
When Mari Lwyd knocks on the door,
In charity answer that knock.'

Midnight. Midnight. Midnight. Midnight.
Hark at the hands of the clock.

Go back. We have heard of dead men's bones
That hunger out in the air.
Jealous they break through their burial-stones,
Their white hands joined in a prayer.
They rip the seams of their proper white clothes
And with red throats parched for gin,
With buckled knuckles and bottle-necked oaths
They hammer the door of an inn.

'O a ham-bone high on a ceiling-hook
And a goose with a golden skin,
And the roaring flames of the food you cook:
For God's sake let us in!
To see the white beer rise in the glass
And the brown jump out of the jug
Would lift those stiffened loons in the grass
Like lambs to the darling dug.'

Sinner and saint, sinner and saint:
A horse's head in the frost.

Go back to your Hell, there are clean souls here,
Go back to your barns of muck.

Go back to your Hell, and leave our beer,
And your Mari bring you luck.
We'll feed you with stones, we'll strip you clean
In the stars, if you're not gone.
But Jesus! why are you all unseen
On whom our lamplight shone?

The slinking dead, the shrinking sands,
And the picklock, picklock, picklock hands.

Midnight. Midnight. Midnight. Midnight.
Hark at the hands of the clock.

VOICE

Eyes on the cloth. Eyes on the plate.
Rigor mortis straightens the figure.
Striking the clock when the hands are straight,
You have seen a god in the eyes of the beggar.

Midnight. Midnight. Midnight. Midnight.
Hark at the hands of the clock.

Faint

'O white is the frost on the breath-bleared panes
And the starlike fire within,
And our Mari is white in her starry reins
Starved through flesh and skin.
It is a skull we carry
In the ribbons of a bride.
Bones of the Nightfrost parry
Bones of the Fire inside.'

Loud and near

'None can look out and bear that sight,
None can bear that shock.
The Mari's shadow is too bright,
Her brilliance is too black.
None can bear that terror
When the pendulum swings back
Of the stiff and stuffed and stifled thing
Gleaming in the sack.'

Midnight. Midnight. Midnight. Midnight.
Hark at the hands of the clock.

The Lamp and The Veil
1945

Yeats in Dublin

in memory of W. B. Yeats

A rich lupin-garden,
A long, amber room,
A bronze head, bookshelves
Glittering in that gloom;
And threads, threads, threads of the sea,
Threads of the birds of doom.

Impression of rain-wet, moving leaves.
A dog upon the drive
Casts a questioning shadow
Where secret flowers connive.
A terrible seabird. Folded wings.
Then the gannet's dive.

'From such a treadle of the sea
Your foot may never come,
Never without breaking
The pattern of the loom:
All the ages go to make
The thread around your thumb.'

'O come back,' the seabirds cry,
'To the raindrops' hammerings,
Down to the ignorant Irish sea
Crossed by encircling wings;
Under the sea dumb grains, great rocks:
Think of these old things.'

But Yeats, Yeats the poet
Under Dublin skies,
After the ten years' journey
On which no seagull flies,
After the waves of silence
I look him in the eyes.

Fresh from the shining sunlight
We came on his dark seat,
Shook hands, paused, were dumb there
Fearing to tire him out,
Though his raised head was noble,
His voice firm and sweet.

'Tell me about that young group
Of Welsh writers,' he said,
'Whose poems in that paper you sent me
The other day I read.'
An image stands on Carmarthen sands
With the black birds overhead.

'The young poets,' he murmured,
'Toil too much. They lay
Something on their table,
And dissect, and wear it away
Till nothing but the grit is left;
But all song is gay.

There must always be a quality
Of nonchalance in the work.
The intellect is impotent
Labouring in the dark,
For a poem is always
A piece of luck.

Who can foretell the run of luck
Or where the luck may fall?
Watching the roulette-wheel
We see the spinning ball,
But where it stops and comes to rest
The place is magical.

The Psychical Research Society
Lately has found
It can experimentally
Foresee that resting-ground
A second before the fall of space
And the death of sound.

Much the treasure-hoarding mind
Values its sum,
But to a breath's vibration
All is held there dumb;
All is reduced to nothing;
Then the luck will come.

Against blinding darkness
A man's blood is thrown,
Striving for that intensity
Which danced before time ran;

That thing, for lack of a better name,
I call 'Eternal Man'.

A poet seeks his deepest thought,
Then finds, when it is made,
A loyalty has held it,
Not by time betrayed,
The very distance measured
By the blood's shade.

In an early poem I set myself
The task to unite
The myths of all ages
In a single night,
To draw their tale, not on the wall
But in the tip of the light.

I might have made it with the myths
Of Ireland alone,
But somewhere in my mind's eye
I saw Priam's throne.
Usna I wanted, but Troy too,
So I put Troy down.'

'Did the idea come slowly,'
I questioned, 'did it unfold
At once, or from the leaves themselves
As from a sculptor's mould?
Was it your mind that saw the words,
Or was your mind told?'

'I made it,' with a slow smile
Said that Irishman,
'Looking at a lady's photograph
Where all those myths began;
So naturally it came slowly.'
And he went on:

'A critic who has pleased me
(Though the best attack)
Says that the style is public
In my latest work;
That near to my youth, with a difference,
Song is going back.

That difference is important
In poem or in play.

Hard as thoughts in the bone to find
Are naked words to say;
Write, get rid of rhetoric;
Cut the dead wood away.

Cast off poetic diction first
And find what is your own.
Learn what reason could not teach
From the marrow in the bone.
Reject false decoration
And make the whole work one.

Today I summon boyhood's reed
But bid that same reed break,
For broken things are powerful
Being bruised and trampled. Blake
And Burns had a public style;
But others found a fake,

The trick and slang of a slippery speech
Trite and second-hand;
Pandering to the popular ear
They did not understand
That truth must cut harder
Than the diamond.'

I asked, had he stirred enmity.
'Yes, my work was banned.
It was the laymen squeaked and squealed
And would not let it stand;
Never the hand of blessing,
Always the felon's hand.

But before my book *A Vision* appeared
The Bishops began to urge
A ban on its publication
Fearing its views at large;
Then they heard it was a guinea,
And they dropped the charge.

The Resurrection would not have been played
But for a general strike.
Men who insist on vessels
Dare not see them break,
Terrified should the dead walk
Or the sleeper wake.

I met, in America,
A holy man who said:
"There will always be miracle—
(He raised his old, white head)
There will always be revelation,"
That old saint said.

A saint. I met his follower then.
He professed belief in all
The tenets of the Church's creed.
Mass and ritual,
Except the immortality
Of the human soul.

Another priest I asked which road
To salvation lay.
"Go to Mass, go to Mass,"
Was all that priest would say.
"It will take just twenty minutes.
Go, and you need not pray."

Then, when I put a question
In salvation's track,
"Read what you like," the priest replied,
"A great or a holy book.
I take when I go praying
A Dante bound in black".'

Yeats justified the parish priest,
One that could curse and bless,
Especially curse, and blame bad crops
On the peasants' wickedness.
'They must have their magician:
He is neither more nor less.'

We from two countries coming
Took tea, and talked of Synge's
Islands, behind us sunlight
And the path of wings,
Before us thought and images
Beaten into rings.

Thought, grief-impassioned, drifted
To Coole, and Lady Gregory:
'Have the trees grown a little
Around Thoor Ballylee?'

One by one he raised those names
Between the waves of the sea.

Lionel Johnson, Dowson,
And political men betrayed,
Murdered by their excess of love
Or by a dream they made;
Synge's mighty statements;
The brightness of the shade.

'We have the folk in Ireland;
The English make it up.
How can a country's language thrive
If an abstract shape
Battening on the vigorous man
Sucks the blood- drop?

When I first went to London
I was looking for a technique.
I had the folk behind me,
My food was there to seek,
But without the subtlety London taught
I could not learn to speak.

I got technique from a man who was
A very bad poet indeed.
He taught me to appreciate
The small stops of the reed;
The Minutiae of a poem
He first made me heed.

What if the labour all seem vain,
What if years are spent
Chiselling and chiselling
The stubborn element?
All is rewarded on a breath
By an accident.

My quarrel with those Londoners
Is that they try
To substitute psychology
For the naked sky
Of metaphysical movement,
And drain the blood dry.

All is materialism, all
The catchwords they strew,
Alien to the blood of man.—'
One ranting slogan drew
That "Poetry must have news in it":
The reverse is true.'

I questioned him: 'How can there be
A national poetry?
What can we make or what resist
When all is like the sea?'
He said: 'You must resist the stream
Of mechanical apathy.'

Speaking of leaders, he affirmed,
'The best is he who knows
The fancy-dress of politics
From his garden-clothes,
Who understands the popular mask,
Those deceiving shows.'

He spoke of de Valera,
A charming, cultured man
Who found upon the platform
True culture under ban,
Then uttered out of vehemence
Words he would say to none.

We talked of national movements.
He pondered the chance
Of Welshmen reviving
The fire of song and dance,
Driving a lifeless hymnal
From that inheritance.

I thought of rough mountains,
The poverty of the heath.
'Though leaders sway the crowd', I said,
'Power is underneath.
The sword of Taliesin
Would never fit a sheath.'

'The leaders and the poets
Are not in unison.
When Hitler struck a medal

He knew that George* won,
But he had not served his movement,
So qualified for none.'

He questioned my French friend,
And his words remain
Shining like pebbles
Under the flow of the Seine,
Where Synge had walked with him,
Where he had met Verlaine.

The work of Péguy he had known,
Claudel and Valéry,
The sacred tapestry of Joan
And Christian charity,
Mallarmé's pupil's masterpiece,
The Graveyard by the Sea.

Spirits whirling about us
Were laid by a look,
Ghosts turned in delicate light
To gold on the edge of a book,
Wound in the shroud of a still page
Which no man took.

Light in the drawing-room,
Daylight on the lawn,
Book-shadows in the corners
Seemed to have drawn
Spirits from the back of the mind,
From conception's dawn.

Yeats and his wife once more
Asked of the Tower
Where I had stood last year
A dumb, low-breathed hour,
Watching the blade of the grass
And the grass-flower.

Then, as the heron
Rises from the stream,
He raised from the haunted chair

* Stefan George (1868–1933).

His tall, proud frame
In that dazzling background
Of heroic dream.

Now, as a child sees
Daybreak on a wall,
His image showed me in a flash
Birth and burial,
The trouble of the lovely song,
Parnell's Funeral.

'I must work,' and 'I must rest'
In one breath he said,
Unconsciously, a blind man
By a blind hand led,
All creation hanging
On that double thread.

My friend and I were silent
Witnessing that thing
Which of the sacred rivers
Had touched the secret spring
Making, in the youth of age,
The dumb stone sing.

With visionary footsteps
Slow, he crossed the room,
He who had made the dead lips sing
And celebrate love in doom,
About him the sages
Of Byzantium.

To that broken vision
What could we bring,
Blinded by the shadow
Of the mounting wing?
Had he not loosed the tongue of dust
And made the dead lips sing?

The river that fed his fingers
A pagan sun would parch
Did not the soul throw writing there
On the vaulted arch,
Clash and flash of irrational love,
A Full Moon in March.

Silence falling from the moon
Beating to brass
The towering labours of the sun
Bids Herodias'
Daughter dance more madly
Till all but love must pass.

Words and the flight of images,
That unerring dance,
Passionate love of wisdom,
Hatred of ignorance.
Words laid on silence.
The tragic utterance.

'I am sorry you have come so far
For so little,' he said.
The music of the mounting wave
Crashed into my head
In which the spray confuses
The living and the dead.

I have seen kindness
In true, loyal eyes.
Who prophesies from the lip of a shell?
What raging water cries?
The blue wave moves beneath me:
Above, the white bird flies.

Sea-Music for My Sister Travelling

for Dorothy

Here with fine compasses I span
The delicate, listening seas that cover ears with pearl,
Divining distances
On the whirled globe where divers pierce the kris
Of light-attracted shark,
Swooping until the dagger finds its mark,
Shooting for bangles wrists and ankles twirl,
Ripped where the sea-jaws miss
By clever swimmers turning in their dark,
Carrying the knife and spike of dawn,
The jewelled clasp

Of dazzling butterfly sea, Caribbean,
Bermuda's pearls, dark African
Lagoons where sprawled, fire-breathing alligators gasp,
Gold fin, bright gill flashed from the quick knife-grasp,
Spinning through rush of crescent shapes
Where blue-net seas gush Tyrian,
Tunnies spawn,
Hunters harpoon the whale,
Far Northward speeding from the South-speeding ships,
White, ever lost, in every wake a tale
Of frost, of fire,
Captured and lost desire,
Of night, the alone, the lost, the never-known,
Left by the foam-bird rising from the flail
Of the cutting ship,
Listening, descending, flown
From water's lip,
White Sibyl shot from the abandoned wheel,
Scouring in daylight for the dead,
Sprung from their sunken figurehead,
Hovering there, whose eyes reveal
The birth of colours, fastening near the Pole
A waste of ice-blocks, aureole
Of death, darkening with wrath,
Aurora borealis, path
Of forms that out of igloos spring at dusk,
Launching long boats to hunt the narwhal's tusk,
White track of bear where seas congeal,
Skinned with green skimming paths of Esquimau and seal.

But I must watch the dolphins at your keel
Weaving all patterns of all unimagined deaths,
Watch, watch the spinning-wheel
Winding the slow thread, snapped off in a trice,
Backward and ever forward spinning,
Binding the end to the beginning,
Turning from shipwreck to the shipyard's vice,
Turning from blue mid-ocean to the river's mouth,
Turning from South to North, returning twice,
Lucky and loth,
Coiled in destruction's great Sargasso growth,
Struck in the cold seawreaths,
Vortex and mysteries of ice

Transfigured into fire,
Coffins of lead, blue archipelagoes,
Mummies with eyes of squids that do not close;
The ritual dancers of the spindrift all
Clash on your ship in frenzy of desire
Meeting above your vessel's fall
Like dancer's cymbals, for the dead
Would with a living vent and scream of bronze
Escape from their bewilderment at once
And pour new deaths, like wine, upon their head,
Released by this from silence' moving thrall;
Those liquid ashes from a funeral-pyre
Fade in a dolphin's gyre,
Eternal sunbeams, wilderness of foam;
Shadrach beckons you to come;
Fingers of the smoking wave
Scatter your shadow where the doomed, unsinged,
Walk in the furnace, fierily
Trespassing the miraculous sea,
Alive in that ecstatic grave
On which no element impinged;
Emerging now, unscathed, unchanged in form,
Swift you fly back
From the same vessel's track,
From icy sea-death and the seven-times-heated storm.
A thousand pigeons cast for home,
A thousand whirling birds fed with white foam
Drop for white bread, and the young whales bound on
Through the fled seas,
Coming and gone,
Prancing to Capricorn
Through the new Past and ageless prophecies,
Coiled in the wonderful wake of the unborn.

In peaceful day, who knows how near you now,
Black, the begetters clash like thunderclouds;
Light in the rainbow from the prow
Hides the ascending death where spirits, torn, begin
To put on light, and shed their parted shrouds.
O, the sea turns, and now your eyes look in.
Now, a born girl above the unborn girl,
You watch the waters spin,
Watch the cold shuttle of the dead

Winding the fearful thread,
Scattered in drift of sunbeams and the spindrift whirl
Tracked with all natures of the impassive moon;
And soon, soon
Shall dolphin's curl,
Crescent of shark and cutting fin
Outrun the figure of your deaths.
Winding your path, O may they dance and leap,
Plunge high and sheer, revel and play,
Turn smoothly then, shout undersea for joy,
Turning through ecstasy of sleep
Slow Fortune's wheel, and treasure those safe breaths
That you, awaking, may stand on that far spray
And from light's maze uncoil the magic seas,
Assembling with new time the perished fable,
Building a town that was a toy
Of paper bricks, the languages
Tumbling from the Tower of Babel,
Where the ship's wheel runs back; where birds deploy
For other voyages
From the dark seaport of your tropic day.

O, at the ship's rail now,
In clustered darkness, grape-black, suddenly
Under the moving, vine-remembering tree,
In later night, earlier by stealth, and starry,
You see the true
Girl of the sea bewildering the storm's crew,
Where fugitive Harpies those deaf men would marry
To rocks where the mind's fears are cast,
Binding Ulysses to the mast,
While she
Springs from the phosphorus darkness with a breath of musk,
Sea-pink, rose-spray, the prow
Breaking her mermaid silence, black sea-crow
Darkening each trough with silence virginal
Beneath the albatross
Of snake-starred, mountainous Africa's Southern Cross,
Darkening the disc
Of ever-widening rings
From your huge anchors cast,
Breath in the violet skies,
Breath of stars' diamonds through primaeval dusk

Hid by Earth's edge from Northern eyes, brilliant at last,
And still she brings
To nothing in the seawaves' clash and fall
Cables of Autumns dropped to Springs,
Grapplers that hook blind water's gliding sands,
Places dissolving, fading hands,
Words, and the moments of seen friends,
Your disc of voices vanishing with the Past.

Flash forward, fin,
Where carrion birds career
Above the carcase lowered by the fleet
Of moving ships, dropped through the water-sheet,
Shuddering, and lost inscrutably beneath
Those winged and hovering looters of the bier
On which the sharks' jaws meet,
Haunting the limpid sea-grave, circled with a wreath
Of vanishing foam, where frail world-bubbles spin
Then break, white beads covering your wake of fear,
Leaving an opal's terror, where night's muttering winds confide
Mute histories to the tide,
But where the sun's blue vulture casts a lidless eye
Over the suffering waters of illimitable green;
The entwining, sinuous, serpentining deep
Clings to the vessel plunging through the lie
And truth and tomb and doom and double-dye
Of tossed foam, tossed and lost, where that Leviathan
And the torpedo sleep.

Who knows so well as I
There are deep sea-bells. Zig-zag swordfish daggering
Rip the plumed exultation of the whale
Whose thousand years are drowned in that blood-spring
Falling through darkness, falling from a wing
To the sea-troughs, ark of the covenant, lowering of the grail
To the mad navel of the million-fated sky.
The emperor of waters, shaped for praise, must fail
Through swordfish-thrust, or sting of the gadfly,
Then drift, and on some sand-beach die.
Knowing these things, the dolphins play
Scattering to chance your sea-thread grave and gay
Flown, yet unflown, a thread I cannot keep
Through the far steadied course, your travel's binnacle
Hovering above a keel of lead

Stretching the Rockies and Australia from a starry tentacle,
World-entering, world-surrounding thread
Following the convolutions of a shell
To the blood-red
Devilish intricacies of sound,
Serpent and lyre-bird purging in a moment
The sacred vanities of the wave-tossed drowned.
Dolphins involve you in their own unknown dark firmament,
Watch with their perfect eyes your sleep
Of nightmare, steep,
Perceiving that live, falling town,
Imagining within
The cobra-hooded wave
Crumbling doors, and by that blast
London hung blinded in the dust,
Fire pulling walls and buildings down,
Green eyes of serpents, the sleek water-skin
Trained from your path to trailing hoses,
A flare of spitting venom rave,
Flickering a tongue of fire in match-blue houses
Till the sea catches from your dread
And pavings close above each left, loved head
Tumbled to dust, where whistling night confuses
The finned and flying unextricated dead
Watching your crystal through the whirl
Of shuddering seas; their eyes are pearl,
Their fingers coral, cramped to save
Your grief from water-raftered night, drowned in their fiery grave.

Rush, dolphins, in your wheel
Of blinding thought, the illuminated prayer
Of water, light and air;
Catch world-surrounding light and music, reel,
Traffic with spun looms, all the mysteries
Of the sped seas,
Flashed lightning, rush-light, gloom no eye can hold,
Rush-light in darkness, spirits in darkness, gold
Of night, pre-natal night, the after-death
Turning upon a single breath
Spiring to God on the sea's circular wall;
Dart, flying-fish, through fold on fold
Of intricate, hurrying light, a dolphin's world
Shining through water-leaps,

Jumping where giant energies abate,
Balanced above a wave, a breath, a fall,
Haunted by preying shapes
Where the twelve cornered winds of the sea-maps
Fly to the centre, to a needle's fate.
That thread the phosphorus sea-serpent grips,
Loud shake the tenebrous timbers of the ships,
Through rending darkness, but the light escapes
Lost on a fish's path: your ship is late.

No sound. What oil may calm the troubled sky
Where cities founder, and the sea is dry?
Or this peninsula, where I,
Fire-watching on your long-left land,
Toiling through water, swimming with one hand,
Fast for your wilderness of baying waters, moon-drawn sand:
I see around me the sun-crazed
Or moon-crazed men, adrift, afloat,
Fainting in an open boat,
Thirst, or the merciless sun amazed
With flaying, blistering fever. Loud they cry,
Naked seamen exclaiming, 'Prophesy,
You who would quench the spiral tongues
On the sea's ladder-rungs,
And raise the mad, wrecked voices from a jumping stone;
Smother that light, through your own graveyard you have gone!'
Yet all is fire, this leaf and they
Whom sun and wind and water flay;
Far out, through lamp and sheet I see
How lives, like fiery ashes on the sea,
Destroy their phoenix in a breath,
Consuming their own death:
No shattering rock may tear
A fibre from the hand which has no like in air;
No wind, no vulture may deride
Surpassing character, superhuman pride.
There each must learn alone
That judgment rests, there where the ash has blown.
O anvil, storm, sheet-anchor, grave and groan,
A fiendish tom-tom cries,
And still the insistent hammer prophesies
All contradictory deaths and births by night
Broken by stars' stampeding flight,

Sea-horses' surge, white bear, walrus and great
Trumpeting Behemoth,
The imponderable christening of their wanton, devious weight;
Samson against the font lifting the gate
And leaping, tautening the limbs and loins of his wrath,
Gathering the pillars, clothed in dust and doom,
Trampling the bloodstained Philistines in the fossil's path,
Blind as the stars, blind path, blind thread,
Fins, birds and dolphins in the flying loom
Whirling about the head
Knowing it knocks against another womb,
Wound in the terrible, wondering music of the dead not dead.

O come, great deaths,
Sea-deaths on sea-deaths, now:
Light tapers in the tombs
Of the cowled sea's retreating catacombs,
Moon-herded waters, cattle for the carrion-crow,
Pricked, goaded to the deep,
Dark, prehistoric sea-bed where life's monsters sleep.
Dolphins that wind, and you that slit the breaths,
Write on the coffin's glass
With diamond grains
Scribbling a tale with diamonds of the stars
On the blown shale's obliterated stains,
On stones wave-moulded, singing, and the hammered-down
Sarcophagus moving through strange waters with a broken crown.
But while the tranquil shuttles deceive and weave
Uncertain treachery,
Spirits unpraised, true baptists in oblivion's wave,
Protect you tenderly.
Their shuddering hearts beat sacred time, and where processions move
You are made safe by their great love;
Town-razing storms, virgins of fire, seize the cramped message-room,
Torch-bearers of alarm
Quenched in the diving swarm
Of phosphorus coruscations, vanishing lamps in bloom
Blown out by spectral lips,
Plunging below the paths and deaths of ships
To the first film of pearl,
Shell of the world unborn and of the waking girl,
Treading time down through rhyme and slime
To the first norm

Of self-engendering flame,
Slow miracle-bed of lightnings and coiled limbs,
Where no pronged martyrs' crucifix beats
Cobbles of a pilgrim's streets,
But the crust breaks in Christ's original radium.

Returning now,
You have the gale for peace.
May giddying lightning play about your prow,
A brilliant storm black bolts and hailstones throw,
Fork-lightning pitch, a wilderness of light,
A coil of deaths, a bodyguard of loves
Freaking the track, flinging the water-fleece
Heaven-high, to sink you deeper in the trough
Where scattering waves
Disperse the night's innumerable graves,
Gold of divine typhoon,
Rammed sea-walls, mounds of rough
Tremendous water, towers of praise,
Fireball and waterspout, the maze
Of clawed, black, velvet waters burrowing from the moon
Spun from death's whirlpool, not to see
Over the breaths and moments, years and days,
The gorgeous power of the demented sea.

Thunder, and still
Hail-hammered mountains move
Processional, to find
Sources of light and peace not in the mind;
Gnarled elm breaks forth; fierce fossil-rock delivers the spring's love.
Thunder, and still
The shore-wind, sweeping from the wave's white hill,
Pauses and begs at the entrance to the shell.
Thunder, and still
Swollen rivers run to find their principle in that first drop
That is not theirs but out of nothing fell,
Moving to time from nothing: did they find it, time would stop.

The frost which fastened on the window-sill
Thaws, and the Spring rains wash the leaves;
Swallows are nesting in the eaves;
The beechwood rings with music of the married dove.
Brief visions blossom from the everlasting well;
Fail will not seed or cell.

The dying bell
Breaks through sound's infinite waves, then snaps their distance off.

What Sibyl cried
Through room, rock, shell and skull, to-day you would come?
To-night
Between the narrow pointers which divide
The close room and the far,
The fathomed world and your unfathomable meteorite,
Erratic in the night, like a new star,
Between blown, blasted Jericho, and houses shattered here,
Between this grief's caught breath and the Great Year
All moons and mysteries are.
Between the appointed lips,
Between death's tide and rocks which guide the ships,
Between the speechless worshipper and John, the unuttered name,
The dark is stricken dumb.
I cannot find a pattern for my fear.
Under the trumpets of your desecration,
Under the dolphins of your consecration,
Under the trumpets blown
By winds converged on the cold cock of flame,
Brass turn-tale, screeching chanticleer,
I sacrifice my nightmares on a stone,
Till their blood mingles with the sun.
They are asleep, the foals the nightmares bore;
Wide-open eyes are sleeping, and they race
Round Earth to the same place;
From threads of dolphins glittering hooves are spun;
Round and round they run;
Blue foals are playing near the close, loved shore.

You will come soon, soon, you will come soon.
The sea is awake, awake. The sea is a bird.
There are fluttering, beating wings. A nameless message
Nods in the shallows. Look, in this cupped hand
The breathing light!
There is a pigeon in the caves. I have heard
A hundred thundering waves, proud, manacled, going
To death, and over them storm-bright, violent plumage,
Terrified, hovering, flown from another land,
Clinging to the rock. Loud breakers, following, flowing
On rainbows and stones, a rock-cupped, miniature lagoon,
Stir the cold oracle that cries:

Come down, come down,
To the terrified darkness, to the dove's red eyes.
Fins flash, the anemone puts quick feelers out;
The seashell turns from the moon.

What tick, what chime?
What loss, what fear, forbidding treachery?
What pendulous event, both chained and free?
Who holds this lead holds all eternity,
Who knows this moment knows the rest of time.
The hammer falls
Transfiguring the whole sky,
Transfiguring short-lived time's futurity
With music of the virginals;
Rest, but no respite: these are moving walls,
And I must lie
Caught in a comet's arm,
Stone-dead within a stone's throw of the sky,
Riding death's orbit on your path of storm.
Lamp of a million leaves,
Words written, or said,
To-night, last night, the uncertain track
Which one thread wandering weaves,
A fiery thread
Shrouded in black,
Signs of the heavens, the Zodiac,
Flood of the crystalline, white, unending Way
Ascending through colossal night
From breath abandoned which believes
The last blown seashell cast up on the bay:
Come down, I say,
Deluge of light, and drown the words' inflection,
Rush through the luminous, coiled, vermilion chambers,
Shatter the labyrinths white,
And ruin all the mind remembers;
Come down, great Resurrection,
Swing up the clarion,
Wake all the dead. What now seems strange?
What furniture shall change?
Sandgrain, doomed grain, cluster of seaweed, carrion,
Root of the starry tree
Under the dolphins of the dead
In whistling night, confusing memory,

Cannot rend from me the doom
Of these real boards, real wreck, uncertain room
To-morrow and forever. What the Sibyl said
Through birds of augury
Walks the sea; then the mysterious call
Vanishes and is gone.
Yet no truth held these warning birds
Like your imagined seawave's fearful fall
Under whose smothering hood
Divined through Earth with cedar-wood,
Your voice and silence are reciprocal,
Vessel impurely understood,
Birth and burial
Of to-night's words and last night's words,
On the world's anvil where a veiled lamp shone.

The Broken Sea

for my Godchild, Danielle Dufau-Labeyrie,
born in Paris, May 1940

I

I trace old history back
To innocent Blake; a knife
Cuts in the cruel wrack
Pictures for waking life.

Where sea-mass on sea-mass hurl
Their merciless strength on the rocks,
The trough, the harrow of stars
Yoked to a sacred ox
Bursts into filigree,
A cold, a moon-struck place
Shaping the grace of a girl
Born of the broken sea.

And calm above disasters
In the confused wake
Of pitiless history
I see the visions of Blake
In their self-bridled power.
Upon the regenerate sea

Among the great Masters
He measured the passing hour.

Your father and mother came
While you were then
Without a form or name,
Daughter of men.

Your father and mother passed
The pictures by,
And the sea's resurrection-blast
Gave back a sigh.

I can see the selfsame day.
She sank to Earth's darkness, kissed,
Tired from that vision, in spray,
From which all lives exist.

2

O weight, O the weight of birth!
O the plunging (silent the answer)
O the plunging (silent the answer)
O the plunging weight of birth!

Between two sirens shaking
The immense, white, memory-crowded, sleeping capital:
Villainous print at a lamp-post,
A long shaft of moonlight,
And the people that walked in darkness crossing the firth
Of sleep and waking, moving in ghostly ritual,
Coming, coming and gone,
Their eyes meeting
A moment, spirits by birth
Wronged, their eyes like keen knives drawn
By chance, death-cheating
Between Notre-Dame and the Sorbonne,
Caught in the draught of lives
Upon the tide of sleepers moving;
A city,
Fishes before dawn
Gasping at the white light,
Perishing in a moment, in a night,
A wave running over the Earth.

'Put out the lamps! Put out
The lamps!' (silent the answer)
The shroud descending
Over the singular lives at corners found
In alleys never-ending,
Found in the deeper dark
Beneath the tapers their great dead befriending,
Found through wired bunks, fire-drowned confusion of the
    founder ark,
The restive weariness and writhing cramps
Of sleepers underground.

O the plunging lamps of death!
O gargoyles of history beckoning!
O people moving beneath!
O birth, O gentle awakening!
O the plunging lamps of death!

3

A cradle in darkness, white.
It must be heavenly. Light
Must stream from it, that white sheet
A pavilion of wonder; meteors; thunderbolts hurled
From clouds; coil upon coil of spiral flame.
The nocturnal flight of the breath, and the ear as still
As a listening shell
Lost in the crystalline heaven; the faint-heard beat
Of life; then a million rainbows caught in the frame
Of parted lashes, lashes closing again
In a darkness of moving threads, the immaculate cradle
Rocked by spirits moving under the world.

Scattered, forgotten, among these waters, this white
Illumination, what story, old as the wrinkled sea,
Brought you, a girl, to birth, in the hour that blackened my
    lamp-stalk
Cloaked on the table, bursting with terrors to be?

Like a book that is washed away, like a scrawled page blown
By stains of the salt-green tides, then left to dry in the sun,
They appear, the unsung, the moving, the lost, the imperfect, the
    met, the known;
All are known patterns to all, yet no other to one.

Cry, where the deathly waters like cymbals meet,
Cry to the deafened Sibyl that the rock above you stands,
Changing the quilt of light to the shroud at your feet;
The pivot of light is hidden, yet walks in your hands.

4

I see a font, and I feel the weight of the petal
Of your little body scatter the rings of the years.
I see the shadow of the arc of the pillars and massy metal
Shrink from the shudder of your limbs, the springs of your tears.

And whoever moves away is still held back
By miraculous water. Your life shines under the fold of the wave.
The taper is burning. Beneath it the robes are black.
I hear the footsteps recede through the colours of night in the nave.
O the plunging lamps of death!

Who is alive in the beam?
Who is alive in the beam?
Awake in the dead of night,
Alive in a night that is dead,
They hear, on the stones of dream,
Walking with a masked light,
Fate with an animal's tread,
Under the moonlit gable,
Under the untolled bell,
The faltering, racing colours, ermine and sable,
Running on treacherous feet;
A thread in the dark, a thread
Under the parapet;
Rats inhabit the shell;
Vapours, crumbling sighs;
And among the buildings' bread
Of stone, the entangled rubble
Of stone and ironwork gleaming,
Crippled fears forewarning
The dawn of innocent light,
Leaning walls foredreaming
Convulsion; then through stubble
Animal black and white;
Tracks interpreting dread,
Black moving on white,
Columns of night and morning
Read by grief-struck eyes;

And the light was masked, they saw but a step ahead.
Black the people in their crowds,
Words unspoken, none was said.
Silence came and silence fled.
White the buildings overhead;
They heard the planes above the clouds:
The entombed living and the walking dead
Catapulted the shrouds, the singed-black shrouds
On Death's deathbed.

There brooding darkness, here a pyre of flame;
The burning of an age.
Works of intricate desire,
The splendour and remorse, the greed and shame
Of tottering Babylon
Flying out golden to the fount of language,
Intense white breath, darkness of passions gone,
And on each page
A number and a name!

The dead, in medieval tombs inurned,
Unfathering worlds beneath the vizor's teeth,
Gargoyle above and sleeping dog beneath,
Forever lost, as Milton said,
Behind the adamantine gate,
Cared not how high the city burned,
For all roads led
From that blue firmament's blinding stream
And every blessed dream
Into the furnace of their fate,
Being torn about with flame,
Themselves too late
To change their nature through the priceless Bread.

Who knows the Furies of the Devourer?
Who knows the lightnings meted and withdrawn
When anger crosses the heavens?
Job measured the dawn;
Elijah was fed by ravens.
Their graves were tended by
The mighty element.
Wheels, wheels of terror
Scream with the suffocated scream of blood.
The obliterated peoples and their little cry

Bind nothing to their shroud.
The flat event
Blots out the great archangel and the cloud.

5

Think by the pounding waves what sudden foam
Gives light to the full moon.
I stand upon the beach and watch them where they come,
Imagining that soon
The tide, heavy with lives, its swords and ships will cast
Out on the shivering silence, and yield up the Past.

Still, still the moon pulls on the waves which magnify
Their lunatic insistence,
Ending by force resistance
To her tumultuous error in the sky.
I see you stir and wake, out of this desolation,
Then, on one leap of faith, I hold a measured nation.

What night engendered day?
What gifts are the dead bringing,
Gifts of joy unmixed?
She the raid killed
Stands in those eyes revealed.
She shadows the lightest singing
Of children at play.
Their indifference to her soul I take for text.
On a cloud my eyes are fixed,
Or a child going her way.

6

Wrenched from the accident,
Plucked from his breast,
The secret none had guessed
In a drop of blood, one drop,
Is spoken plain,
As though man moved in pure element, all time
come to a stop.

Look long upon that stain:
What cannot be said in words,
What cannot be understood
By discs, or coloured flags, or the rings of birds,
Is uttered there in blood:
There is no second country mapped by the stain of blood.

7

In the blood-track of nightmare,
Written with the five last breaths,
Such letters in my sleep I found,
Such fragmentary letters which, if mended,
Might make the eyes of mummies stare;
The folded hands, the fingers bound
Still touching ancient faiths
Yet lived, like goldfish under ice.
I watched, and there, in flame and sound,
Held in the parchment vice,
I saw the fire from which the tongues descended.

I called the witnessing sea; wave on wave replied:
'What should I confess, forbid, or hide?'
World-confusion sent shudders through my brain;
So I fixed my eye on a single death.
Then the abstract countries feared the solid stain
Where the hand was closed on a planet's path.

8

I make you pictures of a woman who died
Unnatural death,
That you may see a country birth betrayed.
She that rose white from spray and had such pride

Forgot the wilderness
From which perfection comes;
Beauty of the sepulchre outruns the foam's,
All breath transfigured by a breathless shade.

And pictures of a man whose blood was thrown
Near the dumbfounded spot,
To prove a lie proud men erect in stone.

What can the wounds' black oracle make known?
Look back, and you shall see the town of Lot.
His country and her country are my own,
Though the waves foam, and cry that they are not.

9

My lamp that was lit every night has burnt a hole in the shade.
A seawave plunges. Listen. Below me crashes the bay.
The rushing greedy water smothers the talk of the spade.
Now, on the sixth of November, I remember the tenth of May.

I was going to fly to your christening to give you a cup.
Here, like Andersen's tailor, I weave the invisible thread.
The burnt-out clock of St. Mary's has come to a stop,
And the hand still points to the figure that beckons the house-stoned
 dead.

Child Shades of my ignorant darkness, I mourn that moment alive
Near the glow-lamped Eumenides' house, overlooking the ships in
 flight,
Where Pearl White focussed our childhood, near the foot of
 Cwmdonkin Drive,
To a figment of crime stampeding in the posters' wind-blown blight.

I regret the broken Past, its prompt and punctilious cares,
All the villainies of the fire-and-brimstone-visited town.
I miss the painter of limbo at the top of the fragrant stairs,
The extravagant hero of night, his iconoclastic frown.

Through the criminal thumb-prints of soot, in the swaddling-bands of
 a shroud,
I pace the familiar street, and the wall repeats my pace,
Alone in the blown-up city, lost in a bird-voiced crowd
Murdered where shattering breakers at your pillow's head leave lace.

For death has burst upon you, yet your light-flooded eyes do not
 tremble
Where pictures for waking life stand in the spray's wild bead.
You are guarded, shrined in the torrent, fast-locked in the cave of the
 Sibyl,
In that terrifying delay of the waters' magical speed.

Asleep to-night in Paris, not knowing I walk your world,
You are deaf to the schoolyard's voices, where, escaped, the children
 meet,
The world of a child's one town, renascent, in rage unfurled
Between Cwmdonkin railing and black-faced Inkerman Street.

Waves, hooded, raging, thunder, hiding contagious guilt,
Tossing, high on the shale, the hard and scribbled stones.
An anchor's dirge is buried under the waters' quilt.
Dazzling sunbeams have hidden the hook and the barnacled bones.

O indifferent grains of sand, O mother-of-pearl of the shell,
I hear the inconstant water, the blind, the wandering one.
The groan of Sophocles, and the groan of the leper's bell
Burst on annihilation: through your window breaks the sun.

I hear the breath of the storm. The engulfed, Gargantuan tide
Heaped in hills by the moles, hurls to the mountain's head
The streets of sunrise. O windows burning on Townhill side,
O light of annunciation, unearthing the unknown dead!

10

Beside the magnificent, quiet, sinister, terrible sea
I hear the pebbles grieve, that eternal Genesis
In the light and stupefaction of foam, where the great white horses flee,
Delirious clutches at sunbeams, delivered of life too soon,
For which your mother does penance, caught in the tumult of peace,
Inhabiting, a rock-bird torn with cymbals, the silence above the moon.

11

You were born when memory was shattered,
Gathered through darkness on a kiss,
Breath dividing and the dry bones scattered:
Waves upon the shore, remember this.

You were born when one who left the serried,
Sheltered ones, ran here shelterless.
You were born when Manselton was buried:
Waves upon the shore, remember this.

I have marked the footprint where she married
Midnight. Aldebaran is
Darker than the brilliance she has buried:
Waves upon the shore, remember this.

12

Crescent she moves,
The cradle of cities,
Kris of their silence:
Now she is high.

Do not insult
The movement of ages
Outrun by the moment
Which is their nature.

She of cold pities
Flies from the sages,
Keeping her love
But for no creature.

Let the fierce fault
Draw the wild vulture.
Search the unending
Looms of the sky.

Cruel, the sea
Is the child of the frailest.
Frenzied, the sea
Has neglected no sigh.

Pulling, pulling the flood,
She applauds, being so bright,
The ritual of blood,
Delusions of the anchored night.

Coldly the moon shines
Never companioning the bone,
Drawing the seawave she refines,
Making that cold edge keen with stone.

Death she may not bring
Down to us who have known
That is an alien thing;
Yet I see in the skies
The betrayal of scornful eyes:
The country of pride would turn the living country to stone.

13

In the wrack of miracle,
In the seawave's plunging spring,
Set your ear to the shell,
Your eyes on that starlike thing
That out of darkness fell;
But do not question again
What words came out of the flood.
Imagine a broken wing
Sweeping to rivers, to Saxony's home, fresh valleys, the
trees in bud.

All that we love is vain,
Vain the beautiful sea,
Until it has cast away
The broken wonder of spray:
That wonder is held a moment, and in that wonder, she.

There fell through darkness a wing
Surging through bright air,
Torn, terrifying,
Lost in the sea-wrack there.
Touch the white edge of the foam,
Identify your despair;
Still the gold threads will come
From light, we know not where.
Break the bubble's dome;
That touch will make you aware
Of death, will laugh at your trouble and comb
Threads of the living hair.

14

The joy of the air is he,
The strength of light is he,
On his own arm he has fallen,
Compelled by sacrifice
To a beauty cold as ice;
He has torn out eyes and tongue
In lust for a hidden Helen,
Because they would not confess
Where they kept the jealous key
To his inaccessible Troy.
That heroic tenderness,
The reckless love of the young,
Captivates every boy.
Know now the dangerous one
True, a hawk in the sun.
O he himself is sung
By death; he has gained his joy.
The rush of broken wings
Deafens the sacred springs;
The sheet of light he nears,
And the memory of these,
The desecration of seas,
Crashes about his ears,
Heaping wrong upon wrong.
Then prance the imagined, white-light horses, where seawaves
shudder, a gong.

15

O what a way we have come
To find a hero's tomb,
And still the patterns deceive us;
Vases of Greece and of Rome
Unweave our nature and weave us
A joy that cannot be named.
What country from love's loom
Breaks into blossoming joy?
Some name it Zion, some
Patmos, the sacred throne.
I know that country at last:
For blood it must not be famed.
There is one blood, and one
Being. Whoever cast
Scorn on a man, has thrown
Truth out, and an idol acclaimed.
The country of pride would turn the living country to stone.

A cry, a shout:
Who ran about
The place I tread?
What runs into my head
From that blind wall?
Noises overhead:
'Jericho must fall'.
Pavings of the dead,
The pavings' trumpet overhead
Blazed; light shone.
But who was it ran out?
What blind threads run
From a gathered shawl?
Compassed by the fold,
The engendering hand,
More than death can hold,
Multiplied a thousandfold
Shook; light blazed.
On her death I gazed
Where those mourners stand.

Why is night afraid,
Petrified with dread?
Fire of that extreme
Anguish, and that force,

Glitters on its course.
A man struck by a stream
Of bullets, and brought down
To the burning town;
A woman death betrayed;
What more is to be said?
'A plane shot down in the raid;
Two of a million dead.'

If you bent your head
Where the two had lain,
Whose death, what stain
And from what country
Would bring to mind again
The seawave's entry?
Better speak it plain:
What stone sentry
Could, if peace were said,
Justify the pall?
Honour to the dead
Shaming these and all,
Did it praise a race,
Would defile this place.

Ah, two cities near!
Keep them not apart.
Living jealousy
Preys not on them here,
Since through heresy
They have but one heart.

Who will say of him he has glorified his land
Who, in a death so splendid,
Surpassing what the sages planned,
Defended love, and his own kind defended?
I can imagine this, imagine all:
We know all truths in Nature when we touch a pall.

16

Maybe from man's first breath
Love was confused with pride.
Shelley heard schoolboys play.
He had looked for a faithful wreath,
But found that war-god's bride
Born of tempestuous spray.

The clash of man with man,
Noise of that wrangling yard,
Haunted his active brain.
Ever since time began
The hero's birth was marred
By ecstasy's fallen stain.
The beautiful son cast forth
Is commanded by the thighs
To fall upon lesser men,
To straddle the dancing froth,
Pledged to her downcast eyes
Where the fountain breaks in rain.
Seeing the iron-hot, fast
Blood which never abates
Till the true life is cast
Back to the primary Fates,
Shaken by that stain,
Drenched with the heat of death,
Prophetic Owen knew
He had not toiled in vain
To kill the heroic myth.
The blossom blossoms anew:
Man breaks from his own death.

Who will count in later time the pities of the sea?
You, maybe, will count them, holding the sun like a flower.
Then the suddenness of the moment will appal you
That can bring so many miseries, sun-starred, from that white dress.

17

O light on the waking lips,
O break of day:
While Earth, ringed with aether, slips
Out of the Milky Way
Into abounding space,
O first and last place,
O drop in the waters' play
Forgotten, remembered by God, sustained by slipping
away!

Why do waves rage?
O why do terrible seas
Clamour, cry out again?

Ah, the surpassing peace
Belongs to desperate men.

True in a faithless age,
They heard the waters trace
Error. They did not turn
But kept their dazzling praise;
They heal us from an urn.

Because they dared to pledge
Against the edge of the waves
Belief, their work is prayer.
Though many outcast were,
Torn with sufferings, care,
Though madness did not spare,
It is their cry that saves.

Passion withheld—what power!
And O, the unrevealed
Is purer than the flower
Waving in the field.

For this, darling, trust
Colour, light and air,
But O, more deeply, the dust,
The parchments hidden there.

No time, if you honour those,
Can spoil your maidenhead.
Gather your life's fresh rose
And cast it to the dead,
That all the ages stand
Dumbfounded in that place,
Love run to time's last sand,
And the light meet the face.

18

I praise the counterpoint
To your tender light of dawn,
A lamp nightly lit
Till it burnt a hole in the shade.
The curtain is half-drawn.
I imagine the coverlet.
Not one skeleton-joint
In the wings of thought shall fade.

I call the corruptible,
I beckon them to this place.
My fist embraces Hell,
And the cities of my hand
Have lepers' tales to tell.
The light on your pillow's lace
Has come from stormy seas.
The moment to which you wake
Was drawn from terrible sand.
Graves beneath you shake.
The groan of Sophocles
And the groan of the leper's bell,
Each one I embrace,
I accept, impoverished, these.
They have left no words to spell
Joy for an orphaned race,
To-morrow's parable;
Yet I pray on my knees
That the light meet the face.

Infinitely that arm
For which all crimes are crimes
Shields you from the storm,
Protects your growing limbs.
Love makes you, though life cease,
The suckling of her peace:
Light is satisfied there.
Words of the truthful say
What your silence says.
Light, where your fingers play,
Flies, fulfilled in air.
Leaf and fruit will share
The stillness you obey,
Grief, ultimate praise,
Words the tombs laid bare,
Words for the break of day.

19

Born in a wailing time,
Cradled by the beam
Groping above and across
A hanging, menaced house,
Born in the topmost room

With a hundred stairs to climb,
Under the silver ships
Intercepted by
The searchlights' travelling rays;
After one siren, warning
Spirits that they will die,
When in the dark eclipse
Souls numbered their days
Between night and morning,
Between the pathless flare
Of blood and hanging flame
Cleaving to murderous air
(Christmas candles named)
And the siren closing the path,
Shroud-rush of the doomed breath,
A cry out of darkness came,
A cry of praise above death,
Your mother's bearing cry.

Quickly, fallen from light,
Fingers laid you on
A pillow bordered with lace,
Asleep under whirling night,
There breathing under the race
Of numberless centuries gone.

Now, that time forgot
In threads of a woollen ball,
You have taken, for better, for worse,
The doll and the universe
To your darkness, and in the shawl
I imagine your waking cot.

Under the eyelashes
Dawn is taking shape,
Inaccessibly white.
You are held by a magic light,
Light like the bloom of the grape
Or the greatest distances.
Wandering the hills of Wales,
Taliesin from the tombs
Treading miraculous grass
From the unknown village comes
Blessing the mountain-pass
In a light piercing like nails.

Dante, who lifts the form
Of man till he bears the stars,
Stands in the trembling beam;
And the great interpreters
Of lyric judgment come,
Compelled by that one theme.

I call Hans Andersen
To lay his book on your bed
Alive with pictured tales,
And to people the patchwork thread
With childhood's travelling men
As true as the house of snails.

Blake from the clouds I call,
Who cried to accusing night:
'All is infinite, all!'
And again, from chaos wild:
'The soul of sweet delight
Can never be defiled.'

Holy witnesses
Of your wondering, waking eyes,
In the stone-struck flash of peace
They seek you darkly out
Asleep like sparkling trout
Under the kingfisher skies.

Caught in the starry course,
They gather your moving dreams
To the sacred river of light;
But I, still under their night,
I lean to the stone-stopped source
And the little pagan streams.

20

Now that the years draw in
All deaths to a single mind,
The sweet adventure of dawn,
The words of Hoelderlin,
And the vision he divined
Of Greece, the Christian dawn,
Of Patmos, islands, hills
Proclaiming Christ aloud
Through all that Nature wills,

The work that he always signed,
Words secret and proud,
Like a lion, like a fawn,
Uniting the gentle and strong,
Though half his life was undone
By a bitter shaft and blind;
Though dust, his black words move
The stars that did him wrong
To his individual love,
The purity of his song.
Fixing his eyes upon
The stillness of aether, he
Man's nature lost and found.
The water leaps on the stone,
It follows its path to the sea,
But never forgets that sound.

And true to the tender ground
On which the sufferer lies,
A voice simple, profound,
To dry tears from all eyes,
Annihilating time
With an intellectual blade,
Piercing the inmost shade
Of Sophoclean death
With deeper meanings crowned,
One of the Cherubim
For truth is its own reward,
More strong than the strongest myth,
World-moving Kierkegaard
Learnt from the Holy Child
The single, abounding love
Whose fidelity shakes the spheres.

Love has drowned the skies.
O brighter than waking eyes,
That splendour, into dust spilled.
Sleep on, that you may move
Through the land their sorrows tilled
To gain love's timeless state,
I have thought to celebrate
The truth no man beheld,
Truth that abides in tears.

Treading the colours now
From a source unknown and sweet,
Treading with printless feet
Grass, and the sleeping buds
That have not burst from the bough
Dove-carried across these years,
You stir. Bright flashes the flood's
Rainbow, alights on day.
You wake to the sun of May.
You wake, and great recollection trembles away.

The Lady With The Unicorn

1948

Music of Colours: White Blossom

White blossom, white, white shell; the Nazarene
Walking in the ear; white touched by souls
Who know the music by which white is seen,
Blinding white, from strings and aureoles,
Until that is not white, seen at the two poles,
Nor white the Scythian hills, nor Marlowe's queen.

The spray looked white until this snowfall.
Now the foam is grey, the wave is dull.
Call nothing white again, we were deceived.
The flood of Noah dies, the rainbow is lived.
Yet from the deluge of illusions an unknown colour is saved.

White must die black, to be born white again
From the womb of sounds, the inscrutable grain,
From the crushed, dark fibre, breaking in pain.

The bud of the apple is already forming there.
The cherry-bud, too, is firm, and behind it the pear
Conspires with the racing cloud. I shall not look.
The rainbow is diving through the wide-open book
Past the rustling paper of birch, the sorceries of bark.

Buds in April, on the waiting branch,
Starrily opening, light raindrops drench,
Swinging from world to world when starlings sweep,
Where they alight in air, are white asleep.
They will not break, not break, until you say
White is not white again, nor may may.

White flowers die soonest, die into that chaste
Bride-bed of the moon, their lives laid waste.
Lilies of Solomon, taken by the gust,
Sigh, make way. And the dark forest
Haunts the lowly crib near Solomon's dust,
Rocked to the end of majesty, warmed by the low beast,
Locked in the liberty of his tremendous rest.

If there is white, or has been white, it must have been
When His eyes looked down and made the leper clean.
White will not be, apart, though the trees try
Spirals of blossom, their green conspiracy.
She who touched His garment saw no white tree.

Lovers speak of Venus, and the white doves,
Jubilant, the white girl, myth's whiteness, Jove's,
Of Leda, the swan, whitest of his loves.
Lust imagines him, web-footed Jupiter, great down
Of thundering light; love's yearning pulls him down
On the white swan-breast, the magical lawn,
Involved in plumage, mastered by the veins of dawn.

In the churchyard the yew is neither green nor black.
I know nothing of Earth or colour until I know I lack
Original white, by which the ravishing bird looks wan.
The mound of dust is nearer, white of mute dust that dies
In the soundfall's great light, the music in the eyes,
Transfiguring whiteness into shadows gone,
Utterly secret. I know you, black swan.

First Joy

First joy through eye and limb
Shoots upward. Groundroots drive
Through shadow and crust a sheath.
I praise God with my breath
As hares leap, fishes swim,
And bees bring honey to the hive.

The yew shuts out that sky
And the dumbfounded well
Hides within its stone
The colours' trance; they shone
Pure, but the stones give cry
Answering what no colours spell.

First joy that sinks in the well
Falters to renew,
Slipping through listening hands
And lips of stone, where stands
Green Neptune, voice and veil
Uncoil from sleep the mysteries of the yew.

On the sands, children pick
Bright shells, who, stooping, know
Nothing of Earth's white dead;
They run with graceful thread

Of light, and are made quick
By earlier streams that sweetlier flow.

Darkness divines great light.
Forced from what no child knows
Passionate joy springs up
Where death has choked the cup;
Even where blind fingers write,
Even where the gravestone's single flower blows.

Returning to Goleufryn

Returning to my grandfather's house, after this exile
From the coracle-river, long left with a coin to be good,
Returning with husks of those venturing ears for food
To lovely Carmarthen, I touch and remember the turnstile
Of this death-bound river. Fresh grass. Here I find that crown
In the shadow of dripping river-wood; then look up to the burning mile
Of windows. It is Goleufryn, the house on the hill;
And picking a child's path in a turn of the Towy I meet the prodigal town.

Sing, little house, clap hands: shut, like a book of the Psalms,
On the leaves and pressed flowers of a journey. All is sunny
In the garden behind you. The soil is alive with blind-petalled blooms
Plundered by bees. Gooseberries and currants are gay
With tranquil, unsettled light. Breathless light begging alms
Of the breathing grasses bent over the river of tombs
Flashes. A salmon has swallowed the tribute-money
Of the path. On the farther bank I see ragged urchins play

With thread and pin. O lead me that I may drown
In those earlier cobbles, reflected; a street that is strewn with palms,
Rustling with blouses and velvet. Yet I alone
By the light in the sunflower deepening, here stand, my eyes cast down
To the footprint of accusations, and hear the faint, leavening
Music of first Welsh words; that gust of plumes
'They shall mount up like eagles', dark-throated assumes,
Cold-sunned, low thunder and gentleness of the authentic Throne.

Yet now I am lost, lost in the water-wound looms
Where brief, square windows break on a garden's decay.
Gold butter is shining, the tablecloth speckled with crumbs.
The kettle throbs. In the calendar harvest is shown,

Standing in sheaves. Which way would I do you wrong?
Low, crumbling doorway of the infirm to the mansions of evening,
And poor, shrunken furrow where the potatoes are sown,
I shall not unnumber one soul I have stood with and known
To regain your stars struck by horses, your sons of God breaking in song.

Money for the Market

Stop where time flies, Earth-winged mortal.
Discern
Where the river flows through the streamers of gipsies and wheels of the fair,
One whose step is dead, yet alive like a child in the fern
Motionless, stunned in the movement of nature, watching a hare.

Winged with Earth, all seasons, sunlight and snow,
Pause, a last leper, a scarecrow, past whom races the flood
Of trees and astounded fields, rivers, clouds, hills and birds that throw
Casting shadows; pull them until through the eye of a needle they go
And assemble with sparkling insects, with cattle chewing the cud.

Money for the market, or barren-birth: which is it? Where
From the clarion-brass of the greedy pursuit does your intimate shadow tend?
What child moves the world who plucks a stray stem whose seeds gravely moving in air
Bring your birth on this path to a silence, the dust of your path to an end?
What is it at once persuades you, true Earth has nothing to spend?

Is it he, watching, who hears
The flow of people, who knows the calamitous drift of their luck?
Is it he, listening, who sees the defacers of life, the maimers of years
Cross the place of two lives, trapping underground mules where a shying foal disappears,
Beautiful pit-blind pony leading a truck?

Stop quite still. A dropped coin spins the world round.
The blind see this river. Yet Midas moves down to the wicked coined light he must keep.
We are rich in the shadow of forfeit. Gain is loss. The lost is the found.
Giving is taking, deep-drawn; sleep is waking and waking is sleep.

Is there a happy town,
A table worth loving not pitched on the jubilant shambles of loss?

In the prodigal height of a barn the straws wander where they are blown.
The beams there rejoice, full of songs till the swallows have flown
Who hide their long wings in the gables grown green with slow moss.

What townsman returning, O who in pride would confess
To have paid his way through the ribboned world? Would not here
Creation rebuke the blind, gaining feet, mossed lanes, starred celandines
 press,
Who paid so much to the calendars, never to this lost year?
What fisherman would not mutter: 'I left them, like lives: they are here.'

I, too, return, Goldengrove. My hook is caught in the trees.
I cast with golden-eyed jackdaws for bait, and a great fish pulls at my gut.
Birds that have flown from a breath's gold bible resting on aged knees
Carry the world in their wings. In their gust, in a breath I am looking for
 gooseberries,
Going in by the glint of a coin through a low door, twenty years shut.

Alone with a lucky farthing,
I drop the engraved, disinherited coin that another picks up.
Then I enter the steep prison-walls of salmon-circled Carmarthen,
Near the market, stocked with gay produce, hung with teapot and cup.

O leaning, tickling time's future from lazy, trout-hiding streams
Where a ladybird flies in the sun,
Deep in grass, deep in grass, I am hidden. Every thread of the river has
 themes.
Fingers stir the steep waters that circling divulge their lost secret of
 names.
Light is shot from their blaze-annulled movement to cobbles where
 castaways run.

Joy leaps in reversal's great splash,
Dome of music transformed to a coracle, overturned by the cast of a fly.
The world is weighed by each ripple. Dante's Vision is lost in a flash
Where a sow has unpeopled Inferno and looks for a sty.
Look. Look. My steep devils are foundering. Still, the forgetter is I.

O scroll on the magical water, lost like a fish's law,
Money for the market is manna that tumbles down;
And the miracle of fishes strips heaven with the colours of stubble, of
 straw,
Of a basket woven by the blind in the eye of the jackdaw,
Unfound till the world-moving pebbles are cast, world-stilled where
 other worlds drown.

Llewelyn's Chariot

Sun of all suns, seed of dandelion seeds,
Sprung from the stem of delight and the starry course,
High at the helm of night, in the van of deeds,
A one-wheeled carriage you drive and a headless horse.
Your Maker makes you his glory, you grasp and push
Through bars the bugle, the mirror, the string of beads,
The doll and the wooden men; with a mighty wish
You ride the brunt of creation's galloping beds.

What golden fleece enshrines at the very prow
Your marvelling head, and summons from ancient seas
Sailors toiling, under the black sea-crow,
What ever-moving, miraculous, wind-faint fleece;
But you kick those puppets, those men of deeds, through the bars,
The tossed men lost, the lost men under the ark,
Seed of spray's seed, swept from the flight of the stars
To a point of light in your look that is almost dark.

Rameses, trumpet and chariot, all you outrun
Grasping your cage where grief is banished for good,
Created nothing, timeless, perpetual one
Dropped from light-years to crawl under legs of wood,
Star-seed, breath-downed, dropped from the topmost sun
To the toppling house near the shed that shadows a hearse,
From whirling, luminous night, to sleep here alone
In the darkness a great light leaves, where a feather stirs.

And I, your listener, stopped on the stairway of breath,
Awake, in the stranger's bed, in the cold, high room,
Calling the sea from Leviathan hollows of earth,
I watch them, castaway toys, while you drive and boom
Your course in the cot to my bed, with the speed of ice,
The giant mirror, the trumpet ringed with a bell,
Till naked you stand, gold-fleeced, shaping, a shell,
All seas to your colour, Llewelyn, child above price.

A Child's Birthday

January, your month,
When sparrows beg for crumbs

Flying to the low suns
Of windows that are kept closed;

They hop again; this day becomes
More fragile through the grimace
Of frost. A child's two thumbs
Press glass, through crystal days
And hushed, windless snows
Seek ancestry, soon lost
In the sun's golden gaze
And lacework of frost.

What sun is there? What race
Of song, caught in the looms
Of flowers? I was doing sums,
Reading in ancient tombs.
Song's ancestry I trace.
I am wrong again; it is yours,
This day and all its hours,
Not, as I supposed,
The property of a ghost,
But to light your Winter-born face.

The Fire in the Snow

White lambs leap. Through miles of snow
Across the muffled fields you go,
Frost-furled and gazing deep,
Lost in a world where white lambs leap.

Into a million eyes of light
You look, beneath that mask of white
Where lambs, wrinkled, without sound,
Bound in the air and print the ground.

You find through crystals white and wet
The buried breath of the violet,
And lost near sunken cairns of stone
Drone-suckled flowers that breed alone.

Your shadow, black on the white snow-field,
Covers the blades your mind revealed.
You linger where grey rocks are still
Covered by a drifted hill.

Your eyes, I know, now read the tract
Beneath snow, where the grain lies packed,
Nor can the Winter sun deceive:
Black shuttles give you their leaves to weave.

Crisp, where you touch the secret loom,
Snow, from the fire-blue sky and from
A black root where all leaves begin,
Flames with a white light on your skin.

Come in. The brilliant, beautiful
Sun has dropped, and the noon-cracked pool
Freezes back. Come, seek from night
Gloom's fire, where the unlit room is white.

I wait, intent, by the firelit stones
Strewn with chopped wood and fallen cones.
Come in, and watch with me in dark
The red spark eating the black bark.

Bright, from fields where the snow lies thick,
From sunk fields to the latch's click
You come; and your eyes, most watchful, glow,
Seeing in the firelight the brightness of snow.

The Coots

A common thief
On the pond of light,
Black as soot
With forehead white,
He carries that loot
Of twig and leaf
To the floating nest;
And in my belief
He would not rest
In his bold advance
Though his path were stoned
By boys who stare
As the dancing foliage
Hides him there;
Such is his trance,
Older than they,

Old as the age
Of stream, or day,
Or the spindled air,
As he stretches space
To the space beyond
And now arrives
Where lilies root
In the drifting pond.
There, in that place,
At the pulse of lives,
At the heart of the rings
And hub of toil,
That other coot,
His mate, is throned.
And he cannot wait
While she leans out
To receive his spoil
With critical eye
And placid wings
That express no doubt
As to why he chose it;
But swims back straight,
Nor sees her dispose it
To let it dry.

The Peacocks

She pecks about in shells and flint,
Fearing the dangerous tail displayed.
Vibrating plumes behind her glint
With sacred eyes. His violence made
Her choose the hard and gritty ground,
The circumspection of her day;
A peahen, pausing on her round,
She hurries, yet has time to stay.
He follows her with giant tail
Eluded by her stone-chilled eye;
The stricken level of her jail
Reflects and apprehends his sky.
Her safety is the natural sun;
The natural earth supplies her needs;

Glimpsing her task and life as one,
She pecks for pods and sunflower-seeds.
Her lord, who hates her gift of sense,
Puts on new glory where she goes.
Her lack of interest makes him tense,
Until at last a splendour flows
Down the divine, contracting plumes,
And there, while she unearths a pod,
His hurricane of light consumes
All but the terror of her god.

Birthday Sleep

Sleep, these ancient hours,
While the reapers thresh.
Sleep, first of flowers,
Infant of this flesh:
The hills for you shall leap,
Winding rivers flash,
Jerusalem rejoice,
And the mountain-ash
Move above your sleep,
Move above your sleep.

Great the mystery stands
Over the dumb tree;
Gift of buried hands
Whom no eye can see
Yet the sages love,
Rest within her silk,
For the moving breast
Cannot give you milk
Till you hear the dove,
Till you hear the dove.

Then this giant weight,
Vessel of her womb,
Birth will dedicate
Falling through the loom
Near the reapers' sound,
Heaven and Earth in dance
Moving, as the babe

Leapt with radiance
And our life was found,
And our life was found,
Where knees touched the ground,
Where knees touched the ground.

Sardine-Fishers at Daybreak

Lifted on linen, I feel
In the full moon's white lake
Death in the wake of the keel,
Threads that strain and break
Before the breaking of day.
Noise knocked me awake,
Flight of the Milky Way,
Then hammering heels, a wake
Of heels on the cobbled town,
Clogs clattering down
To the harbour, a march of death,
Flight of the lives under breath,
From the shooting light, their race,
Pulled to the meeting-place,
Caught in short nets, they shun,
Gasping, the livid sun.

Snared sunbeams, flashing, show
A forest of masts, a fire
Of colour; and, mounting higher,
Tall rods that flicker and glow
Moored at Concarneau, where
A reflected clock tells time.
Rapier-like they climb
From the bright boats anchored there.
These wait for a priest to bless
Their going; and the folded sails,
Bound for the coast of Wales,
Point, in their idleness,
North, where sardine-boats dress
In nets near the Point each tree;
And octopus-dark below,
Where blood-red tunnies go,
Audierne, the silent sea.

Before dawn, hard to discern,
From the jetty, cold as a cairn,
Thumping with motors, go
Ships from Audierne,
And hang their nets low.
Slow from the grey quay, slow,
Without sails they pass.
Then three in a dinghy row
Out on the sea of glass.
One stands in the dinghy, seen
Flinging meal as to fowls.
The moon is white like a queen.
He gives a sign; and with owls'
Noiseless flight they steal
Back to the silent keel.

Flat, flat as a lake
Is the sea, silent, a wonder.
That silence who can break?
They are the silver under
Breath, and all shall die.
Rough hands take
Over the slippery, sly
Sides of the ship blue nets
Of fish that fall in a heap
On the deck, bright winding-sheets
Coiled in the wake of sleep.

Their touch no hand reveals
Through the strange, cold element
Until they fall in creels,
Killed by the daylight, spent.

Where three hundred ships meet,
Miles out at sea, a silent fleet,
Before light breaks, blue nets,
Gossamer, fine as lawn,
Are dropped from their threaded floats,
Dropped from the sardine-boats
By hands familiar with dawn.

From under the waking sea
Ascend the brilliant heads
Of sleep. Mysteriously
I watch them, caught in threads,

Tugged like a silver river,
Hauled by rough hands over
The burdened side of the ship,
Terrified, shuddering, shy
Incarnations of sky,
Hover, tumble down
To the sleek boards, wet and brown
Under a rust-brown sail.
They lie about rope and bale,
Flounder, splash, and are still,
Cast on a mounting hill.

Ah cold, where no two lives meet,
Light's fine needle quivers.
Under sea a white film hovers,
A caul whose haul discovers,
White as a winding-sheet,
Gasping in death, night's lovers,
Flight of hid stars. The sun
Is rising, rising. The sun
Is rising, waking from sleep.
Look, they sparkle and leap,
Vanishing, one by one.
With heaving force they are drawn
Over the spanned ship's sides
By hands grown old with the tides,
And dropped there, trophies of dawn,
Shaken, taken,
Frail, lit, forsaken,
Falling dead at my feet.

Sky is brightening while they are spent.
Four men are standing afresh
While one is crouching, bent.
The crew rip open the tent
Of light. With a knife they gash
The brilliant, awakened sheet.
They are shaking the silver fish.
Caught, I see them flash,
Fastened, glittering, steep
Into blue threads drawn
From darkness, wrung from sleep,
Falling in that bright heap,
Hung in the webs of dawn.

Swallows over the Weser

Dark in their dipping and rising the swallows fly over the Weser.
Here in the buttercups lying, we watch them, nor long to be wiser
Than day, but to fly like the swallows, to dip and to rise, were a deftness,
A daring, a language of movement, a gracefulness, something surpassing
Ecstasy. Keen the wild swallow can see the quick waters beneath her.
We through the buttercup-grasses can see the black star of her shadow
Scintillate now on the water and cut like a scythe through the grasses
Green in the sun. Here to lie, here to dream on the Summersoft meadow
Watching their wings in the sunlight, their wings that transfix the bright
 aether,
Diamondly flying, is lovely. Low diving, they skim where the branches
Of sycamore darken the river, jade leaves in a thunder-light glassing
With terror the marble-dark mover, caught up where the sun-dazzle
 blanches
Their underside shot on a wheel, revolution revealing each feather,
Then gone: O the dark and the fair one, the gloom and the glory, not
 either
Still for a moment! But we, lying back, see the flash and the damask,
Blue sash of their darting, their distance, then fragile, the far-away fleeces
And movement of wind-gathered clouds; so we watch them through
 goldcups that wither
Fly over the ferns of the weir, where the water like quicksilver ceases
Or burns in a dragonfly sailing, now lost in the light of the morning,
Touching with fingers this doom of the close thing eternally passing.

Ophelia

Stunned in the stone light, laid among the lilies,
Still in the green wave, graven in the reed-bed,
Lip-read by clouds in the language of the shallows,
Lie there, reflected.

Soft come the eddies, cold between your fingers.
Rippling through cresses, willow-trunk and reed-root,
Gropes the grey water; there the resting mayfly
Burns like an emerald.

Haunting the path, Laertes falls to Hamlet;
He, the young Dane, the mover of your mountains,
Sees the locked lids, your nunnery of sorrows,
Drowned in oblivion.

Silvered with dawn, the pattern of the bridge-vault
Dancing, a light-skein woven by the stream there,
Travels through shade the story of your dying,
Sweet-named Ophelia.

Dense was your last night, thick with stars unnumbered.
Bruised, the reeds parted. Under them the mud slipped,
Yielding. Scuttling and terrified, the moorhen
Left you to sink there.

Few, faint the petals carried on the surface,
Watched by those bright eyes ambushed under shadow,
Mouse, bird and insect, bore you witness, keeping
Pace ever silent.

Here, then, you lingered, late upon the world's rim,
Matched here the princelike, stopped, and were confounded,
Finding that image altered in the water's
Bitter remembrance.

Passion recalls the tumult of your story,
Midnight revives it, where your name is printed;
Yet from the water, intimate, there echoes:
'Tell this to no man'.

Bride-veils of mist fall, brilliant are the sunbeams,
Open the great leaves, all the birds are singing.
Still unawake in purity of darkness
Whiter than daylight

Dream the soft lids, the white, the deathly sleeping;
Closed are the lashes: day is there a legend.
Rise from the fair flesh, from the midnight water,
Child too soon buried.

Song

Do not tempt me from this sky
That yet seems to you a stone;
A hand, if on the dead it lie,
Shall put out the sun and moon.
There no envy more can come,
There the ambitious insect dies;
Secret is the written tomb;

There the moment's lifetime flies.
They who mourn here known the love
Nature is not worthy of.

Fidelity to the Dead

The withered leaf is blest, and the bird with shrunk claw in the shingle.
Under the shawl the life-yielding hand has caught the passionate thread.
Immortal silence transfigures them. O ultimate faith found single,
O light of intense meditation, from you the timid have fled.

Love steals from the fortunate man and gives to the heart it bereaves.
Dark thunders descend on Prometheus. A light over Earth is shed.
How, with love's great example, could I fear what the blind Fate weaves?
Love is fidelity to the unfortunate dead.

Fidelity to the Living

Tenuous life, I have wronged you. You are the leaves, the sun,
The light, the bird at peace in the sky, though pulled by a
plummet of lead.
Out of dark books I accused you. O look at her face: there is spun
A thread of light from her silence: she holds that beautiful thread.

The mother lifts her child to her breast. O what infinite, tender
Frailty! She laughs near his eyelids: O, above Solomon blest!
The great, magnanimous leaves have opened. Plucked from their
judgment in splendour,
Even now, by the very thread which binds them, they are at rest.

The Return of Spring

The Spring returns. Green valleys, the sparkling meadows
Crowd gold, under larks, wry-rooted, the gorse, deep-scented.
Lovely it is to live, to turn the eyes seaward,
To laugh with waves that outlive us.

And marvellously the sundering, receding seawaves
Pound the resounding sands; they knock at the hour-glass.

Thunder compels no man, yet a thought compels him,
Lost, neglected, yet tender.

Why in the wood, where already the new leaves mending
Winter's wild net, cast fragile, immature shadows,
Do I tread pure darkness, resisting that green dominion?
What is the thing more sacred?

Taut branches exude gold wax of the breaking buds.
Sweet finches sing. The stream has a hundred voices
Unheard before. One leans on the grass like a bridegroom,
And death slips under the bride-sleep.

Wait for no second Spring in Bishopston Valley.
Once, once only it breaks. If you plunge your fingers
In the stream, all secrets under the Earth grow articulate
In a moment, and for you only.

Diamonds of light, emeralds of leaves, green jewels:
For me the unnoticed, death-touching script is more passionate.
Cover the tome with dust; there dwells the redeemer,
Deathlessly known by the voice-fall.

O Spring, the box of colours, blue sky, green trees!
Has the brook ears? Donne has delivered his sermon.
Not easily you beguile the pulse, the footprint
Vaulted with intimate music.

Yet you return, bring beauty to Earth. I see
The skill and wonder you practise upon our eyes.
Break the veiled branches. Still, in the single leaf
It holds you, silken, a garland.

O returning child, not knowing why you were born,
Not understanding world's beauty the dead sustain,
The sharpness of colour, the clearness of water are yours;
The love there shadowed you know not.

What first I feared as a rite I love as a sacrament.
The Spring returns. I look. There is no dissembling.
The brook falters, runs on. I divine those meanings,
Listening to tongues that are silent.

Foal

Darkness is not dark, nor sunlight the light of the sun
But a double journey of insistent silver hooves.
Light wakes in the foal's blind eyes as lightning illuminates corn
With a rustle of fine-eared grass, where a starling shivers.

And whoever watches a foal sees two images,
Delicate, circling, born, the spirit with blind eyes leaping
And the left spirit, vanished, yet here, the vessel of ages
Clay-cold, blue, laid low by her great wide belly the hill.

See him break that circle, stooping to drink, to suck
His mother, vaulted with a beautiful hero's back
Arched under the singing mane,
Shaped to her shining, pricked into awareness
By the swinging dug, amazed by the movement of suns;
His blue fellow has run again down into grass,
And he slips from that mother to the boundless horizons of air,
Looking for that other, the foal no longer there.

But perhaps
In the darkness under the tufted thyme and downtrodden winds,
In the darkness under the violet's roots, in the darkness of the pitcher's
music,
In the uttermost darkness of a vase
There is still the print of fingers, the shadow of waters.
And under the dry, curled parchment of the soil there is always a little foal
Asleep.

So the whole morning he runs here, fulfilling the track
Of so many suns; vanishing the mole's way, moving
Into mole's mysteries under the zodiac,
Racing, stopping in the circle. Startled he stands
Dazzled, where darkness is green, where the sunlight is black,
While his mother, grazing, is moving away
From the lagging star of those stars, the unrisen wonder
In the path of the dead, fallen from the sun in her hooves,
And eluding the dead hands, begging him to play.

Rhossili*

Pushed out from the rocks, pushed far by old thought, long into night,
under starlight,
At last, tired from my coastal labouring, I come to you, sleepless Rhossili.
I have cut through the mirror-bright sea in the long, slender boat with two
paddles,
And ground in the sand. Dawn breaks. I stare, amazed, at the marvel.

Coiled sand, gold mountains, grass-tufted dunes, unending, rising,
descending,
And the cat-spotted, wind-crafty tide, spitting serpent-white tongues
drawn slack,
Soon reaching the barnacled wreck, quivering, recoiling, bending
Stung eyes to the rasping whisper of gongs, of songs that will not run
back.

Rhossili! Spindle of the moon! Turning-place of winds, end of Earth, and
of Gower!
Last one, shivering like a shell, cold with thought that is fiery and new!
A tent-pole. The cries of seabirds. And over our fingers the power
Of perplexing starlight, entangling our threads in the field soaked with
dew.

Worm's Head! The rock of Tiresias' eyes! From the world's very verge
I listen to the locked bell-ringers, the impetuous thunder and crash
Of the flying, flagellant waves, torn into two by the surge
From the strata of winkle-stuck rocks, and caverns where claw-mussels
flash.

Terrified, the nesting-birds mount as I climb. Mantles of fugitive blue
Drain blood, and the bull of the sea falls pierced in the spindrift dance.
Up from the mirror of the waters to the summit a seabird flew.
I creep to the verge of the pard-breathing tide. Cries turn round the
rock's turning lance.

Flat on my face I lie, near the needle around which the wide world spins.
Three eggs are balanced there, mottled in cushion-soft, quicksilver grass,
on the final rock.
Far out in the deep blue water the razorbills fish, and their skins
Dazzle, where they flutter blown wings drenched white, nor scatter, nor
break their flock.

* Pronounce Rhŏ-silly

I watch them like bright-winged ants, on the deep, unresting swell
Where they rise and fall, fly clear of the crest, or hover with sea-touching
wings.
High overhead wheel the herring-gulls, each with a plummet; they drop,
and a bell
Rocks in each bird, swung away by a thread, spun out from these
rock-rooted things.

Sheer down they rush at my head, crazy with fear for the loss
Of their locked, unawakened young, hidden in those brown shells
On a perilous ledge. They scream; and their wings divide and cross
In a shuddering shadow of piston-like bones, in a rain of farewells.

From the navel of rock, birth's pinnacle, the hovering wings hurled wide,
Flying out and ever returning to this unseen point of fear,
Watch witchcraft, the snakelike movement of the enchanted tide.
I reach to the razorbills' verge. My fingers clutch the rock spear.

Light screams: Look down at the mad, mazed frenzy of the destroying
moon!
Gasp at the cockle-sucked heaven! Tide-blown the castaways lie
Peeled to the parched and weary grains where the beaked ships spin and
are gone.
Blood-light on the wings of the sea! O the bull and the dragonfly!

The Sibyl keeps watch for Tiresias. In the dumb yet singing rock
The brother of light is dead, or sleeping, transfixed like a shell in a cleft,
In a thunder of floundering timbers, where pine-logs and rum-barrels
knock.
Sun-dazzled the book-leaves have opened; but only his vision is left.

Look! The sea-threads! Thought begins there! In a million rainbows!
The zenith
Stares at the long flat beach, no bend, no break in the dance
Of sandgrains and seawaves, drenched in gold spray, where the downs fly
on to Llangennith:
Dolphins, plunging from death into birth, you are held by the Sibyl's
trance!

The Feather

I stoop to gather a seabird's feather
Fallen on the beach,
Torn from a beautiful drifting wing;

What can I learn or teach,
Running my finger through the comb
And along the horny quill?
The body it was torn from
Gave out a cry so shrill,
Sailors looked from their white road
To see what help was there.
It dragged the winds to a drop of blood
Falling through drowned air,
Dropping from the sea-hawk's beak,
From frenzied talons sharp;
Now if the words they lost I speak
It must be to that harp
Under the strange, light-headed sea
That bears a straw of the nest.
Unless I make that melody,
How can the dead have rest?

Sheer from wide air to the wilderness
The victim fell, and lay;
The starlike bone is fathomless,
Lost among wind and spray.
This lonely, isolated thing
Trembles amid their sound.
I set my finger on the string
That spins the ages round.
But let it sleep, let it sleep
Where shell and stone are cast;
Its ecstasy the Furies keep,
For nothing here is past.
The perfect into night must fly;
On this the winds agree.
How could a blind rock satisfy
The hungers of the sea?

The Spoils of War

The world is weaned from this one dead by the thread of a shawl,
How little a pin
Unfastening the fold and fuse of light in Lucifer's fall;
The world is weaned from a point in the estuary of the grail,

This pin, this point over and under the Bristol Channel's wailing,
Piercing the sky carried in the breast, flung to the maniac grin
Of brains and shattered windows. A mad child sucks at her wall.

She sprang, luminous on a wish, to the trivial
Tread of her gallows-drop, reaching for a cushion for her child in the
shelter to sleep on,
Crossed her own tombstone, then all the stars ran in
And the world shot back like a ball;
Dropping from nowhere through a whirlwind of skies and eyes,
Casting the vesture and tidings of those calamities,
To a shrouded, most mute place, to her inmost call.

And the pavings, crying they were crossed, ring out
In a skipping-rope world of to-morrow's names and games,
That they were crossed, crossed, certainly crossed by the same,
Same feet. O gag those echoes down, lest the bloodstains shout.

Cover the crypt of her footprint, running from the sleepless, sheltered
one,
Pitched into light, under the wind and whine of bombs,
When the pavings flew up to the stars in a volley of tombs.
Night is burnt white in the dirt of a street in Manselton.

Many run past her, and five stoop over her, the faceless, breastless one,
The steeples unpinned from her holy shadow, in the dead position.
Wild weddings, peals of bells in their hard, hard eyes proclaim a
desertion.
Wounded to the death of Earth, she forgives those restless ones.
Divorced from her darling, O at last no ropes are rung.
Look on her face; mine eyes dazzle; she died young.

Unveiling the Statue

for a French friend, before the fall of France

I. GRIEF AT MECHANICAL DEATH

Friend, no temple is true
Built in another's eyes.
The Adam Angelo drew
Leaves in the burning skies
No ashes for hands to strew,
No place for memories.

But should that phoenix rise
From a crippled engine's fall,
Or should the outrageous seas
Drown you under their swell,
I grieve for the great disease
That turns a people pale.

I summon serene typhoons,
Earthquakes, storms of sand,
Glaciers calving like moons,
All plagues of the sea and land,
To still the eyes of pontoons
Dilated over the drowned.

But O, how forgive the small-drawn
Annihilators of faith,
In the holy skies of dawn
The bullet's tragic path
Breaking, where couplers spawn,
A man's short-circuited myth?

Lying quite still in the field,
At rest, on the sunny day,
With a book your hands half-held
And the words you met half-way,
Your pupils flash, fulfilled
With a faith no years can betray.

I imagine all visions, all
In your deep, world-filming eyes,
Murdered, blinded by gall.
Blinding vitriol flies,
O enters the pupil to kill
The sailing galaxies.

Are you the victim of
Those couplers, Venus and Mars,
Stretched, to serve their love,
Bound to the wheel of the stars?
Heaven's axle whirling above
Is plunged in the temple, the hero's.

Who laid the mechanical trap?
Necessity, not God.
Now on a mother's lap
Must the child pure milk had fed

Sucked from a sacred pap,
Renounce all imagined good.

'All things' and 'Nothing' become
Two fates you juggle with,
Balls that dance on a plume
Till a bullet snaps the myth;
But grief, grief is the sum,
Grief at mechanical death.

2. PRAYER FOR A REAL DEATH

Where order is all reversed death shrouds the breath love had nursed:
This knife of all-taking death that is all in a life,
This laughed-off shrapnel shattering the breastwork and vision, Christ's craft,
This guile of the small, momentous bullet smothered in a smile,
This splinter splicing breath short in the rain of a metal Winter,
This flowing of sound and shape to a mound unshaping, unknowing,
Show form in deformity growing,
The tree of life and the stalk of death in graft.

Infant, come down; O give me my real death that I may be washed in the font
For this death is a copper-smith's cloud, bombs' smoke, and a woman's deceit,
The street in a man passing over the man in the street.
Fetch nails and a hammer and wood of a sycamore-tree, storm-stayed,
To make good this last, lost boon machinery hastily made
For noble Adam, unmourned by these inattentive feet.

3. THE THREEFOLD SHIELD

Victory enters with drum and trumpet, pomp and panoply, dividing the wind with flags.
The defeated is prey to his monster, Andromeda chained to the crags.
Job in dust and ashes has a throne of bone and rags.

The hero has mounted his horse; he speaks to the unknown people, tramples the unknown hill.
Eyeless Gloucester stands at the place where men are beetles, where seabirds are shrill.
Dagon is god in Gaza, Samson a slave at the mill.

Fierce is the music, loud the shouting of Tamburlaine tearing the throats of kings.

Antigone sees her father; a great light Oedipus brings
Out of the trodden darkness; the mountain speaks through the springs.

4. TEARS

There the perfect pattern is
Though here these cruel cords are strung.
Above the moving mysteries
The fountain's everlasting song
Alters not a drop or breath;
Inviolate the music mocks
The groan of mutilated death
Broken on these mortal rocks,
Paradise of paradox
That terrified the virgin Thel
Alone in all the sunny flocks
Who saw where tears of pity fell.

5. THE URN

That the perceiver pause, his passion treasured in a searching eye,
I call from this dry place to the unfeeling urn whose figured eyelids
tremble,
That this cold statue to a man may laugh at its identity,
Marvelling how shedding of hot blood becomes a theme for marble.
Where like a veil the tantalizing web of secret misery is hung,
Violence of battle glitters in stone eye and quiet tongue.
From this time's sand and theft I call to the great Givers,
From this dry tongue of time I call to the two rivers.
O, he is still as water where the sand flies.
He is standing there, I see him pause:
I have stood still in the temple of your eyes
Where the cruel light flows suddenly back from us
To the still room, the proportions of the vase.

Four Sonnets of Resurrection

in memory of David Lewis

PAPYRUS

I with papyrus fingers, bathed in myrrh,
Under the sad, laid stones where children play,

Taught by the syllable, for love of her,
Doomed to a spiral crypt, illumine day.
Under twelve winds, four seasons, and five seas,
I throw on darkness death's eternal forms,
The elaborate sycamore, casting strange keys,
And twisted mulberry, which hides silkworms.
Their wind-born utterances I weave around
This sacred letter of a word untold
In all the winds' wild music, till the drowned
Dragged the moon down, and saw their lives unfold.
Then their souls cry, and in the tomb of sound
Glitters the waters' book, whose thread I hold.

TEARS WEAR TIME DOWN

Tears wear time down, the heart beats out its urn.
Known lands' last grains unseal prodigious doors.
Sand grabs the light and folds the flying shores
Where a wave rides, but tells no tide's return.
O navel of night and sea, heart of the shell
Where the skies' moonlight, raving in still walls,
Moves like a rainbow back through numberless falls
Sucked from the beach to each domed wave's blind bell:
You tell me that no ghost is truly laid
But spinning on a dolphin's eye will turn,
Turn, turn, till all things are re-made.
What should we know, cast in the span we made,
Being of small dust gigantically born,
But that the earth lies broken on the spade.

DRIFTWOOD

Why do men cling to driftwood? Christ, if resurrection be,
The least last grain in the hour-glass holding the twin skies
Bids fair to plunder light. Then the flood comes. Blood dies.
Blood dies. That echo seething back, blind mast, mad, sightless tree,
Rocks, and Fate's whistling, shattering breakers hit the shuddering scree
For sorrow, for silence of him. Whose hurt is there, then? Will fast eyes
Break to the knock of sunlight? Will May come? O, how shall mankind
rise,
He fallen? Mankind being one, how can he wake, till the last footprint
walk upon the sea?
O strong, great hand, fold, fold the waters. Ear, catch back, faint,
sea-shell secret, voice and thread.

Trust the fourth Fate of wood. Transfigured by the deafening spray,
The pagan creeds fly back, staining white stones, and overhead
Wheel the dark birds of Fate, while rainbow dolphins play.
Through paths of sea and air, all oracles, vultures for their dead,
Forebode black message, but lack that word his stillness spangled—O
hear it—dares to say.

FOUNTAINS

Fountains avenge, springs of eternal Winter,
Dust's worlds with worlds of sound. How fresh they are
Whose fingers are about the urn of care:
I see their arms circling the giant water.
Fallen lives flow gently to the listening ear
Hearing forever the mute, lovely pipe
Where judgment, lost in the miraculous drop,
Flies to the metaphor we cannot hear.
Then, in marled dust, in foul and ghastly mould,
The white roots of that vision veiled in ground
Of violet light, caught in the blind webs wound
By horrid spiders, chain the pulse I hold.
Then catch I dead leaves Winter has struck cold,
Voice of their vision, finger of their sound.

The Dove and the Gargoyle

Steep vertigo's staggering revenges above the stones,
Yet hardly an inch under the talons,
Gargoyles yet guard their avenged, vertiginous dead,

Scarcely projecting a millimetre from their vizored age
Under the dove's miraculous language,
Iron-deaf, listening for the last word a thought in armour said.

The walkers are betrayed by those shining monitors
For whom the moving Earth weaves sculptors
Better and more fitted to vie with the birds.

Stop, then, and quail beneath their tyrannous eloquence,
All you, save one whose tongue is tense,
Transfigured by God with a message that has no words.

Then look: the talon transfigures the Gargoyle's iron
With the rush of the unknown
Sky-grail, whose image alights on their shadowed, heraldic hate;

Aurora borealis of the sky falling
To the architecture of the wing,
Rocking the giant cathedral where movement lies in state.

O ruby eye, I know your talon is already a ring
On a dead archbishop's finger,
Who on the brink of annunciation did not dare

To surrender the archives' treasure under the hovering vane,
And receive the directly given,
Suddenly revealed authority of the safe, perilous air.

Westminster Bridge

Since the light lifts what memory's architecture destroys
Where silver-grey, dust's pencil writes a moulded, suffering tale,
The lids must close to see, where a mute fountain plays,
True lovers rise from scribbled names, men, women, girls and boys.
The waters are sick, the clock ticks death, dull rumour's cart of days
Carrying the plague-scarred over the river, roars like ale
Mulled in a mill-race, traffic-throated at the bar of noise:
How should my pulse find words in the stone, translated for Wales?

But light, light, the dazzling one, the innocent, replies:
They have quarried buildings of your bare hills. These figures around an
urn
Cross the bought flood; they fix you with their bartered eyes.
The bridge is a treadmill; alone the bathers, naked, are born.
Yet all is unique, all sacred, where the anonymous garment is worn.
The true, the afflicted, are one, coin-cankered in dubious disguise.

Crowds

Why should the living need my oil?
I see them, and their eyes are blest.
No. For those others I must toil:
I toil to set the dead at rest.

Yet when I watch in solemn tides
The drifting crowds, each life a ghost,
I mourn them, for their truth abides;
Nor is one loved, till he is lost.

Reprisals of Calm

for a friend lost at sea

Born without ambition,
Born on the seventh day,
When arduous love's fruition
In works accomplished lay,
He heard the living streams
Falling from stone to stone
Where light unuttered seems
To break from all that's gone.
Sunlight, wind and storm
Coloured the ripening skin
Where the leaf's starlike form
Dropped into origin.
He was most near light's wing,
Butterfly's damask tip
Making the blossom swing,
Recoiling where bees dip
To a new burning centre
Dilated in the leaves.
Let the true quietude enter
Since the wild space it leaves
Is less significant
Than that which hardly stirs.
So, news of this event
Beating upon loud ears
Had scarcely been discerned,
Yet, of a sudden, he
The balance overturned
By which men hear and see.
A boy, alien to these
Who, earth-renouncing, find
Above the pastoral trees
An eyrie of the mind;
And then, a boy who plays
The music Mozart made:
I burn within his days
To feel the unfolding shade.
For he, who brought no feud
To the surviving grass,
With a voice subdued

Broke like a looking-glass
The thunders of the tide
And left my lips to say:
What passion do you hide,
Light on the windswept bay?

Lover and Girl

You have opened the graves
And unbarred the door of the sea.
You have turned the barren waves
To blossoms upon life's tree.
Why seems it the ocean no longer accuses and raves?

'You were changed by me.'

You were patient as flame
Lit for the souls of the dead.
The barren women came,
Knocked, and were comforted.
What word was it passed when you gave me that power to
reclaim?

'Nothing I said.'

When we stood by the sheaves,
I looked, and, no longer estranged,
Saw the chestnut ripening in leaves
Wild breath disarranged.
Who drew my eyes forth to the loom till they saw how it
weaves?

'I said you were changed.'

Yet the mystery goes
Still deeper, that brought it to pass.
In the grave you transfigured the rose,
Springing changed in the grass.
Where found you this lightning that alters the bloom where
it grows?

In what burning-glass?

Green Names, Green Moss

The grief-rung, searching bell
Vaulted with footprints flying
Proclaims the pangs of hell
Altered by the dying.
They are gone in. I wait
By the grave's single flower
Where mosses ruminate
On birthday and death-hour.
What earthquake undermines
The general burial-ground,
Altering the proud lines
To a parable unfound?
The mourners all were wrong
Who followed them from towns,
Under the tempters' song
Of eunuch bells and gowns
To these twin tenements,
Obscurity and Fame,
Cold seed of great events
And sleep's last epigram.

Swing, life-leaping bell;
Strike, in the mourning trees.
No ravisher can tell
Their secret histories;
Not one can you reclaim,
But side-track their loss
Until the last, loved name
Is covered with moss.
Yet every moment must,
Each turn of head or hand,
Though disfigured by dust,
Incorruptibly stand;
If they are nothing now
Then they were nothing then.
Blinded with thirst I know,
Beneath my foot lie men
Each laid in his own caul
Too intricately still
In the rock of his soul
Where the pure fountains fill,
Too sacred to be touched

By memory or bell.
Out of wild hands that clutched,
Their lives, vibrating, fell.
The echoes breed children
Where the round bell swings.
A crippled coupling tune
Old Charon sings
As with an ivied oar
He rows across.
I can see them no more,
Only green names, green moss.

The Conception

First is the vision. Yet, since God decreed
A living witness, prone beneath the groom,
Are not the stars of heaven like this one seed,
And does not Earth revolve within the womb?
What mandrake screamed? What shudder shakes the tomb?
What infant crying out in mortal need?
What sacred pattern, leaping from time's loom,
Breaks, for the opulence of the breast to feed?
Imprisoned life, lie safe in these curled arms.
My eyes have said you are not, yet you are.
O faith here carried, yet appointed far,
Why should you fear this night, the clustered swarms,
Who hide the ordained tranquillity of forms
Locked in the circuit of your ripening star?

The Burial

Go to that place where men can look no more
At what on Earth shone brightest. As this wave
Leaps to great light, then, scattering, seeks the shore,
So your fame rose, that sinks into this grave.
Go where dissemblers can no more deprave
The dazzling love, nor knock that hidden door
Closed on the shrouded body the womb gave,
Dark as Christ's hem, as no dark looked before.

Yet must the buried shine, if any shines:
So sleeps the seed; so shrinks in rigid fold
The chrysalis, and hides its patterns old:
We touch, but cannot see its waking lines.
Honour this dust. The presence God refines
Even here is sunk, whose promised flesh is gold.

The Betrothal

I must die first, to look into those eyes,
And yet no lover ever found his bride
But with that look. Brave children were denied
Until I saw the grave where faith must rise
Out of this dust. Then moved the enamoured skies
From mountains humbled to the dust-grain's pride
Through sleep, and took the bone from Adam's side.
Wisdom I saw not, yet my act was wise.
For she, about whom heavenly bodies move
In that strict music of all sacred things,
Made peace with Earth. Her stillness was my love.
I was a bird then, needing no more wings
Than this late vesture, and my guarded ring's
Perpetual evocation of the dove.

Gravestones

Look down. The dead have life.
Their dreadful night accompanies our Springs.
Touch the next leaf:
Such darkness lives there, where a last grief sings.

Light blinds the whirling graves.
Lost under rainwet earth the letters run.
A finger grieves,
Touching worn names, bearing daughter and son.

Here the quick life was borne,
A fountain quenched, fountains with sufferings crowned.
Creeds of the bone
Summoned from darkness what no Sibyl found.

Truly the meek are blest
Past proud men's trumpets, for they stilled their fame
Till this late blast
Gave them their muted, and their truest name.

Sunk are the stones, green-dewed,
Blunted with age, touched by cool, listening grass.
Vainly these died,
Did not miraculous silence come to pass.

Yet they have lovers' ends,
Lose to hold fast, as violets root in frost.
With stronger hands
I see them rise through all that they have lost.

I take a sunflower down,
With light's first faith persuaded and entwined.
Break, buried dawn,
For the dead live, and I am of their kind.

Birds of Joy and Care

Look where in light the lark
Dares diamond heavenbreak, high
Mounting above the dark,
And fills the sky
With sparkling printless notes the spectres perish by.

That sun-exalted sound
Leaps like a fountain, shed
On five brown eggs the ground
Lays bare in dread,
Cloistered by windblown grass where clumsy cattle tread.

Torn from the breviary
Of graves, the monk's-hood mind
And coffined aviary
Of wings confined,
Ascending to receive that gift no thought could find,

Praising the suffered light,
He makes all heaven the field
Of his inspired delight,
And shows revealed

The glorious christening fire whose covenant Christ has
sealed.

That ecstasy were man's,
But evening brings unrest.
He sees the ptarmigans
Guarding their nest,
And hears a plover's cry fall wounded towards the West.

Plumage rides the air
All day, all night, for lovers:
Birds of joy and care;
The haunted plovers
Darkly express the doubt a hidden fear discovers.

Rending low heaven like flails,
Like tearing silk, they fling
Terror to earth; one trails
A broken wing,
Deception and disguise on humans practising.

Birds cry all night, all day,
Spring night and Autumn night,
Then the moor's moult of grey
Alters with snow to white.
White on that whitening ground, the mountain grouse unite.

So thrive the ptarmigans,
Flock, and match earth to feather.
Saint Francis with blind hands
In larks' sweet weather
Pulls to the breaking year seasons and birds together;

Preaches to them aloud,
Then says: 'O Christ, hear me:
Your angels in the cloud
Take from this tree
The harp they play that gives these wings their symmetry.

Pledge with your heavenly ring
These birds, by faith made wise,
That though the songs men sing
Follow the fashion's guise,
They still may cleave to heaven, and sing with praising eyes.'

The Healing of the Leper

O, have you seen the leper healed,
And fixed your eyes upon his look?
There is the book of God revealed,
And God has made no other book.

The withered hand which time interred
Grasps in a moment the unseen.
The word we had not heard, is heard.
What we are then, we had not been.

Plotinus, preaching on heaven's floor,
Could not give praise like that loud cry
Bursting the bondage of death's door;
For we die once; indeed we die.

What Sandro Botticelli found
Rose from the river where we bathe:
Music the air, the stream, the ground;
Music the dove, the rock, the faith:

And all that music whirled upon
The eyes' deep-sighted, burning rays,
Where all the prayers of labours done
Are resurrected into praise.

But look: his face is like a mask
Surrounded by the beat of wings.
Because he knows that ancient task
His true transfiguration springs.

All fires the prophets' words contained
Fly to those eyes, transfixed above.
Their awful precept has remained:
'Be nothing, first; and then, be love'.

Arakhova and the Daemon

for David Cochrane, killed on Parnassus 1929

She, on the path where he had gone,
Even now assembles rock. To touch
The pulse of water that runs on
Is to have lost and found so much.

Was it not there that he caught hold,
Where Delphi hears the hidden spring?
And there Prometheus' fire like gold
Under the edge of that great wing

Suddenly caught his nineteen years
As thundering, whirling waters go,
Into whose stream the mind's eye stares
Where the light gathers all we know.

Light on Parnassus: there, keen-brained,
He struck it from the flint he held,
And halfway up the rock attained
A sky no other man beheld,

Wrought of old cities like a skein
Gathered from gate and buried wall,
Whirling about that single vein.
What mountain eagle watched him fall?

His crooked climbing, out of joint,
Possessed the Sibyl in her cell;
And still she looks to Cochrane's Point
Silent, as though her brother fell.

There in Arakhova men say
He climbed by moonlight; others guess
That the sun dazzled him. He lay
Long near a precipice. Pages press

Life, like a flower. A myth is laid
Mute, where these guardian trees surround
The chiselled stone a workman made.
Under that rock his bones were found;

And seventeen years are gone, where now
Light, like a new-found blossom, breaks.
I ponder this, much marvelling how
His daemon haunts the path she takes

Who never saw him. Yet he struck
Fire from the rock with all he said.
His daemon so transforms that rock
That the rough world, not he, is dead.

Lace-Maker

Lined, wrinkled face,
Fingers of Samothrace
Making so secretly move
In a fragile pattern of lace
Your untranslatable love:

Dark, withdrawn from delight,
Under the water-bowl light
On a cushion spread in your room
Pricking the stretch of night
With secrets old as the womb:

Patient, you toil alone.
Eighty years are gone
Since first your fingers tossed
Those bobbins one by one
In a craft that is almost lost.

Flashing in failing skies,
Gay Kitty Fisher's Eyes,
As they call these Buckingham beads,
Restore that far sunrise
To your pensive widow's weeds;

And your shadowing, birdlike hand,
Migrated from a young land,
Brings, like a midnight lark,
Whiter than whitest sand,
Light running out of dark:

Fine sand, too quick to tread,
Crossed by the sea in your head
In a hundred thundering tides
Breaking in foam, the thread
White, unlost, like a bride's

Beautiful, gathered lace,
Foretelling the lover's pace,
That lover of foam, the hot
Sea, for one hour, one place,
One moment, caught in a knot.

No sooner come than gone:
So light, it is not weighed down

By any thought that will stay.
You have seen time's flood that would drown
Surpassed in butterflies' play,

Yet intricately surpassed;
For rather you chose to fast
Than sell that delicate stream
Of lace on the altar cast,
A gift, for night to redeem:

Lace, fragile, fine,
In a magic, a moving design,
A silence, in which I see
Through the sea-engendered vine
A glory, not of the sea.

The Butterflies

High, lost in light, they pair,
Butterflies blue, so fair,
Blind in stopped flight,
Twined on a thread,
Then drop where light, effaced,
Shuts, in the dread
Secret of sepalled air,
Their petals chaste.

Hid, meadow-masked from sight,
Hushed near the pulse of light,
They magnify
With round big eye
Antennae'd, that gold place
From which the sky
Seizes their still delight,
Inventing space.

Suddenly they spring up,
Blown from a buttercup,
Alight, elude,
And reunite;
They mingle their blue wings
Dazzling the sight,
Like a blue wind, then stop,

Sit, and are kings.

That crooked life would seem
Vain, did no falling stream
Chime a strange year
Time-changing here,
And yew-tree with no sound,
And murmuring weir,
Catch on a weaver's beam
The thread they wound

Past the farm wall, where grieves
An aspen, whose wild leaves
Toss, where roots brawl
On fosse and wall,
Gathering their green and white,
Strain, feign to fall,
And cast across the eaves
A changing light:

A dancing thread, how much
More fragile, hard to touch,
Brighter in flight,
More light than theirs
Or spiders' threads in air.
Fugitive players:
It was a pain to watch
A twine so fair

Flying, so quickly gone,
Stretching their dalliance on
From plot to plot,
Not to return,
Past hedge and flowering rose,
Falling in turn,
As though the hour had shone
For none but those.

The Sinner

Softly she fell, and with her tears she washed
His feet, fast weeping, and dried them with her hair,
Kissed, kissed them faster, fainted, and kissed them afresh.

Her love, her lost life, the miracle loved most, lay there.
Light! She had found Him, sleepless, redeeming time there,
O deeper than language, in a circle where all was hushed,
While their heavy eyelids sold Him to birds of the air;
And in each new falling of her tears her fault was refreshed.

O, seeing her spikenard, to whom much was forgiven,
Spilt from love's box, anointing the limbs for heaven,
What horror repels her accuser? Who rears that stone
Shaped in the fountain of her magnanimous womb,
To disfigure her love-name and shut the mouth of the tomb,
For whom the unnumbered candles cannot atone?

A Necklace of Stones

I sing a placeless and a timeless heaven.
Time has no tongue or bell where I descant.
Space has no exile from the sweetening font,
No girl of stone His hands have not forgiven.
House of the husk and room of the Eleven
Track precious springs. There travels what I want
Like water from a mountain, and my chant
Flies where the penury of streams is given.

What grains of calculating, sun-parched lands,
What shells long hidden in the moon-drawn sea
Disturb the astronomers who sift the sands
And count the stars? The necklace that I see
Touches her neck, yet ignorant is she:
All is transfigured by a touch of hands.

A Christening Remembered

for Rhiannon

Water of life no prophet could divine,
Whose eyes now know a month more light than shade:
The font in your awakening is waylaid,
Where fell that christening moment from the vine.
If I look deeply there, I see time fade
And light grow perfect, dark; and darkness shine.

Again I see the curve her body made,
Bearing you like a pitcher doomed to wine.

That ancient miracle makes moist your lip
With Cana's feast; and babblings none could spell
Recall great buckets that a chain let slip
Down the dark, echoing walls of some deep well
Where a stone, plunging, woke you from your sleep:
Your angel spoke the moment that it fell.

Blake

Blake was immortal. When his eyes were bent
On mortal forms he knew that Earth was heaven.
The stones of law were love's negations graven,
And Christ was each forgiving lineament.
He touched with his two hands the firmament,
Found there that peace by deathless judgment given
That pulls time back to make the reckoning even
Between the abounding ages and time spent.
Who murmurs 'Not again' must know he lies;
'Now is undying' was Blake's eternal theme.
He knew that thief who mocked Christ, and despaired,
And that good thief who looked for Paradise;
He knew the evil and the noble dream,
The eternal heaven that breaks on lòve declared.

The Listening Days

Morning of light, I wake.
The waves and watersprings,
Birdsong and leaves that shake,
Proclaim created things.
The laughing wind lifts branches through the air;
All that I touch is truthful, and is fair.

Now, in the height of noon,
No shadow here is seen;
But shades will lengthen soon,
Stretching across the green.

He pours down thought and fills me with lost light;
Yet who loved day, that loves not starry night?

The words we speak are low:
They linger near the path.
We are upheld, I know,
By those who died in faith.
They are about us now who can fulfil
All when the wind has dropped, and when the boughs are still.

Zacchaeus in the Leaves

Silence before
Sound.
Sycamore:

A tree
Predestined to beauty.
Blown leaves. Antiquity.
Light lost. Light found.

The myth above the myth.
The imagined zenith
Of youth in youth.

Light on the leaves in wind
Flying. The silver-sequined
Goat-leaf, dark-skinned.

Sycamore leaves; coiled thick,
God-dark, Dionysiac,
The ascending trunk. Pan's music.
The sap made quick.

Wind-gathered sound. The flow
Of lives. Wood-sounds. Wood-hollow.
Hades locked below.

Sap leaps. The springing race
Threading the magic surface
Drops to one place.

A sign to us!
A tree, and then a tree
No more.

Silent Zacchaeus,
Ageless one.
The buried sun,
And the key it bore.

*

Light found in every age
The leaves of Spring
Fading from lineage,
The seed, the wing.

From what dark scent
Of waters breaking
In night most innocent
Of dead men waking,

From what laid bone
Rose man's belief?
What Sibyl wrote upon
The breaking leaf?

Sibylline words.
The buried lives.
Lost among nesting-birds,
The burden of the leaves.

The myth above the myth,
Pan above Zacchaeus;
Zacchaeus climbing,
Mounted above his youth,
Alone in time
Seeking the heavenly death.
The crooked he had left,
Yes, and the wise,
To climb the tree-trunk,
To sit in a cleft
And see through his eyes
Not what they saw,
Not what they heard,
No leaf, no claw,
No wing, no bird,
But light surpassing
All known green,
As if all drunk
And sober stirred,

Known, unknown,
Where seen, unseen,
Were one alone;
Jesus passing,
The Nazarene.

Lovers embraced
And their eyes were solaced;
But Zacchaeus gripped fast

The tree-branch, crouching,
Watching the myth
Moving, the myth
Move to the zenith
Not found in youth:
'If His eyes see us,
If His eyes see us,
Dazzled above men,
Though we are buried then,
The myth above the truth.'

Who stilled the pipes of Pan?
What marvel weaves
Death, deathless, pagan,
Turning the Sibyl's leaves?

Firm, yet betrayed no more,
The young lie with the young.
Leaves of the sycamore,
Lifted on wind, give tongue:

'I have supported one
In my own right
Who watched the procession,
His eyes full of light.

I can fade now,
My thought heard or unheard.
Did he not leave my bough,
And said no word?'

*

Slow the procession was coming. The drinkers remained
Sitting cross-legged, close to the dead who were chained,
Beggars of light. Only the man in the tree
Looked on the road, and saw where light was ordained.

Among the quick and the dead is the point divine,
Moving; among those talking, the drinkers of wine,
The shuffling of feet, the running of time, the gust
Of windblown leaves, no, not the Muses, the nine,

Have seen the universe race through the leaves and thrill
Because it has found the point of predestined will,
There where the fountain breaks from lips that are dust.
Stop: the great branches are moving. Now they are still.

The Song of the Good Samaritan

I sing of the Good Samaritan, of
Pity and the Fixed Stars. Him the Awakeners bless
Who heal the Earth with silent tumult of love.

There came the configuration of ages, less
Than his moment of deepest shadow. I sing of his
Leap into God, of the trial of gentleness.

Night. Death. And forever the distances
Woven by the pulse, that infinite loom of heaven;
Then out of the water a kiss, a leper's kiss,

Given through the dark. Look up! The moment is given
To the dog derided and scorned; and a look outpaces
The beautiful horses mythology thought to have driven.

Look. Look up! Frozen light! The Gorgon grimaces
Of the stone-blind heaven freeze blood in the marvelling child
Standing alone on the bed near the strange toy-faces.

Constellations! Look! The Fixed Stars! Blind meteors whirled!
Night's pattern, the clustered myths! On the Milky Road
Towards milk-white Jericho stumbles one from the world

Leading a mule, borne down with its dusty load,
To the shade of a tree, to a trough. The mythologies shrink,
And the nameless image is healed of its murderous goad.

Font of the fingers, water where asses drink,
Winged horses above you scattering, manes of the Norn,
And heroic Pegasus, leap into light from the brink.

Swallows quiver, rounding the magical horn

Of fullness, emptied for John's wild honey. They break
Light with their wings, and the era of love is born.

He broke the classical falsehood, summoned awake
A world from dust with the secret worlds of his tears.
Shut in those heavens he heard the mythologies shake.

Their violent haunches taut, their delicate ears
Coiled to a point, a horn growing out of each head,
They know they are crystal, their breath the smoke of the spheres.

Centaurs, unicorns, wondering, weaving a thread
From the loom of silence, coiling all ages at once
To a hero's masterful, measured, arrogant tread.

And music sprung from the rock, from the pagan dance
Of firelit bodies, heard in the cataract's head;
A prince of warriors, Venus guiding his lance.

Those heroes gather the spaces through which they have sped
To ivory silence or toil of intractable bronze,
Resurrecting the ravisher's cup, the wine of the dead.

Yet the buried see them as the unforgiving, spun
From cruelty's frenzy back through a minotaur maze,
A battle of Centaurs fled into the blaze of suns;

Fled, fled, in a furious pattern of praise
From the throat of light, a thunder of galloping feet
Riding the rim that acclaims their arrogant days.

What vision startled a prophet in that hard heat
Of the wayside's ultimate shadow? He bent to hear
The spheres from a donkey suffer their proud retreat.

Then, as he looked on those features, sphere upon sphere
Shone round the loom of the hand. No name had this
That buried and raised all time in the spring of a tear.

And he heard through heaven the retreating distances,
Timbrels, the long gold trumpet, the Pharaoh's car,
Heroic song, gold idols, the pagan dances.

Even as a child I began to say: How far?
Parting the curtain, the winding-sheet of the dead.
The loom of the hand has the pathway of every star.

Disappearance of the proud horses! Circling in dread,
Stampeding in light, he heard the mythologies shrink,

The rushing stars, their reverberant, thundering tread;

From a little worn-away trough where asses drink,
One by one, and above them, finding the sea,
Swallows pass, and their world ripples over the brink.

'O moment,' he breathed, 'frail as the branch of a tree,
This act is secret, eluding all fabulous joys.
The wound I suffer, the joy I am bearing, is he.

For they were movement itself, but mine was a choice
Between those visions acclaimed by pride overthrown,
And the downcast, intimate eyes, the source of the voice.

Dip, swallows. The Centaurs already are stone,
And the water listens, finding continually crooked
The path the asses have paced, the thread you have flown.

Now, if I speak, my words can belong to no book
For my fingers mingle the language of water and dove,
Ending, here at the source, the journey they took.

Out of the dust I raised this image of love.
Moment of darkness, moment, still you are mine,
Though the proud-winged, galloping horses disdainfully move

From the wounded god, the arena of dust and sand.

And only the tilted loom is lucky, divine,
Where the mocked, unpremeditated bowl of the hand
Makes the world nothing, pouring in oil and wine.'

The Cave-Drawing

Excavator, explore rock from the great Ice Age
Moored by this anchor of bones from the sailing sky;
And find this agonized beast, figured forth where centuries fly,
Marked by an arrow, man's prey, overtaken in rage
At the dawn of life. There, drawn to his far cry,
Stab the unstrict measure, find only that chase for gauge
Where stag or bison speaks a momentous language
And beckons us late through the labyrinth of his eye.

For delicately, upon silver, he found the fleeting line,
Untutored here, of deer that eluded knowledge.

In the shadow of an eagle they sprang from the spear of the
hunter. Their image
Danced; it flew from his wrist as the aquiline
Wing-beat shuddered; they were luminous, caught in the wedge
Of triangular wisdom, flung from the flint's edge fine,
Stretched on a sunray, making that eagle shine
In quartzlight, stream's light, falling from ledge to ledge.

He witnessed the bison bounding through dust from a crimson sun.
For us he made light sing in the dark of his line,
Arrested motion, all animals pierced and crystalline:
He, he alone had found it, his look trained down
By luck their lightning emergence. This was his mine
Of mineral wonder, making the skilled hand run,
A hunter, spearlike, outspeeding all ages begun,
At which we marvel. Pagan, pristine, divine

Met in the rock where his hand, like the hand on a sickle reaping,
Narrowly moved, in the age of the mastodon,
Bridling the horses of sunrise, curbed, yet able to stun
The rock with vision; such was his flint-line creeping
In the heavens on its early path, for his toil seemed one
Measure of light. He arose from night to the shaping
Of a life the glaciers had left. Rigid gloom escaping,
He watched the day-hawk wheel where no wheel was known.

Then the night-rain stopped. Five colours, a mist-formed rainbow
spun
From the dawn of time, to potter and painter sweeping
From the lost Ice Age, was hung there, all colours of morning
keeping
On the edge of sleep, to attend the Syrian:
Antelopes flying on the rim of the world unsleeping,
A bison pierced, an eagle dropped from the sun,
Deer like a river flying, suddenly gone,
And again like a vein behind the iris leaping.

The Yew-Tree

Is there a cause why we should wake the dead?
Should they not sleep, safe in the sepulchre?
I, a man walking, one alive to fear,

Hear these deep, holy boughs and berries red
Sweep the dark graves, then stop where seem to tread
Long-vanished mourners from an earlier year.
Late-leaving, then, from each fresh grave I hear
Love's nearmost: 'O, who will lift this lost, loved head,
Crowned with flowers fading, whose quick colours pray?'
Then none makes answer; yet, soon, bodily
Reaching to God, I hear that good thief say:
'Lord, for no wrong Thou diest, but justly we'.
That word kills grief, and through the dark-boughed tree
Gives to each dead his resurrection day.

The Lady with the Unicorn

About this lady many fruitful trees.
There the chaste unicorn before her knees
Stares in a glass to purify her sight.
At her right hand a lion sits,
And through the foliage, in and out, there flits
Many a bird; then hounds, with deer in flight:
Light is her element; her tapestry is light.

There is her mediaeval music met.
On the high table-top, with damask set
To charm, between the chaste beast and the strong,
An organ which her fingers play
Rests, and her pretty servant's hands obey
Those pipes with bellows to sustain their song
Attuned to distant stars, making their short life long.

This ended, gathered from some leafy way,
That servant brings her flowers upon a tray.
She lifts them to inhale their magic breath.
Caught in that breath's elusive maze,
She marvels. On a stool a monkey plays
With flowers from wicker trailing, strewn beneath,
A heaven of fragrance breathing through their mask of death.

Next, her right hand upholds that coat-of-arms
Seeming love's guardian against war's alarms,
And with her left she grips the upright horn.
This touch, while birds through branches peer,

Consecrates all the beasts as they appear,
Frisking among dark foliage to adorn
Her fingers that caress the constant unicorn.

A lion rampant grips the upright pole.
Her serving-maid now proffers her a bowl
Of peaches, damsons, almonds, grapes, and sweets.
This lady savours one, and sees
How white of almonds, red of mulberries,
Is each a praise no other tree repeats,
Now strangely on love's tree engrafted while she eats.

The senses leave a chain upon her tongue.
That place is hushed, from which the light is sprung.
Curtains are hung, embroidered with strange art.
The letters 'TO MY SOLE DESIRE'
Crown that pavilion with a band of fire
Whose folds the unicorn and lion part,
Revealing in their midst her love-awakened heart.

O sovereign balm to heal all mortal illness:
Long let him look, and still he will find stillness,
Her one betrothed, who sees her museful face.
This lady, with her flowers and hounds,
Woven in light, in air, in wooded grounds,
Transmits a glory wrought about her grace,
Caught in a sacred bond within the encircling space.

Let him look softly, with some seventh sense
Breaking that circle's hushed magnificence,
And see what universe her love controls,
Moving with hushed, divine intent
Through the five senses to their sacrament
Whose Eden turns between two silent poles,
Creating with pure speed that harmony of souls.

Where is the heart of mathematic space?
Throned on a mystery in that leafy place,
This lady's fingers hold, where distance flies.
The Past and Future like a skein
For her betrothed to wind, and loose again.
Lion and unicorn forbid disguise.
He looks, and she looks forth: there are no other eyes.

The Death Bell
poems and ballads
1954

The Strangled Prayer

Look down at midnight when my strangled prayer
Calls through night-leaves the shades of ancestors,
Midsummer night, Eden of windless air,
Coiled with strange creepers where the moth-wing stirs.
Conscience fights echoes, footprints on worn stairs,
And my ten fingers separate the stars.
Bless my strained heels. I drown in a child's hair.

The boards are full of voices. Through my vow
Insects run out. The cricket chirps Amen.
Plumb on the floor I kneel. Stark moonlight now
Touches the skin and pricks desirous men;
They dance, they leap, they gratify the moon.
Bones makes a circle round my naked moan.
Above this sheet the Pleiads and the Plough

Are white with ancient music. Mars is red
With violent fury, glowing with vine-must.
The crested darkness hovering overhead
Has eyes of serpents. My great prayer is crossed
By all the travelling beasts. My proud loins lust.
Snatch up, untwist me, twelve-tongued Pentecost,
For Nature makes me mortal in her bed.

Time's Deathbed

I went to bed with time.
Through the blue dark, sublime,
I watched Orion rise
And all the stars' fireflies
Through distance climb.

Quite still I lay awake,
Hearing time's spectre make
Dynastic moan, more far
Than midnight's millionth star,
For love's dead sake.

Softly the curtain flapped
As though a ball had dapped
And then bounced out again;
And through my brain
Thoughts travelled and were trapped.

The universe enshrined
Stared from my mummied mind;
I heard my beating blood:
One near me stood.
I smiled inside the wind.

I listened. Time like sand
Slid through a hidden hand;
Although no step was heard,
It seemed a shadow stirred:
My dark was manned.

Then, while I listened still,
A voice from near the sill
More low, more wavering
Than curlew's call in Spring,
Made my flesh thrill:

'Possess new time, possess
New time, or nothingness.
The spoils of sleep
That other gives. I keep
Spoil-spurning nakedness.'

Desire contended there
With one so fair,
My pulse stopped as I turned
To that new life which burned
With upright hair.

Then sprang a sweat of fear,
For where soul thrust a spear
Blood rose immense,
The light was so intense,
The shade so near.

Then, when all thoughts were summed
And the small flies had hummed
Around the passive bone,
I gave so great a groan
That time was dumbed.

Deeper and far more tender
That groan to my life-lender
Floated, than songs of praise,
For the firm pulse of days
Was locked in my surrender.

Once more the Near One spoke:
'Lie still. Your fist then broke
The hour-glass that has cursed
Man from the first
With superstition's cloak.

Time built your room three-walled
Where Fear, a nursling, crawled,
But at the fourth wall I
Bring the starred sky
And the scented world.'

Confusion of the dark,
Snuffing of the spark,
Unclothed the shades
For which we had used spades
In the priests' sad park.

Confusion tenebrous
Brought spoilers covetous,
But naked in the sheet
It was uniquely sweet
To lie so generous.

Pledges to Darkness

I. NEFERTITI

Grave Nefertiti keeps that principle in mind
Which covers with cold fire the calm, stylistic face,
Leaving loved lute with wheat-ears near the rigid hand
And gold wine-vessel, when her mask, depicting the sped race,
Truthful in its last look, transcends the Zodiac,
The features rarefied, through tenderest darkness seen,
Thrust forward, lifted out of life, the hair caught back,
Unsheathed in true perfection, flashed forth like a queen.

No shallow memory clings to the gold-painted veil
From thoughts unworthy of death. Who cares where passion went?
The first and last, in their most natural, cannot fail;
Always the moment's pledge is stronger than event.
Things of less tension are not life; but O, this dust,
This silence, through revolving worlds is kept the same.

The abstract darkness must not see her, but she must
Through night's miraculous pupils see herself as flame.

Close to her sleeping mask the bird-beaked Mysteries brood;
There the transfiguring workmen like small insects toil,
Each beating out in gold the sacred from the crude,
Teaching the Shades her tongue, protecting their new spoil.
Art by the blade is made attentive to the sheath,
Matching her fire with phoenix, date-palm, hawk and dove,
Supporting her raised glory with their weight beneath,
Annihilation of all but detail wrought through love.

Break not for love of death the vigil of that queen.
Who could translate her stillness to a waking world,
A room by daylight changed, yet where a god has been?
Dust falls, time's atom falls, into a portent whirled
Of luminous, killing language where men lack the key;
Yet she, she clasps with folded hands her hidden scroll,
Her eyes being set in death, being taught with joy to see
That radiant Master guard the stations of her soul.

2. EGYPTIAN BURIAL: RESURRECTION IN WALES

Leave within reach of this dead hand
A little food, new coins, a vessel carved with grace.
Let the fine bracelet touch the sand
To hear if time still move.
A narrow ship must take her now
Where subterranean waters race,
Born of our tears. Yet she must keep one vow.
Under the low lamp fit death's glove
And lay the hands in place.

Those hurrying waters fly so near,
Yet she is fixed; her features bear no stain of time.
Her fire-translated eyes appear
Like salamanders seen.
No element in conflict must
Darken their discs with crime
Or spoil those edges where a craftsman's trust
Paints and prepares a rigid queen
Through death and sleep to climb.

Memory returns. Unbounded longings press,
Yet none has power the exalted passion to uncoil

That is her script and body's dress
Guarding the circle known.
There Art has mastery, for the Shade
Distinguishes the paints and oil.
In death she knows, fine things are finely made;
Through these the flower, when most alone,
Returns to its right soil.

Yet she, assembling in the light
Earth's broken hieroglyph, must watch the Nile confound
Antiquity with present sight,
Vision consuming death.
The letters in their melted state
Grind out, where Usk's new moon goes round,
Her life's completion. All of her is fate,
Her faith, her necessary breath
Breathed back, where light is sound.

Yet now she whispers close: 'Dispense
No precious ointment here; my body has cast all.
Here, if the taper burn intense,
It may instruct your eyes
To seek that holiest treasure laid
A Syrian widow once let fall.
This contrite darkness never has betrayed
Love's perfect secret whose disguise
Sleeps in my lettered pall.'

Dear love, could my true soul believe
The wide heavens merciless, I still would not forsake
The man-tilled earth to which bones cleave
While horses race across
The neighbouring field, and their hooves shine
Scattering a starlike wake.
Magnanimous morning, if we change no line,
Shall pierce stone, leaf and moss,
And the true creature at light's bidding wake.

The Turning of the Stars

There is a moment when Apollo's tree
Is Daphne still. The Past is not the Past
But wound within a ring

So finely wrought,
It knows each path and avenue of thought.
Downward he looks, through heaven and earth, to see
The sunlight and dayspring
Caught in her eyes, all uttered love surpassed
By that first heaven which knows her timelessly.

There is a touch, before the wall of bark
Echoes the music of those timeless hands,
The pivot of the god
Like light revealed
Where all the stars seem fallen in one field,
And secret, where the underleaf is dark,
Language is understood
Green as a spring, translated for all lands,
A touch to which rivers of leaves must hark.

Look. In the midnight heaven two stars draw near,
First the awakening laurel pressed by lips,
Her mortal destiny,
Her walk, her grief,
Then her ascending star of true belief;
Opposed, of differing glories, they appear,
Each on its axle-tree
Whirling, two heavenly bodies, to eclipse,
Pitched into darkness by love's greater year.

Miraculous, the flight of measured thought
Crosses the rebel fire of burning youth;
A choir of tranquil heads
Moving sublime
Through Raphael's heaven, from distance into time,
Inspired the pupil Perugino taught
To paint heaven's periods,
His mind being in its silence fixed on truth:
Unrest in calm, calm in unrest he sought.

Galileo, spun, recanting, to the stars,
Through the smoked glass of time presumed to watch
With monstrous emphasis
The disc of light
Edged by the rim of that great wheel in flight;
Copernicus proclaimed, we turned like Mars;
He checked the sun by this.

Alighieri, fixed yet flying, knelt to match
The speed of distance to the burial-vase.

Circle on circle, purgatorial years
Whirl against time the union of the blest.
A man may bind the stars
To his own bent
By faith protected, till that grave ascent
Find a new pivot for the moving spheres;
Or this may come to pass:
One intense moment may consume the rest,
A flash translate blind mortals into seers.

So love descends: the star which blots out heaven
Moves in the morning of our making hands.
Where Raphael's heavens project
On Mary's dread
The Infant Christ, a halo round His head,
He seems, the firstfruits of their sleep, to have given
To living intellect
The life of faith their death in faith demands;
His broken bread affirmed the sleepers' leaven.

About us garlands of earth's natural green
Quicken with may and hide the blackbird's clutch.
Leaves cover up the well,
And buds begin
To break, and hide the fountain's origin.
Spring behind Spring, star behind star, unseen,
Revolve in seed and cell.
Vision fulfils the source of visible touch.
Invisible dancers make our feet serene.

There is a power that holds me by a chain,
So ancient is the love that guards this book,
Inscrutable that praise;
I see the crash,
Fleece and spent fury, Sodom's deluge-flash;
I see the wide world sink, and rise again,
Hung in pure night, ablaze
With million worlds united in a look
Where boundless glory astounds the eye of the brain.

Verse is a part of silence. I have known
Always that declamation is impure.

This language best fits prayer,
The crystal night
Teeming with worlds in mathematic height.
Prodigious darkness guards its undertone,
And though that wheel of air
Seems to leave nothing earthly to endure,
The likeness, not the original, is gone.

Music of Colours: The Blossom Scattered

O, but how white is white, white from shadows come,
Sailing white of clouds, not seen before
On any snowfield, any shore;
Or this dense blue, delivered from the tomb,
White of the risen body, fiery blue of sky,
Light the saints teach us, light we learn to adore;
Not space revealed it, but the needle's eye
Love's dark thread holding, when we began to die.
It was the leper's, not the bird's cry,
Gave back that glory, made that glory more.

I cannot sound the nature of that spray
Lifted on wind, the blossoms falling away,
A death, a birth, an earthy mystery,
As though each petal stirring held the whole tree
That grew, created on the Lord's day.
There is no falling now. Yet for time's sake
These blossoms are scattered. They fall. How still they are.
They drop, they vanish, where all blossoms break.
Who touches one dead blossom touches every star.

So the green Earth is first no colour and then green.
Spirits who walk, who know
All is untouchable, and, knowing this, touch so,
Who know the music by which white is seen,
See the world's colours in flashes come and go.
The marguerite's petal is white, is wet with rain,
Is white, then loses white, and then is white again
Not from time's course, but from the living spring,
Miraculous whiteness, a petal, a wing,
Like light, like lightning, soft thunder, white as jet,
Ageing on ageless breaths. The ages are not yet.

Is there a tree, a bud, that knows not this:
White breaks from darkness, breaks from such a kiss
No mind can measure? Locked in the branching knot,
Conception shudders; that interior shade
Makes light in darkness, light where light was not;
Then the white petal, of whitest darkness made,
Breaks, and is silent. Immaculate they break,
Consuming vision, blinding eyes awake,
Dazzling the eyes with music, light's unspoken sound,
White born of bride and bridegroom, when they take
Love's path through Hades, engendered of dark ground.

Leda remembers. The rush of wings cast wide.
Sheer lightning, godhead, descending on the flood.
Night, the late, hidden waters on the moon's dark side.
Her virgin secrecy, doomed against time to run.
Morning. The visitation. All colours hurled in one.
Struggling with night, with radiance! That smothering glory cried:
'Heavenborn am I. White-plumaged heart, you beat against the sun!'
All recollection sinking from the dazzled blood.

She woke, and her awakened wings were fire,
Darkened with light; O blinding white was she
With white's bewildering darkness. So that secret choir
Know, in the thicket, and witness more than we,
Listening to early day, dew's voice, the lightest feet,
As though Saint Francis passing, told who they were,
Fledged of pure spirit, though upheld by air.
I think one living is already there,
So sound asleep she is, her breath so faint,
She knows, she welcomes the footstep of the saint,
So still, so moving, joy sprung of despair,
And the two feasts, where light and darkness meet.

Testimony

She testifies to that first truth
The hour-glass cannot hold.
Her voice recalls the voice of Ruth
When she to Naomi told
A pledge too dear for time to break

Or Earth to render vain:
Dark is the radiance doomed to wake
This Danae to the rain.

Delicate as the foal whose hooves
Seem moving on the sky,
Clear as the questioning moon that moves
And feels the waves' reply,
Fragrant as when Spring rains renew
The lilac and the lime,
Rich as the Earth which Adam knew
Before the birth of time:

In every form I see the stamp
And image of the fair,
And yet Copernicus's lamp
Was always burning there.
How could interpreters divine
The depth of eye and hand
If the lost myth that made them shine
They could not understand?

Put out that lamp, and let her be
Cut from the sacred cord,
From bright Eternity set free,
Weaned by a pagan word;
A life courageous, short and great
As in the days gone by,
Spun by the strong, blind-fingered Fate,
Restore, and let her die.

No use! The measure of her days
Sinks, to outlive the moon,
Shines like the widow's cruse of praise
And is restored as soon,
That watched Elijah on the bed
Bowed in the might of prayer
Bring back the breath into his dead
And give her son to her.

What's faith? Her movement in repose
Hangs by so fine a thread.
The fountain fills and overflows:
What patience there is shed,
Making her plunge of glory seem

A prey to hungry time,
Whose planets through the elliptic beam
Back to their stations climb.

Niobe

'O Niobe, con che occhi dolenti
vedeva io te . . .
Purgatorio, XII, 37

'Rachel weeping for her
children, and would not
be comforted, because
they are not.'
Mat. II, 18

If we shall live, it must be from this rock
The stream shall break.
How many centuries must be endured,
The face in rock, the face folded in sorrow,
Seen and remembered like the breaking wave
Falling upon the shore of recollection,
Seasons of sleep revolving in the grave,
The mother in her wall of rock immured,
A day like any day, but with no morrow,
The Pole-star and the needle of affliction
Drawn from these waters through the boundless night,
Fixed, while the edge of light
Toils, through the spindrift and the moaning buoy,
To cut this diamond of eternal joy.

Is this the place?
It is.
Is this the place?
Not here,
But near to this.
Is this the very rock?
Not Niobe, whom Dante on his way
Saw with such sorrowing eyes, but Niobe,
A rock unyielding in the whirling spray,
Still anchored in the footprint of her loss,
Like a blind woman waiting to be healed.

This is the rock: it has a woman's shape.
Until her grief transfigures the whole sea
She must wait here: no second birth shall come.

Ah dumb Piétà, fixed beneath closed eyelids,
Strong vision pledged to seek the unchanging light
Of angels, true above a changing world!

Bereavement has a life, a tapestry
Begun and ended with a single thread,
Whether upon the shore of Greece or Wales,
Whether in London or in Nagasaki,
A woman stands, pausing to count her dead.
Stillness finds there a time akin to sleep,
A pageant moving under watery veils,
Where Past and Future meet. The drapery
Of one bereaved remembers Niobe,
That vision coming at the end of sleep
And bringing death which is the end of sleep.
She, too, can show the lineaments of God.

And through that arc of blue, victorious light
Has left the silence of the battlefield,
Bringing from Marathon the death of Winter,
Declaring all things new which have a life,
Not waiting for the life which death revealed.
Mountains and broken marbles cast their shadow.
Quartz in the rock. Extinguished are the barrows.
Here the sea breaks; it scatters in wild spray.
Rock hears the knock of light, shields the dumb heart
        from day,
Divides the cloud, splinters the sun's keen arrows,
And sees him riding on with empty quiver.
After the loss, the hunger,
After named death on death, she grieves no longer.
Memory itself turns rock; that heart-sprung river
Ebbs in cold veins away.

Sea-holly, thrift and thistle crown her head,
Soft bloom of thistle, honeyed sea-pink blowing,
Dry-petalled, crisp, cold as the coral's bed,
Sprung from a sponge sucked dry from waters flowing.
There might the phoenix rest,
Feathering on ashen rock a fiery nest;
But still the rockflowers break, remorseful, red,

Like blood of children sacrificed in vain.
The wind blows through them, and they live again.
She does not live.
She is the quartz and shadow of her dead.
She, from her pangs a weary fugitive,
Hears not the sea, but sleeps heartbroken here,
Sleeps through the turning tide, the turning year,
Weaves and unweaves her magic thread of hours.
Her hands clutch victims, overthrown
In violent sleep, and clasp a stone
Entangled in the roots of barren flowers.

There is a light upon the waters now
That makes the lands all gay.
The warm sun softens earth.
The Spring returns and brings the longer day.
Birds shake the singing bough;
Quick buds put forth.
Thick blossoms weigh their branches to the ground.
Fruitful images abound.
Yet that low harp whose strings dead fingers play
Tells instantly these joys are purchased by
Deaths in the dazzling sky
Too ancient and inscrutable to know.
Blossoms are weaned from snow
By sleight of heavenly hand.
All things have passed through music; swift or slow,
Rooted in loss they stand.

Across the fields wild curlews call,
Spring's amorous, wavering cries.
They rise,
They fall,
Reaching the sea, lost in the blinding spray
Spending its light against a rocky wall.
And here, where no miraculous birth shall rise,
Her faith is fixed, and keeps the waves at bay.
Thistles take root in rock; they root in mould
In rifts of rock, hiding the rock-heart cold
Giving no access to the balm of healing,
No access to the pious hands of hope.
Who seeks her sorrow can but blindly grope.
Who touches, touches stone that has no feeling.
No consolation hers, who will not be consoled.

This woman had the mark of strong desires:
Love and maternal frenzy spurred her on
Until her only ones
Outshone the splendours of the sun and moon
And made their mother jealous of her pride.
There was no woman prouder of her sons,
There was no mother prouder of her daughters
Than Niobe was once.
Behold her changed, remembering their pyres.
Long is her second state: her first was brief.
Where are they now, on whom Fate's shadow falls
From inaccessible walls?
Fallen, all fallen, white seawreaths in the waters
Moving and changed, the scorn of every tide.
If the rock woke, what heart could bear her grief?

She shall not wake.
Her daughters and her sons shall not grow old;
Nor shall the bond between them break:
The water-course runs true, though it runs cold.
Her the sharp moon-shafts and the sunlight spears
Can strike no more; but from the treacherous mirror
Of night's and noonday's hopes and fears
She sinks through one dark universe of tears.
And there her conscience cries:
'One thing is terrible: to die in error.
Die quickly, Niobe, die!
Death is to enter again the changing circle.'
—'No circle, none, am I,
Who am rock, am not the sea.
What can the changes bring, ever, to me?
Let time ebb back: in me an anchor rests,
Far safer here than among the waves' white crests.
Here, where the cormorant stretches wings to dry
And stares into the sun,
I know an age of sorrow is begun,
And Atlas-like, I bear the moving sky.'

Look at the rock.
Look, look: there is a seagull in her body.
The veins are brilliant and the bones accuse
The seawaves' shock.
The low wind has a guilty song.
The sun has treacherous rays.

The sun's hands with the Winter's death are bloody
Time's seething wash its hungry groan renews,
And every stone cries out an ancient wrong.
Her crystal-gazing glass has drained the days
To the last minute, where the soul can praise
What is still faithful, but no longer strong.

The winged grief taloned in the place of death
Is she.
The frozen wintry stream's enchanted breath
Is she.
She is the stinging herb, the barb that rends.
She is the anchor of the winds and clouds.
She is the crag that bends
The stormcloud to its point that forms the floods.

Who knows the threshold of her secrecies,
And who can enter
The place that grief has forced with its own tears?
Where grief is true, it is the Earth that dies:
The image of one loved outweighs the Earth.
Why should she read the sundial's old degrees
Who knows a timeless birth,
Whose heart is fixed in rock beneath time's centre?
She cannot, like old trees,
Stretch forth a pattern from unwounded years.

Almost,
Almost she bears her children now again,
Weaned of the rocky ghost
Or born through anguish out of her own brain,
As though a fixed, a trance-like rage must breed
A supernatural seed.
She stays. She goes not; yet, as we look, is gone.
See the sad quartzlight glitter in the stone.

And she's the pivot and the pin of fable
Clothing the gods with mortal jealousies.
Bright is her midnight, but her day is sable,
And there is land beneath her windy seas.
She's the cornelian where the lost flesh hides,
Crossed and re-crossed by sorrow's hundred tides.

And she's dumb Winter of the stricken years,
And she is Job without his messengers.

Death in our life, Job, Winter, Niobe,
O mountain-rock that first imagined sea,
Tragedy, we have learnt from lives that pass,
Can, like a note of music, break time's glass;
And we, on whom destruction like a sword
Hangs, in dark fission and the atomic cloud,
Marvel to see the spirit of your grey spars
Guarding a glory nature had denied.
If death is measured by the truth we hide
And solace by the love that moves the stars,
Under time's cry, the seabird's constant flying,
Dropping your plummet to the utmost deep
Where worlds and grains turn over in their sleep,
Teach us the folds of truth, and your true dying.

Climbing above the Cave

Rock-rung echo, wrung from this moving
Step-quickened speaker, Antaeus-born light,
My cave-crossing shadow, lucky living,
Inverted, vertical, binds in flight
Fossil to wind-flower, stone to air,
The spaceless dead in their speechless rock
To a spirit hung on the windy stair,
Stunned by the dull waves' crash and shock.
Great hollows, then, make the fine strings speak;
'You were born to a musical order, die
To a musical order; seek, then, seek
Notes that were true in the Past.'

Here I
Unsheathe a dagger to pierce the sun.
I have trapped the winds, lassooed the sea,
Tread intricately this track where none
Hears what I hear, sees what I see,
All wedges, ledges being betrayed
To the last pressure of foot on stone.
Here time is stopped, and the crouching shade
Knows for an instant the unknown,
How my hand's companion, breaking the crust
Of violent hunters hidden beneath,
Signals an insurrection of dust,

And a mounted skeleton in the teeth
Of the waves and the whirlwind spurs his host
Into thundering seas.

My praying step
Can make rocks fast, uproot the coast,
With the faith of a prophet softly keep
Sea, mountain, and giant air
Dancing, forever changing, born
In a moment, then no longer there,
Lands that a wishbone laughs to scorn
Where the parched flint has eyes.

Yet here
Luminous tides and breeding winds
Tell me suddenly I am near
Darkness, the door of my hidden friends,
Where stone is a fading wonder, moss
A monument; there the glacier thrives
Dropping stalactites' marble gloss,
Quick as a shower of hail where knives,
Edged on the whetstone, turn.

For there
Fins cut the surface, flashing free.
Dolphins, leaping to light in air,
Turn, and bound on the wheel of sea.
Wave through the cave-mouth glorious swims,
Gathering from darkness my true day,
Wrenching from rock the eternal limbs
Where the soul's fathers, anchorites, pray.

A Prayer

If I dare pray for one
Gift in the coming age
That might protect my son
On every shifting stage
Keeping his joy as true
As now he feels in play
Fetching the ball I threw
Or pitched from day to day
Safe in a cot where sleep

Finds him still clasping toys
Until I step and stoop
And loose them with no noise,
I pray that he may have
Recourse in argument
After the falling wave
To what remains unspent,
That he may stoop and dare
To gather for his own
In that loud, hostile air
One word's deliberate throne,
I mean the uncounted praise,
The bridegroom's calm return
For which all nights and days
In speculation burn.
There where the breakers fly
Scattering their bridal lace,
Where instantly joy's eye
Rejects the commonplace,
Let him find strength to throw
Compromise to the winds
Though constancy forgo
All but his truest friends,
And patiently repair
The drift of broken vows,
Creating from despair
His Christ-appointed house,
That in the testing hour
Of hostile circumstance
His soul may put on power,
The impotence of chance
Revealing in his hold
On envy's taunting mind
Like Samson, tranquil-souled,
Who remained strong, though blind.

The Caryatids

for Rhiannon asleep

How still the Caryatids
Hold up their sleeping urns

Above the dreaming lids.
Hark, and the wash returns
Of time's remembered wrack.
Loud the wave breaks, and loud
The dragging wash ebbs back,
Threading a moonlit shroud.

In dread of lightning now
A towering breaker brings
Blackness beneath the Plough
And scatters seabirds' wings
Sleeping upon its crest.
The wild Earth wanders there
Stunned by the moon's unrest
Where seaweeds like gold hair

Cling to a dazzling shell.
Cold are these waters, cold
The tales no lips can spell
Asleep in that white fold;
Yet the grave arms how strong,
Supporting, while seas broke,
The balanced urns of song
Under the lightning-stroke.

Aggressive candour plays
Already in your eyes
Teaching you daring ways,
Lending your bold replies
An elemental charm
Pure as the light of dawn.
And how could I disarm
A truth so finely drawn

From the dark sheath of sleep?
You are not six years old;
Yet the first wash will keep,
Whatever life re-mould
With brush or palette-knife
Afterwards on the page.
And I, who watch your life
Against the uncertain age

Momentously at rest,
Already see divined

The joy by which we are blest
Moving in eyes declined.
How should I pray? My prayer
Found in closed eyelids stands
While seawaves pierce night's air
And pound the unyielding sands.

There all the reckoned grains
Obey the rock-like Word
Whose lightning love remains,
Waiting to be restored.
And still how patiently
They watch above your bed,
Nor touch the form I see.
Like footprints on the sea,
How near is love to dread!

The Dead Shag

Shag: a mummified bird.
The sea-flash never is still.
I have watched long, long,
The craning neck that stirred
To the fisherman's lightest sound.
Jet-winged skimmer of sea
Sped from the leaning hill;
Under my net I found
A blackened piece of a tree,
Touched through the brilliant curd
Of spray, a cold black thing;
Then at once I caught the thrill
Of a wing in the fire-wake charred.
Shag: a mummified bird.
The sea-flash never is still.

I did not expect that knot
Of black in the hollow pool.
I have watched long, long,
This glancing fisher-bird, shot
With every silk of the rock,
Rising in foam, then sheer
Dive through the spindrift spool

Under the herring-gulls' flock,
Always to reappear
In an unpredictable spot.
The light in the eye had set;
As I touched the rigid flesh,
Under my net it stayed
Sunken, the eye of jade
Seen through a narrow mesh.

Taut, hard to forget,
This under-water bird
Glistening, glistening low,
Would vanish under the net
Of waves, where vision would rest
On beams, till at last a speck
Emerged, a questioning head
Buoyed up between crest and crest.
I have watched the straining neck
Streaming on wind to set
Its wonder back in a wedge,
Then, its orbit ended, stop
On a ledge that overhung
Plumb chaos, where seabirds swung
But only their shades would drop.

Near to that meeting-place,
A guano-whitened rock,
Listening, listening low,
Hidden flat on my face
In grass, I have heard the wail
Of bird by eel-dark bird
Surveying the pitch and knock
Of the breakers' punishing flail,
Where the lightest trespassing word
Would prompt an exodus race,
A movement start like a shot
Each anchorite from its mark
To safety out in the bay.
I have lost the light of day
If once I have lost that dark.

The Heron

The cloud-backed heron will not move:
He stares into the stream.
He stands unfaltering while the gulls
And oyster-catchers scream.
He does not hear, he cannot see
The great white horses of the sea,
But fixes eyes on stillness
Below their flying team.

How long will he remain, how long
Have the grey woods been green?
The sky and the reflected sky,
Their glass he has not seen,
But silent as a speck of sand
Interpreting the sea and land,
His fall pulls down the fabric
Of all that windy scene.

Sailing with clouds and woods behind,
Pausing in leisured flight,
He stepped, alighting on a stone,
Dropped from the stars of night.
He stood there unconcerned with day,
Deaf to the tumult of the bay,
Watching a stone in water,
A fish's hidden light.

Sharp rocks drive back the breaking waves,
Confusing sea with air.
Bundles of spray blown mountain-high
Have left the shingle bare.
A shipwrecked anchor wedged by rocks,
Loosed by the thundering equinox,
Divides the herded waters,
The stallion and his mare.

Yet no distraction breaks the watch
Of that time-killing bird.
He stands unmoving on the stone;
Since dawn he has not stirred.
Calamity about him cries,
But he has fixed his golden eyes
On water's crooked tablet,
On light's reflected word.

Woodpecker and Lyre-Bird

On gorse displaying that greenish
  Glittering enamelled plumage,
    Startled, he skimmed rock, leaving
      A stone-grey socket of light.
He had seen me, sudden to vanish,
  Gone, bequeathing an image
    Of weighted brilliance, achieving
      In loops its ponderous flight.

Too shy at heart, of a hurt
  I would never do him possessed,
    He cut through those rocks like a cordon.
      I looked: again he was there,
The green-sunned wings, head alert,
  Keen talons and scarlet crest
    On a cry evicted, low burden,
      Too rich, too heavy for air.

Why did the ancients fear them?
  Wisdom belongs to the birds.
    They seek for their preservation
      A wit they teach to their young;
Fly when a foot comes near them,
  Make light of sibylline words,
    Turn leaves with a murmuration
      Or naked cry of the tongue.

Where the woodpecker chances to rest
  He changes hollow and fold,
    Makes fallow and rocky places
      Vibrate, as though to a bell.
They ruffle the ground who best
  Refine the horizon's gold;
    The design of outer spaces
      In the inmost they excel.

Primaeval music is most
  Itself that escapes the throng,
    Catches fire from a thorn,
      Of the nearest leaf takes hold.
Taliesin, body and ghost,
  Compelled his muscular song
    To gather glory unborn
      From a glory already old.

This lyre-bird holds to man
The covenant caught in a leaf,
All space, all distance treasured
By the architectural wing.
Lost art's unsearchable span,
The poem is shaped by belief:
If the song is justly measured
The dead may be heard to sing.

A Book from Venice

Books are like water. Silver, laughing river
From Venice, making light play after two hundred years;
Yes, here are Dante and Guido, the companions,
Fountain ascending.

They rise from sandgrains where they seemed forgotten.
Sound here through leaf-light hooves of early singing,
These Tuscan poets. Fresher breaks their morning,
Found at the sea's edge.

So shine, serene one: plumage of two eagles
Fading, like specks, beyond the Tuscan mountains.
Then, where one plunges, all the married ages
Fall from the hour-glass.

Ah twofold vision, marvel of the print-fount,
Woven light vanishing, yet returning ever,
Binding the Past, a water-thread of music
Veining the ear-shell.

O eyes of sleep, life of lost ages,
O thread of fingers, craft of careful printers,
Light in eyes lost, so near and yet so distant,
Breath on this opal:

Wave on wave breaking, endless enchantment,
Thunder of sea-spray, the constant horizon.
O ring of lives, O Earth unchanging,
Song, the newborn one.

Light in the nautilus, nimbus of distance,
Glory of the foal's eyes asleep in dune-grass,
Lost as the skylark, through that blue ascending,
Light of the word's fall,

How have you chained me, with the voice of exile
Evoking the centuries, vanished like gondolas,
Gone with the sea-flash, inconstant, brilliant,
Printing on aether

Praise of linked sounds, particular creation,
Spun of pure glory, labyrinth of stillness
Carrying all secrets to their final cadence,
Ageless as morning.

Epithalamion

FOR MICHAEL HAMBURGER

There are no waters that shall tell their tale
Though white and falling like a bridal veil,
So secret is the pulse of man
That beat before time's river ran
And shall, when it has stopped, in light prevail.

To-night is glory, when Saint Valentine
Shall tread out thoughts and crush his grapes to wine.
Delicate instruments must wake
For the dumb heart's impulsive sake
The attentive harmony of pure design.

Unfold the tapestry where images
Move on the fabric base and are at peace.
Let wine and torches then revive
Their deathborn mystery made alive,
Escorted from the sacred rites of Greece.

For now the branches of two ancestries
Are broken down, and become grafted trees.
Now calculated shades must move
Towards the new centre of their love
And printless sundials learn the unknown degrees.

What myth-embroidered darkness black as pitch
Now makes the unfolded tapestry so rich,
Or why should those assenting shades
Rebuke that phoenix which upbraids
Time's patient needle and laborious stitch?

Far back, the sacred pattern still is found,
Two lovers walking on the verdant ground
Through avenues of suffering,
Controlling the deceit of Spring
With their dropped voices' distance-mastering sound.

But ask what mystery isolates a man
From time, or how that separation can
Bring closer to the living heart
That contemplation which, apart,
Had seemed eccentric to its cause and plan.

Where lay his work if nature was the norm?
Perfection was the soul resisting form.
He watched its utmost passion grow,
Controlled by Michelangelo:
The Sistine wonder shook him like a storm.

Then, in the labyrinths of solitude
Seeking a place where no man might intrude,
His mind was checked by its own shade
Where intellect and music made
A book by mutual intercourse renewed.

When night had buried all that he had learned
In sleep, with looms and libraries inurned
And fossil carvings from the silt,
Over the starry waters' quilt
At dawn the unpredictable returned.

And so it fell; before his lover's eye
Moved she the firstborn is remembered by.
Dawn broke the shivered glass and, steep,
Woke Adam from his second sleep,
And all creation hung upon a cry.

The swallow now is home. The singing sea
Beats to a whirlpool wild virginity.
Andromeda has lost her chains
And where the astounded rock remains
A myth is born of myth's captivity.

Her lover, poised above the timeless pole,
Sped by the hour when lightning struck his soul,
Now plunges his heroic spear
Through the subdued, devouring year,
And time the dragon falls to his control.

From truth how is it possible to hide?
What clouds conspire the lightning will decide.
Though desolation gave him wings
Their brightest hour is that which brings
Darkness to rock and radiance to his bride.

The Shell

Who could devise
But the dark sea this thing
Of depth, of dyes
Claws of weed cling,
Whose colour cries:
'I am of water, as of air the wing',
Yet holds the eyes
As though they looked on music perishing?

Yet the shell knows
Only its own dark chamber
Coiled in repose
Where without number
One by one goes
Each blind wave, feeling mother-of-pearl and amber,
Flooding, to close
A book all men might clasp, yet none remember.

Too far away
For thought to find the track,
Sparkling with spray
Rose, green and black,
The colours play,
Strained by the ebb, revealing in the wrack
The myth of day,
A girl too still to call her bridegroom back.

There falls the weight
Of glory unpossessed;
There the sands late
Hold the new guest
Whose ponderous freight
Draws the pool's hollow like a footprint pressed.
Its outcast state
Suddenly seems miraculous and blest.

Turn it; now hold
Its ancient heart. How fair
With lost tales told
In sea-salt air
Light's leaf-of-gold
Leaps from the threshold up the spiral stair,
Then lost, is cold,
Bound in a flash to rock with Ariadne's hair.

Art and the Ravens

Art holds in wind the way the ravens build
Breeding, flying, and still the thread holds fast.
Birth cries out, flying; and where the cry is stilled
Substance gives way, the talon grips the Past.
At the rock's foot fossils and wrecks are cast.
Still the cry wanders, though the cry is stilled.
Art holds in wind the way the ravens build.

Stand to time now, my Muse,
Unwavering, like this rock
The mated ravens use,
Building against the shock
Of dawn, a throne in air
Above the labouring sea,
Yet fine as a child's hair
Because great industry
Accomplishes no art
To match the widespread wing
Riding the heavens apart,
A lost, yet living thing.

Stumbling their rock-rung way,
I startle them. They drop
Over the verge of day,
Buoyed by the sea-wind up.
Then, seeing my shade molest
The gaunt and threadbare place
Where hangs their windy nest,
See with what towering grace,
As wave's ninth wonder whirls
Its fleece against that wall,

He superb wings unfurls
With talons poised, to fall.

O great, O guardian strength,
Vertical power of wings,
True plummet found at length
By devious reckonings,
Your skirmishings protect
Love's brood, the hidden young,
By piercing intellect
High in the balance hung.
Far down, the breakers prove
Accomplishment all vain
Till art, the body of love,
Is won from death again.

One raven floats away
To scour the wrack and glide
Raucous above the bay,
Returning soon in pride
To perch upon this crest
Whose hollows fill the air
With voice on voice at rest
Lost in the breakers there.
And then both ravens give
Their dark fair-weather cry,
Watching the wild earth live
From those twin points of sky.

O dark, interior flame,
O spring Elijah struck:
Obscurity is fame;
Glory and praise are luck.
Nothing can live so wild
As those ambitious wings
Majestic, for love's child
Defending ancient springs.
Drifting in light, they stall.
Winds' conflict keeps them true.
Sunbeam and breaker's fall
Confound them. They cut through.

Art holds in wind the way the ravens build
Breeding, flying, and still the thread holds fast.
Crag falls to crag; and where that cry is stilled,

Under black wings the talon grips the Past.
At the rock's foot fossils and wrecks are cast.
The sky is falling: distance is fulfilled.
Art holds in wind the way the ravens build.

Taliesin in Gower

Late I return, O violent, colossal, reverberant, eavesdropping sea.
My country is here. I am foal and violet. Hawthorn breaks from my
hands.
I watch the inquisitive cormorant pry from the praying rock of Pwlldu,
Then skim to the gulls' white colony, to Oxwich's cockle-strewn sands.

I have seen the curlew's triangular print, I know every inch of his way.
I have gone through the door of the foundered ship, I have slept in the
winch of the cave
With pine-log and unicorn-spiral shell secreting the colours of day;
I have been taught the script of the stones, and I know the tongue of the
wave.

I witness here in a vision the landscape to which I was born,
Three smouldering bushes of willow, like trees of fire, and the course
Of the river under the stones of death, carrying the ear of corn
Withdrawn from the moon-dead chaos of rocks overlooking its secret
force.

I see, a marvel in Winter's marshes, the iris break from its sheath
And the dripping branch in the ache of sunrise frost and shadow redeem
With wonder of patient, living leaf, while Winter, season of death,
Rebukes the sun, and grinds out men's groans in the voice of its
underground stream.

Yet now my task is to weigh the rocks on the level wings of a bird,
To relate these undulations of time to a kestrel's motionless poise.
I speak, and the soft-running hour-glass answers; the core of the rock is a
third:
Landscape survives, and these holy creatures proclaim their regenerate
joys.

I know this mighty theatre, my footsole knows it for mine.
I am nearer the rising pewit's call than the shiver of her own wing.
I ascend in the loud waves' thunder, I am under the last of the nine.
In a hundred dramatic shapes I perish, in the last I live and sing.

All that I see with my sea-changed eyes is a vision too great for the brain.
The luminous country of auk and eagle rocks and shivers to earth.
In the hunter's quarry this landscape died; my vision restores it again.
These stones are prayers; every boulder is hung on a breath's miraculous
birth.

Gorse breaks on the steep cliff-side, clings earth, in patches blackened for
sheep,
For grazing fired; now the fair weather comes to the ravens' pinnacled
knoll.
Larks break heaven from the thyme-breathing turf; far under, flying
through sleep,
Their black fins cutting the rainbow surf, the porpoises follow the shoal.

They are gone where the river runs out, there where the breakers divide
The lacework of Three Cliffs Bay in a music of two seas;
A heron flaps where the sandbank holds a dyke to the twofold tide,
A wave-encircled isthmus of sound which the white bird-parliament flees.

Rhinoceros, bear and reindeer haunt the crawling glaciers of age
Beheld in the eye of the rock, where a javelin'd arm held stiff,
Withdrawn from the vision of flying colours, reveals, like script on a page,
The unpassing moment's arrested glory, a life locked fast in the cliff.

Now let the great rock turn. I am safe with an ear of corn,
A repository of light once plucked, from all men hidden away.
I have passed through a million changes. In a butterfly coracle borne,
My faith surmounting the Titan, I greet the prodigious bay.

I celebrate you, marvellous forms. But first I must cut the wood,
Exactly measure the strings, to make manifest what shall be.
All Earth being weighed by an ear of corn, all heaven by a drop of blood.
How shall I loosen this music to the listening, eavesdropping sea?

Cantata for the Waking of Lazarus

There sang a fountain in a Syrian courtyard leaping
Near to the place where Lazarus, the loved of Jesus, lay,
Lazarus, four days dead, alone in shadow sleeping.
Some say that in the sepulchre where mute he lay
There on the burning rose of resurrection-day
His eyes were sleeping fixed, although his veins were cold.
They bathed his feet beside the eucalyptus tree;

They gave him simple burial, neither myrrh nor gold;
Yet did the fountain-drops cry out that he could see,
Cry out that he could feel although his hands were cold;
The fountain cried that he, in that grave shadow sleeping,
Alone could see God's face, and blind with sun were they
Who climbed the mountain slowly on the rocky way.
Now did the sun climb heaven, but one who cast a shade,
Seeing a white crowd near the tomb-mouth with much weeping,
Prayed for him with closed eyes; with love's great strength he prayed:

Lazarus dead, rise up: for you the doves obeying
The voice of light within the water's utmost crown
Change all the drops to glory. In their cloud delaying,
Pity at last the rich, consumed by their renown.
A winding-sheet has veiled the silence of love's glory,
Earth purified by love, no life not full of light;
Sleep in the sepulchre, believe that ancient story,
That ancient sun believe, on Moses' tablets raying,
Yet see these petals breaking near the source, and white
Roses on thorny stems, and white acacia swaying
Where glinting birds alight above the ringing cup.
Crumble this crust of birth to throw to ring-doves playing.
Rise through the waking Earth; Lazarus dead, rise up.

Come to me, God, who sleep, who know that holy stave
Sung when hands laid me down within the fallen tears,
Wound in a winding-sheet, a caul about my ears,
Who must endure this dark, the freshly covered grave;
The Romans drove you out, they hunted you with spears,
Yet you have pieced my flesh, have knit me, bone to bone,
Have kindled here this force, behind the sombre stone,
To wake, yet not to wake, who hear that holy stave.

Then, as the people passed, the fountain ceased from leaping,
While yet unwakened by the Son of God he slept.
By this were many gathered near the tomb-mouth with much
weeping.
Then did the fountain stop. That moment, Jesus wept.

Then sang those little birds upon the very stone
Where the dead spoke for that first time and all the folk drew near;
So great a marvel had not yet on Earth been known,
For the young man came forth, and it was he they knew;
And they drew back amazed; it shook their hearts with fear
To see the young man walk. Then that white retinue
Knew that their own last resurrection had come near.

Come, O Redeemer, come; come down, and make Earth new.

Love, newly born, come down: for you the fountain playing
Leaps into light, then spills, and fills the basin's brim.
Water gives life to stone, and light renews our saying:
For you the sages wait, and listening cherubim
Support the fountain's weight around its marble base.
For you the ages wait, old prophets are not still
Around this font of birth; they strain to see your face.

For you his winding horn a Triton's lips are playing;
His crooked eyes in water watch the fountain fill.
For you the doves of light return from their far straying,
Too long away, too long, in that Italian town.
Open my eyes at last, my eyes long shut with praying,
And let me see your eyes: love, newly born, come down.

Ballad of the Rough Sea

I like the smell of the wind, the sniff,
Said a man on the top of Dover cliff.
I like the voice of the sea, the sound,
Said the fossil-man asleep in the ground.
And I want to look over the sea,
Said the man on the cliff-top free.
I want to look over the sea,
I will look over the sea.

The sun fell slant on the cliff's white face
And the waters ran under the sails in a race
But the fossil-man in his bed of chalk
Turned in his grave and began to talk:
O what's the good of a man in a rock
Who will not wake when the seawaves knock?
I want to stand up in the rock,
I will stand up in the rock.

O the seagulls are crying, the seagulls scream
That the sea is cruel and blue and green
But to-day the waters are white with spray
And hark in the boats what the fishermen say:
'It's a rough grey day with the tide coming in
And a haul of herring's a slippery skin

For the waters are deep and the nets are thin.
It's a rough grey day with the tide coming in.'

The fishers were fishing in little boats
From Cap Grisnez to John o' Groats
When the man in the rock and the man on the cliff
Met, like a shadow sheer and stiff.
They were shooting their hooks from the side
And the wind coming in with the tide.
They were leaning and looking over the side.
They were shooting their hooks from the side.

There's a phantom above the seawaves' roar
Screams, and a man has come through the door
Of the chalkwhite cliff, and star and sea
Are locked in the fear of a fisherman's knee,
But louder and louder the white waves hiss—
They will never come out of this.
Till the stars fall and the stone mouths kiss
They will never come out of this.

Come up from the sea, you sandy shoals
That lurk where Leviathan swims and rolls!
Like the pointed limpets stung by foam
Bared by the black wave leaping home
Come up from the sea, you crags,
Where the soaked straw-pillow sags,
Come up for the wreck's black-timbered rags,
Come up from the sea, you crags.

'O wandering water white and free
As the runaway stag that hides in the tree,
As the runaway stag that flies from the horn,
Fly to the low roof where we were born
And pull the door from the hinge and throw
The seven wild windows all in a row
And the tables and chairs in the room below
Through the white sea-jaws throw!

There are loaves of bread in the wooden chest
And safe on the hooks the white cups rest
And high on the shelf are sugar and tea
But cold is the darkness under the sea.
There's a floor unsafe beneath
And the sea has a wolf's white teeth.

O sweet would it be to beg and breathe.
There's a floor unsafe beneath.

O gallows-man on the cliff-top free,
Why do you fix your eyes on the sea?
O man in the rock erect and stiff,
Why are you pale as the dead white cliff?
O is it your thought and is it your wish
To help us to catch a creel of fish?
The waters to-night are devilish.
O tell us your thought and your wish.'

I have left in a room my rope and pin.
I will open your eyes when the sea rolls in.
I have left in a cave my bony skull.
I am waiting to hear the cry of a gull
For a seagull is crying aloud
That the sea is white as a shroud,
That, whiter than whitest moon or cloud,
The sea is white as a shroud.

'Go back to your rock, go back to your room.
We are men of heart, not men of the tomb.
Not the sea's twist nor the wind's alarms
Shall pull us down from the New Moon's arms,
And our ships are good black teak.
Go back, for we must not speak.
Go back to the crevice, back to the creek.
Go back, for we must not speak.'

Ballad of the Equinox

Pwlldu*—an eternal place!
The black stream under the stones
Carries the bones of the dead,
The starved, the talkative bones.

There the great shingle-bank
Props a theatrical scene
Where guess the generous dead
What lovers' words may mean.

* Pwlldu—Welsh for 'black pool'—is pronounced 'Poollh-dee'.

When the sun and the moon are level
And the sky has a fish's scales
I stand by the foxy foam
On that groaning shingle of Wales.

Beyond Hunt's moonlike bay,
That pockmarked crescent of rocks,
White horses, dead white horses,
Priests of the equinox,

Deride my lonely curse,
And the moon rides over, pale,
Where the wicked wet dog in the hearse
And the devil in the wind prevail.

The wild wind screams they are mad
Whom the sun and moon delight.
I have followed the curve of the stones
Into this lonely night.

And I hurl a stick to the wave
And watch it slowly come,
By all the tides of the grave,
Stopped, like the tick of the foam.

Here, brought by foam, it lies,
A spent and weary log,
A crab with a million eyes
And a cast-up, wicked dog

Its marriage witnesses
On the sterile porch of Hell.
And yet I know this is
The last dead miracle,

Mightier than the mole
That draws with the strength of ten,
Yoke of great oxen,
Yoke, and mover of men.

Though itself a barren thing,
It has been where none has been,
Knows what no actor knows
On this theatrical scene:

'O unsatisfied!
O terrible and alone!

Come to the edge of the tide
And find what none has known,

That the allegorical shadow
Of the lover will not swerve
Though the moon drive him to madness
With its sailing curve.'

Pwlldu—an eternal place!
The black stream under the stones
Carries the bones of the dead,
The starved, the talkative bones.

Ballad of Crawley Woods

Who guards the secret of this wood
Dropping from hill to wave?
What monster bids a virgin good
Rise up from his own grave
And walk the road and then return,
Taught by the moving leaves?
What legend from a lettered urn
Heaves when the forest heaves?

A whispering, violent, vaunting wind
Can turn the branches pale,
Can make the eyes of hazels blind
And blasphemy prevail:
'Rise up, rise up, Rhossili Sands,
Beat on a pagan drum!
You with a missal in your hands,
Put down your book, and come.'

*

A skeleton rose near Crawley Woods,
Heaved the gravestone back.
Dock-leaves covered his ankle-bones.
The night around was black.
'Now that the dark is thick,' he said,
'No footstep on the road,
I, that never found human love,
May find the love of God.'

'O cock your head, O cock your head,'
The lovely darkness cried,
'There goes that horseman riding;
We love to hear him ride;
Galloping from Rhossili Sands
Along that edge of spray,
Spurring the horse beneath his hands
To April's bridal day.'

'My mind runs back to summertime.
I kept a sacred fast.
I, to an ash along a wall
Rooted in the Past
That put forth leaves of living green
Although it lay there prone,
Returned from windy Paviland
To live my life alone.'

What branches rouse above his head?
What noise of wind and sea?
About him all the quick and dead
Are keeping company;
And past him leaves and spectres race,
Each with a secret bride,
Seeking in earth a dancing-place,
In roots a place to hide.

What sudden terror shakes the trees,
What thunder-clap of whips?
'Under the wind with kisses,
Your weight beneath my lips!'
What do the whirling dead leaves say,
Vanishing to the South?
'Under the night in your dear arms,
Ah lift me, mouth to mouth!'

'O cock your head, O cock your head:
Married by a chain,
These the storm that whirled asleep
Now whirls awake again.
Very fine chains they carry,
Slender chains of gold.
All these the night-winds marry
Must wed beneath the mould.

O, had you kissed the fresh green leaf,
Not the leaf that was bound,
You would be riding fast asleep,
Riding under the ground
With Paolo and Francesca
Whom Dante found in Hell.
Every whirling withered leaf
Leads you to some cell.'

'Where goes Rhossili's rider,
And where, these restless dead?
I trespass everywhere I walk
On some lover's bed.
Who roused this hunger in my sleep?
Who prised me from my mound?
Why does my soul imagine rape?
Why do the leaves run round?'

*

Now this is the Ballad of Crawley Woods;
No more is there to say.
Now let the rich man give his goods,
Nor keep the poor away,
But think of him who lies there still
And wishes all men well,
Hearing the branches on the hill,
Hearing the breakers' bell.

Though long he lay in death's embrace,
That tree and wall were true.
The rose in that rose-window
Knew every leaf that grew.
For him each single drop of dew
Trembled, a world of praise.
The secret of the dead he knew
None but their Christ can raise.

Ballad of the Three Coins

I know this road like the back of my hand
From birth to the lonely sea
With a windblown dog and a bottle of sand,
And I count my curses three.

The birds of the sea hang high in the air
And the land-birds crowd the tree.
I go, they cannot tell me where,
But their cries were torn from me.

A mile beyond Red Chamber
Flashes a light of broken skies.
The mother-of-pearl of the winkle-shell
Runs back to drowned men's eyes.

I take this first of the paths which run
Seaward from the thorny wood.
Flocks of starlings darken the sun,
And the moon is in my blood.

Swollen shoes, a pole and a pack,
And three considered coins;
A pain in the head, a pain in the back,
And a great pain in the groins.

They say the dawn brings learning
And the midnight, love.
The sun and the moon should teach me;
The stars should dig my grave.

But the bones that are I are the bones of a man
Walking between two lives.
The three coins of the Furies
Leap on the road of knives.

The first coin spins in the light of Dawn.
I see it glint and burn.
There is eager thought in those patient eyes.
Athene, O, your turn.

'Go to the field and you will find
A woman milking a cow.'
Beautiful dawn, instruct me:
Dawn, and the olive-bough.

I passed a field where they buried a man.
A dark priest in a cowl
Prayed above his body,
And over him swept an owl.

Then I came, I came to a five-barred gate
Where a slow sight held me still.

A woman was gripping the teats of a cow,
A bucket waiting to fill.

The curse of Earth is the curse of the beggar.
Intellect breaks his sleep.
No books in the world will slake that thirst,
So swift it is, and deep.

I raised the white milk high on my head
Where it shone like Solomon's crown.
That world would have stood for ever,
But the second coin pulled me down.

The second coin spins in the light of Noon.
I see it glint and burn.
There is jealous arrogance in those eyes.
This is Juno's turn.

> 'Go to the stream and you will find
> A queen where the light is strong.'
> Beautiful noon, instruct me:
> Noon, and the cuckoo's song.

I went, I went to the faltering stream,
And a rare sight held me back.
A woman bathed from the water's edge,
Stopped me in my track.

I fixed my eyes on her. At once
Jealousy ran through my blood.
Her proud beauty was the sun's,
Her brood the eagle's brood.

I could not cross the stepping-stones
For jealousy jumped on my back.
I cursed the crone on my great back-bone.
I cursed her white and black.

O stint and glint of the jealous flint,
O pride of the flashing crown!
What was the good of a haughty queen?
A beggar cannot lie down.

At last I managed my way across
That crooked, evil stream,
And I found a stone with a little green moss
And a lost, illegible name.

I stretched my legs and my heart was still;
I fixed my eyes on a tree;
When the third great pain got hold of me,
The worst of those bad three.

O let me be, you women!
O my coins were curses three.
The first I carried, the second I buried,
The third I'll cast to the sea.

The third coin spins in the Starlight.
O where are the first two gone?
Come down, engendering darkness.
A wild dog leads me on.

What rest is there on the love-starved Earth
When the sea is starved for love?
Beautiful Night, instruct me:
Night, and the turtle-dove.

'Run down, run down to the yellow-white foam,
A naked girl you will see
Who will take that last coin from you,
The worst of those bad three.'

To the beach I went, I went to the rock,
I stood where the limpets clung.
The salt blood sprang at my heart's great knock,
And now the salt wind stung.

What have I come to win from death
Girding up my loins?
Swollen shoes, a pole and a pack,
And the last of three bad coins.

What if, when I come to the yellow-white foam,
Nothing I can see
But a bottle up to its neck in sand
And a wet dog peeled by the sea?

O what of Athene's halo
And what of Solomon's crown?
And what of Juno's jealous love?
A beggar cannot lie down.

But now by the yellow-white foam I stand,
And all is altered, all is changed,

All that logic of the land
Ravished and deranged.

The barren bears the fruits of the Earth
And the fruit bears barrenness.
The sun and the moon know nothing,
And between them I know less.

Ballad of Hunt's Bay

It was a grey and ghoulish day;
The rocks were hidden or taken to pray,
But the 'Maid of Ireland' kept her way.

The Sabbath! A tree-log lying at rest;
A flying priest under each white crest;
A searcher under the raven's nest.

The waters ran white in their shivering bands
Baring their teeth, tore streams to strands.
Oystercatchers screamed on the sands.

The wrack was crowded with bundles of straw,
Jettisoned palliasse, planks, and raw
Ropes entangled with wing and claw.

Galloping grains; motionless flint;
A black stick holds my eyes intent,
In a moment spanning the ocean footprint.

'Who are you, Sir? What finds you here?'
—'I am Sir Vulture, to bring you cheer.
  I sing this song to the hermit's ear.'

A flash in the shell and he was gone:
Sea-horse and rider of horse were one,
But the 'Maid of Ireland' still kept on.

Sucked by bells, the shingle ground
Out of the ebb a deathlike sound
Of nail-torn sea-wood, bones of the drowned.

Seagulls rose, and their shadows cried:
'He that spoke and was at your side
Lied not. Wait for another tide.'

Day is shrunk to a bubbling seed.
Double your back to the smell of the weed.
Black in the pools the wet planks bleed.

Time reflowers in an earlier mould.
Stones and pebbles are smoothed and rolled.
Seabirds are scouring the beach for gold.

Scrabbled bark, and a bone picked clean;
Two sharp rocks, and a log between.
Under the surface, hands unseen.

Fingers picking the holes of the coast,
Riddling water, their needle is lost;
They quiver about us, ah haunting host!

Many timbers, many and one.
A host of fears in the rising sun.
Near me the circling waters run.

Under the stupefying wave
A limpet grips their slippery grave.
Flat ghosts in sackcloth crawl through the cave.

Hands closed on the task they did.
Skill is asleep in the light of the lid,
And the fast green waves have something hid.

Floating there, where rings of the pool
Unwind forever their wonder's spool,
Are wooden parts of the sunken tool.

Under the drifting wood they walk.
A stanchion rusting, thrusting a stalk.
Screws scraping sand grind dead men's talk.

Bewildered spray and a broken vow.
Silk of the pool, is it then or now?
The moon is milking the old sea-cow.

What foundered ironwork? Smart and cold
Is the tar on the stinging wood I hold,
Stained with a word no stars foretold.

A hiss, a flash, and a weed blown back.
How can a voice come out of a sack,
Or breath from pieces of wood gone black?

Voices, inch-shallow, I mark and miss.

The cormorant flies from them. Cold shells hiss.
Land shudders back from the dead's white kiss.

He crosses the water a second late,
Flees with his shadow, low and straight,
And the shadow touches his wings like fate.

'O cross the water, far and wide,'
Cries the floating wood and the breath inside,
'Fly to my mother—
my lost—
my bride.'

'O cross the water to cupboard and hod,
To loaf and cup,' sings the breath of the god
Through the broken stick, my divining-rod.

And blind with fury the sea runs in,
Nailing their hands to a rustgold tin,
Guilty, and white with the breath of men.

'Maid of Ireland,' unseen Maid,
Why is the pulse in my hand afraid
To touch the sea-wood, soaked with dread?

Stunned, the oystercatchers escape
White from the rock, like birds in sleep.
There is no secret the rocks can keep.

What shipyard town where the sea-log lies
Sees the morning founder in their eyes?
Is there a book to keep their sighs?

Sighs of sailors, lusty, strong,
Tossed to the boomerang beat of a gong,
Lost in the fall of the curlew's song.

True is the teak and the pitchpine, true
The wood of the hatch, and every screw.
The sea spits white the curse of the crew.

And long, long after, caught in a cleft,
A slumbering mammoth of wood is left,
Eyeless, limbless, dumb and deaf.

Spirit laid in the long dumb wood,
Floundering, sleeping, left by the flood,
Freed by the wave, by the ninth wave's hood,

Ride till you come where men are cast
To a music binding Future and Past
Heard by Ulysses, lashed to the mast.

'Who are you, Sir? What brings you here,
Looming out of the path they steer?'
—'Cover your eyes. Their hour is near.'

I hold in my hands the broken stick,
And the voice in the fork cries out, 'Be quick!'
—'Be slow. I, too, have a bone to pick.'

Who in the mist at my elbow stands?
O blenched waters, crystal sands.
—'I launch them out of your waking hands.

I am the bone the salt winds bleach.
Me the widows of hope beseech.
I am the rope that did not reach.'

Who is it flies
Blinding my eyes,
In a moment spanning the ocean footprint?

Stick, stick,
Broken stick,
Why do you breathe? Why do you glint?

'I see a chain of white hands thrown,
But the voice in your fingers is your own.
Leave me. Let me lie on a stone.'

And I fling the broken stick away
With the world and the ocean under its sway;
And silence pulls the thunders away.

Ballad of Culver's Hole

What feet are heard about these rocks
This highest tide of the year?
White spray of the equinox,
You chill the heart with fear.

Two boats close in from East and West
On a little boat that feels

The lucky weight of Culver
Gripping the stolen creels.

Is it the rope of Culver
Where the shag has the wit to dive,
Dragged through the shivering breakers,
That makes these rocks alive?

A great, round barrel
He has rolled up that grey beach.
Voices like claws are closing in,
Almost within reach.

In a moment he has vanished.
The gully's packed with dread.
Where is he hiding in the rocks,
The man they took for dead?

'Between this headland and that point
He surely ran aground.
Who saw the cunning hare stop dead
To cheat the flying hound?

You up there, on the cliff's dark brows,
You who stand there stiff,
Where does Culver keep his house,
Perched upon what cliff?'

'We know nothing, we know nothing,
Never found his nest.
Ours is the crooked haystack,
The white-washed farm at rest.

We hear nothing, we hear nothing,
Only seabirds' cries.
Call his name to the rock, and then
Hear what the rock replies.

A white-washed cottage, a house of stone
Might not hold your man.
Out of a nest of bleaching bone
The brightest fisher sprang.

We have seen the kestrel hang in the air
And where the ravens glide
Have combed the rocks for laver-bread
And the cockles in the tide.

But danger haunts the upper ledge
Here where the seagull flies.
Why do you ask us gently
With murder in your eyes?

Watch, watch your footing.
The stones in the ledge are loose.
Under this hollow cliff the sea
Is hissing like a goose.'

'Let two upon the green turf go
And two upon the rocks.
A great tide is running,
On the door of death it knocks.

It roars to have him hammered down
With nails to the sea bed.
Where is he hiding in the rocks,
The man we took for dead?'

'The equinox is rising;
The sky to the West is black.
The sea has drowned a hundred pools:
Should we not go back?'

'To think, that fish was in my net
And now has got away.
He beckons for the sun to set
And the waters fill the bay.'

'Go back, go back, and leave him
Before it is too late.
The sea has drowned a thousand pools.
We cannot fight with Fate.

The great rock and the little rock,
They slip beneath the wave.
These breakers have drawn blood before,
Their lilies strewn a grave.

The mole beneath the giant sea
Is heaping mound on mound.
Make for the ship, come quickly,
Or we shall all be drowned.'

'The dark is helping the digging mole
To cut our exit off.

Who could smoke out a smuggler's hole
In a sea so blind and rough?

God rot the guts of Culver
By whom the good man dies.
He laughs behind a wall of rock
Where every rock has eyes.'

Now each rock wears disguises,
Each darkened stone deceives,
And louder the wave rises
With a noise of rustling leaves.

But before the long wave hit the ground
The shag had the wit to dive.
Those greyhounds covered at a bound
The hare they left alive.

Their noose is for that goose of the sea,
But they have not caught him yet.
A barrel rises slowly
Just where the sun had set.

Ballad of the Trial of Sodom

God came to Abram
Abram the man
Who knew no glory
Could resist God's ban,
And God said: '*Abram,*
I come to destroy
Sodom, Sodom,
Sodom, Sodom,
That golden city
Of sin and joy.'

Thunder. Thunder. Thunder. Thunder.
Death is terrible, a thing of wonder.
First is a lethargy that no man likes,
Then comes the moment when the lightning strikes.

Then Abram, trying
To save that place,
Thinking of the dying,

Fell upon his face.
'Lord, if there were fifty
Righteous men
In Sodom, Sodom,
Sodom, Sodom,
Men who were steadfast,
Would you destroy it then?'

Heaven knows what payment
An advocate should ask,
But old man Abram
Had the hardest task.
He looked at Sodom
And he heard God's voice:
'Sodom, Sodom,
Sodom, Sodom;
Hide not the city
That my hand destroys.'

And Abram was trying
To save that place.
He lay for a long time
And could not lift his face.
'White though the lightning
Where the thunder rolls
Towards Sodom, Sodom,
Sodom, Sodom,
I shall not destroy it
If there are fifty souls.'

And Abram pondered.
He could not make amends.
It lightened and thundered.
He counted up his friends.
'Lord God, have patience.
May flesh be left alive
In Sodom, Sodom,
Sodom, Sodom,
That doomed city,
If the fifty lack five?'

The Lord God darkened
Like a fiery cloud.
Abram waited
As he lay there bowed;

He saw Hell's demons
In a midnight dive
In Sodom, Sodom,
Sodom, Sodom.
*'I shall not destroy it
For the forty-and-five.'*

'Lord God, have patience.
Destruction is just;
To hide the accursed
In the darkest dust.
But should there be forty
In the temple found
Of Sodom, Sodom,
Sodom, Sodom,
Then would you brand it,
Raze it to the ground?

Abram breathed.
A long breath he took.
He thought of the temple,
And the temple shook.
Monsters of sacrilege
Sprawled where it stood
In Sodom, Sodom,
Sodom, Sodom,
*'I would not brand it
For the forty good.'*

And Abram knew,
Abram knew,
This was the hardest
Peace for which to sue.
'Lord God, forgive me
That I should speak again
Of Sodom, Sodom,
Sodom, Sodom.
Would you spare the city
For thirty good men?'

Thunder. Thunder. Thunder. Thunder.
Death is terrible, a thing of wonder.
First is a lethargy that no man likes,
Then comes the moment when the lightning strikes.

And Abram counted.
Try as he would,
He could not make the number up
To thirty good.
The Judgment's answer
Came upon him then:
'Tell Sodom, Sodom,
Sodom, Sodom,
I shall not destroy it
For thirty good men.'

Abram was silent.
Abram was dumb.
He heard Hell's demons
Beating on a drum.
He saw men carried
Under long, slim poles
Through Sodom, Sodom,
Sodom, Sodom.
'Lord, would you save it
For twenty souls?'

This was the last time.
This was the last.
Now for the brimstone
And the blinding blast.
He saw huge darkness
Like a hangman's hood
On Sodom, Sodom,
Sodom, Sodom.
'I still would spare it
For the twenty good.'

'Lord, Thou art just.
Lord, Thou art just.
How should we utter
Who are less than dust?
Yet so wicked
Are the hearts of men
In Sodom, Sodom,
Sodom, Sodom.
Still would you spare it
If the good were ten?'

Fearful the silence,

Fearful the span
Stretching that moment
Between God and man.
Abram sweated
His life out then
For Sodom, Sodom,
Sodom, Sodom.
'I shall not destroy it
If the good are ten.'

Abram the father
Counting up the cost
Saw faith plainly
And knew that he had lost.
God looked at Sodom
In that pleading place,
Sodom, Sodom,
Sodom, Sodom.
Down looked Abram,
And he lost his case.

Ballad of the Two Tapsters

Two tapsters traded on Thames's side
When the tide of Thames ran dry.
Their swaggering barrels were big with pride,
But the wine was hard to buy.

They had corks and taps and a counter of wood
But the running wine was gone.
'The old moon's money has gone for good,
But the new moon has not shone.'

'I saw her shining, I saw her shine,'
A tapping beggar cried.
'She carried her fortune, I made it mine,
And sleep upon Thames's side.'

He told how he slept and saw in the mud
The gold and the silver lie,
And a great round barrel, huge as a flood,
Through a corner of his starved eye.

He had watched men trundle it out of the rut
And over a plank; it fell.
He heard the wine run into the butt
As the sea runs into a shell.

Two tapsters traded on Thames's side,
But the trade in the wine went ill.
They were down to their last white penny;
There were shadows and dust in the till.

'O where can we get new wine to sell,
And where can we get it soon?'
'Our barrels are dry as a swollen cork,
Though round as the round full moon.'

They fetched an empty barrel,
They rolled it upon its side.
They propped it against the window-sill
And they pushed the window wide.

Just as the dark came stealing
And the moon rose white and still,
They laid it high on its rolling rim
And left it there to fill.

In a room of fragile moonlight
Under a cask they hide,
And they soon hear mermaids singing
Like drowned men under the tide.

Asleep like rats in the yellow straw,
They dream of a sinking ship,
White horses, a wake, then slipping,
A waggoner cracking his whip.

Now from the window leaking
The flood of light seeps in.
They hear the rattle of wheels on the street
But not one rap at the Inn.

Then up leaps the younger, and leaning
Out of the window, cries:
'Here comes old Beatwind driving
With the glint of gold in his eyes.'

'O where are you going to, Beatwind?'
'To Putney's market of wine.'

'And have you got a corner on that cart of yours
For a butt or a barrel of mine?'

'What wine would it be that you might sell,
And how shall you pay the fee,
Who are banned from the vineyards of Rhine, Moselle,
Champagne and Burgundy?

O what have you got in that barrel?'
He gave them a bargaining frown.
'It will cost you the coats on your bankrupt backs
To get this barrel to town.'

I dreamed last night of a dancing-girl
And the bands on her arms were gold,
But the bands on her ankles were silver:
O what may the great cask hold?

Two tapsters laugh in the sunlight,
In the Winter sunlight cold.
'Now, waggoner, wager your cart and horse,
Here's a barrel your men won't hold.'

Then two men tried to take it,
And four, and six men tried,
But the strongest sinews seemed like straw
That floats on Atlantic's side.

I dreamed last night of a dancing-girl
And the bands on her arms were gold,
But the bands on her ankles were silver:
O what may the great cask hold?

Be warned, you Thames-side traders,
If gambling men you be,
You cannot bend to the shores of the world
Or strive with the great dark sea.

The Death Bell

'It tolls for *thee*.' – Donne

THE SUPPLICATION OF SILENCE

Hold fast the impatient bell
And let my soul have time

To count and ponder well
What steps he has to climb
To see what Simeon saw
And those three travelled kings,
Love that fulfils the law
Figured in limbs, not wings;
Whose hands uphold the throne
By that last promise given
That before day had gone
He'ld be with Him in heaven.
Pause, while I set my prayer
Against contending lust;
Then, on the doubting air
Give tongue, majestic dust.

For this bell tolls to birth
Him who hears: 'I, if I
Be lifted up from earth,
Will draw men unto Me.'
There in one height are met
Old age and swaddling-bands.
Before his life had set,
Simeon in his two hands
Caught up the babe, and praised
God, to a hidden lyre.
Love's resurrection blazed,
Changing, as by a fire,
All tongues to his true song.
That Pentecostal gust
Now kindles like a tongue
This dark, this simple dust.

Hold back. Do not release
The bell before its time.
Let the long rope of peace
So pregnant in its chime
Through distance gravitate
From pole to silent pole,
Counting with all its weight
The effort of the soul.
Since death and birth obey
One measured harmony,
Shall not the lyre outweigh
The grief-enfolding sea?

When through the bell-rope's span
The music of the just
Has raised the living man,
Give tongue, majestic dust.

Questioning eyes now see
The finite distance move.
How may the company
Of stars preserve his love?
Or who can match the speed
Of whirling nebulae
To the Samaritan's deed
Performed in sympathy?
Not twice, but only once
The evolved in nature stands,
Whether it move in suns
Or pass through living hands.
Now that the starry field
Lies fallen, and the crust
Breaks for the grain to yield,
Give tongue, majestic dust.

THE TOLLING

All is conjecture here
And affirmation there.
Here is the bell man-rung
And there the angel's tongue.
Ah, could the skies reveal
Two spirits in one peal;
But great design has hid
Foreknowledge from the lid.
Here is the reckoning
But there the austere scales swing
Where last is counted first
And confidence reversed.
Yet in the bell we pull
Love's nightingale and bull
Compel a deeper tone
Than either could alone.
Both in the window make
True colours that shall wake
When the last trump is heard;
But Matthew set his word

So firmly that I trace
In dust an angel's face.
The nightingale's dark pain
Heaven's midnight can unchain
Of which this earth's a shade,
And the long love delayed
By that ecstatic tongue
Is always pure and young.
Yet in the bull an old
Earth of momentous mould,
Out of the red marl wrought,
Matches the Maker's thought.
There where a strong shape died
Void air is dignified.
The dying Laocoön,
Tense with his sons in stone,
Wrestling with Fate, blind thralls,
On resurrection calls.
He who, his strength being spent,
Still remained reticent,
Darts his sublime unrest
Into the marvelling breast
Because he did not speak.
Even thus far went the Greek.

Man in his mortal state
Can bear the heavy weight
Of earth and heaven and hell
Compounded in a bell
If he discern the glory
Of John's deep-thundered story
By which a thorn-crowned head
Sinking, to raise the dead,
Has pulled unbounded space
Down, by the weight of grace,
Whose deep-rung moment wins
Forgiveness of all sins.
The impulsive, pagan earth
Gave that proud hunter birth
From whose uplifted hell
The blood of Abel fell.
Yet heaven, since time began,
Loves a reluctant man.

I sigh, for thought has proved
That each, who was so loved,
From stillness can increase
Strength which belongs to peace.

The last, most solemn fires
Teach us that no desires
Can bless as theirs can bless
Who give the wilderness
That dignity of line
From doctrine pounded fine.
In death the fourfold man
Still rules time's bell, and can
Teach the competitive
The loss by which we live.
Deep conflict is the forge
From which their faiths emerge
Who give to humankind
Mind that is more than mind.
The hour when such men die
Translates the galaxy
And keeps, where stars abound,
The selfsame holy ground
Reclaimed from ancient rocks,
Preserved by paradox
Through time and whirling space,
Lost Eden's latter place.
There is no bell that swings,
Though swift as angels' wings,
But answers to the mould
Fiery, primaeval, cold,
In which it first was cast.
Though resurrection's blast
Thrill the resounding nave
And call from niche and grave,
Where sunbeams fall aslant,
Each holy celebrant,
There is no temperate flight
Can raise mankind to light
Save where the font is laid.
Cooled and prepared by shade,
Each must achieve his own
Deliverance from stone,

Pulled by the world to make
True answer, nor to break,
But rise to heaven through weight,
Weaned of an earth made great
Crowning with man-pulled ropes
Those efficacious drops.

I that was born in Wales
Cherish heaven's dust in scales
Which may at dusk be seen
On every village green
Where Tawe, Taff or Wye
Through fields and woods goes by,
Or Western Towy's flame
Writes all its watery name
In gold, and blinds our eyes;
For so heaven's joys surprise,
Like music from mild air
Too marvellous to bear
Within the bell's wild span,
The pausing, conscious man.
Who questions at what age
The dead are raised? To assuage
The curious, vision smooths
The lids of age, and youth's.
Even man's defeated hopes
Are variants of those stops
Which, when the god has played,
No creature stands betrayed.

Yet now the bell falls dumb.
Already he is come
Into that other room
So near to his first home.
And I, who set his age
And this last pilgrimage
Against youth's eager quest,
Turned to his point of rest,
Ask what daemonic force
Still holds man to one course.
There is a power from Fate
Which none can estimate,
Held in the godlike reins.
Nothing but dust remains.

How can a stone bell teach
To all men or to each
The ascending fall of those
In whom heaven's scales repose?
Not even the full-starred night
Can put conception right
Till bone be knit with bone.
Then shall their loss be known.

NOTE ON THE DEATH BELL

At the beginning of the poem the bell is unrung, and it cannot ring, or cannot ring with satisfaction to the soul, until it is told its right argument by the dust for which it tolls. For every argument but the silent prayer of the dust itself, expecting resurrection, is an evasion of truth, swayed by a too optimistic hope or a too impatient despair from its true music. That music is understood by Simeon, who in his old age lifted the Christchild and saw the light of salvation, when the image of transient man ceased to be transient, and the weight of life in his hands put on immortality and became a weight of glory.

When the bell tolls, the impossible is made possible, and the transfigured wisdom of angels is made accessible for a moment to the blind devotion of the mourners; for man is made to know, through love, more than he knows. The soul of the dead has not died, and it may be recalled by the silence of love itself. Within that silence the voice of the nightingale, remembering the soul as soul, promises undiminished ecstasy, and the voice of the bull, remembering the soul as body, reminds the mourners of the dignity of death; both contribute to the force of love at the committal.

The pathos of pre-Christian love lies in its incompleteness, the prophetic nature of pre-Christian death in its reticence. Thus, Laocoön represents the bull's thirst for resurrection, and Abel, the nightingale's. Their deaths, and all future deaths, are simultaneous in the bell's tolling.

The bell itself is more than an instrument. It is involved with all for whom it has tolled, and its resonance has the power to beckon everyone whom its sound has touched. Before it rises, it must sink to its full weight at the end of the rope, and lie there, as the dead body must, under a single thread, expecting resurrection. The harmony within the bell, and within the dead body, is musically controlled, and depends upon the mercy and judgment of heavenly scales for its peace. These scales are discernible everywhere in nature, but they may be discerned only by the intuition, not by the reason. They reveal that unredeemed man, through acquisitiveness, wills his own perdition, but that redeemed man, falling through time deliberately, is raised by loss. Whether in Eden or on the banks of the four Welsh rivers named in the poem, the resurrection of the body is assured, not by the instinct of self-preservation, but by the moment of loss, of the whole man's recurrent willingness to lose himself to an act of love.

Cypress and Acacia
1959

Ode

Truth is simple: out of the mouth of babes
Flows the living word to correct the proud.
All great acts are serene and
Born in the bands of acknowledged glory.

Ugly and ignorant voices have compelled
Countries to hear; eloquent men have sown
Misery with their gestures.
Covetous men are afraid of silence.

So, when these islands faced a tyrannous power,
Death approached in the air; towns, churches, fell;
Seas rendered up their victims;
Noble and innocent souls were martyred.

Tragedy once was dignified by the dance.
Life could overturn fate, an heroic tongue,
Still refusing betrayal,
Feel in the dark the accord of angels.

Joy is woven true on a tragic base.
They who feel, where they stand, the worshipping dead,
Seek for all words responses
Deep, and attuned to a heavenly music.

Chargers pranced. The procession children enjoyed
Held in check what none might entirely know,
Mist of their wakened mornings
Changing all they had dreamed to wonder.

Then caparisoned horses mounted moved
Down the historic streets to the city's heart.
Then did heraldic London
Seal one day for the summoned ages.

Watchful gargoyles brooded while listening ears
Hearkened to echoes of war in stirrups and hooves.
Doves wheeling high above them.
Lighting, restored preservation's murmur.

God's true fear, the rebuke of power, attended
Her the trumpets proclaimed and the moment crowned
Throned by the Thames, just past this
Century's noon, in the midst of Summer.

Then, as the mantle fell and the crown was lowered,
Set with emeralds, rubies and precious stones,
Minstrels bade the anointed
Keep, like the morning star, her stillness.

Still, to the just who wait at the end of time,
All then passing is constant in their gaze.
All our intent is sacred;
All that was early is judged, is measured.

Dust in the Balance

Why should pure spirit in ribs of bone be trussed,
Why should clear vision pine in jails of eyes,
Why mortal ears divine immortal skies
And heaven interpret to the listening dust?
What need of man's proportions have the just,
Or of his temples spirits already wise,
Or thought, or script, or toil to harmonize
And curb love's horses, held by reins of lust?

Come down, sweet cadence, come; I grieve alone.
By this closed word all distances fulfil.
Hearing those abstract senses mock the bone,
My soul is like a lute when it is still,
That played when mockers tore His cloak apart
Who gave them all, but not His beating heart.

Pegasus and the Child

When you are labouring, technically proud,
Like Ajax, or that great Greek charioteer,
Caught up in dazzle of your soul's career,
Think of the child here drowned, the simple shroud;

Who played where now the blackened water blanches
For (April come) the wagtails have returned;
Yes, and the kingfisher her joy's June burned
Will come, unseen, and break familiar branches.

So near the low leaves hang to that green pond
That Pegasus discerns those milking cows

Ambling to drink there past the white-washed house
Where place and sunrise keep their ancient bond.

(They break the water, you the starry height.
Your soul transcends them; they return to Earth.
Yet your ambition and the pains of birth
Each other need, like figures in a rite.)

When you are labouring, then the secret spurs
Will press the pace, and goad the winged horse faster.
Late is the script, and early the disaster.
Great is the argument, but frail the verse.

Loiterers

This my birthplace? No, friend, this is Xanion's,
He, the owner of that yellow barley.
Mischievous chicory was all I planted:
Blue-eyed, we played here.

O, could the mayfly of memory wing back
Through bee-bustle and waspish digressions,
Certainly here it would find us standing,
Left in this cart-rut.

There the house glinted, near the tilting hay-rick,
Down through rose-ramblers to the prosperous earth-mould.
There the sky flashed to the windows, and the windows
Flashed to our young eyes.

Dawn's early singers, missel-thrush and skylark,
Still mark the track we followed to the cornfield.
Foxgloves in midge-light hid the turning river
Swept by the swallows.

Fallen is the house to the earth-mould, fallen.
Quick, for we lag here. If the dust is pollen
Robbed by the butterfly, stolen by the mayfly,
Why should we sigh, then?

Three Harps

Ambitions playing:
The first, inseparable
From gold-edged printing
On Daedalus' table.

Desire for flight;
Chariot-usurping skill.
The god of light
Torn from the godlike will.

What tears of amber,
What pre-natal force
From dawn's dark chamber
Fired me on my course?

Three harps: one
From emulation drew its strength.
The rising sun:
A harp at arm's length.

The second word of day;
The second word:
A harp a hand away
Held by a human cord.

By cypress taught and yew,
My soul I made
Write old ambition new
And qualify the laurel's shade.

I set one grave apart,
Gave speech to stone:
'Come back to my sad heart
And play this harp of bone.'

Little for the sun I cared,
Little for renown.
I saw the unknown, unshared,
True grave. So I lay down;

Lay down, and closed my eyes
To the end of all time,
The end of birth's enterprise
And death's small crime.

Then at once the shrouded harp
Was manifest. I began
To touch, though pain is sharp,
The ribs of the man.

Poets, in Whom Truth Lives

Poets, in whom truth lives
Until you say you know,
Gone are the birds; the leaves
Drop, drift away, and snow
Surrounds you where you sing,
A silent ring.

Lives of the dead you share,
Earth-hid, in tender trust.
Passion builds the air;
The beautiful and just
Through your tongues' ecstasy
Can hear and see.

Christ, where the cold stream ran
Which now lies locked in doubt,
A proud cock-pheasant can
Stretching its plumage out
More praise you than the rest
With his gold crest.

So hear those shepherds come,
Drawn by a secret fire,
Though Vergil's voice is dumb
Proclaiming to the lyre,
Through time by Winter torn,
The boy, new-born.

The abounding river stops.
Time in a flash grows less
True than these glittering drops
Caught on a thread of glass
Two frosty branches bear
In trance-like air.

Stoop; for the hollow ground
Integrity yet keeps

True as a viol's sound
Though the musician sleeps.
Strong is your trust; then wait:
Your King comes late.

Taliesin and the Spring of Vision

'I tread the sand at the sea's edge, sand of the hour-glass,
And the sand receives my footprint, singing:
"You are my nearmost, you who have travelled the farthest,
And you are my constant, who have endured all vicissitudes
In the cradle of sea, Fate's hands, and the spinning waters.
The measure of past grief is the measure of present joy.
Your tears, which have dried to Chance, now spring from a secret.
Here time's glass breaks, and the world is transfigured in music".'

So sang the grains of sand, and while they whirled to a pattern
Taliesin took refuge under the unfledged rock.
He could not see in the cave, but groped with his hand,
And the rock he touched was the socket of all men's eyes,
And he touched the spring of vision. He had the mind of a fish
That moment. He knew the glitter of scale and fin.
He touched the pin of pivotal space, and he saw
One sandgrain balance the ages' cumulus cloud.

Earth's shadow hung. Taliesin said: 'The penumbra of history is
terrible.
Life changes, breaks, scatters. There is no sheet-anchor.
Time reigns; yet the kingdom of love is every moment,
Whose citizens do not age in each other's eyes.
In a time of darkness the pattern of life is restored
By men who make all transience seem an illusion
Through inward acts, acts corresponding to music.
Their works of love leave words that do not end in the heart.'

He still held rock. Then three drops fell on his fingers,
And Future and Past converged in a lightning flash:
'It was we who instructed Shakespeare, who fell upon Dante's eyes,
Who opened to Blake the Minute Particulars. We are the soul's
rebirth.'

Taliesin answered: 'I have encountered the irreducible diamond
In the rock. Yet now it is over. Omniscience is not for man.

Christen me, therefore, that my acts in the dark may be just,
And adapt my partial vision to the limitation of time.'

A Man with a Field

If I close my eyes I can see a man with a load of hay
Cross this garden, guiding his wheelbarrow through the copse
To a long, low green-house littered with earthenware, glass and clay,
Then prop his scythe near the sycamore to enter it, potted with seeds,
And pause where chrysanthemums grow, with tomatoes' dragonish beads.
Stooping to fasten the door, he turns on the path which leads
To his rain-pitted bedroom of cellos, and low jugs catching the drops.

If I open my eyes I see this musician-turned-ploughman slow,
Plainly follow his tractor vibrating beneath blue sky,
Or cast his sickle wide, or reach full-length with the hoe,
Or blame the weather that set its blight on a crop or a plan
To mend his roof, or cut back trees where convolvulus ran,
Or attend to as many needs as the holes in a watering-can:
He would wait for the better weather; it had been a wet July.

This year his field lay fallow; he was late putting down his seed.
Cold December concealed with a sighing surplice of snow
His waste of neglected furrows, overgrown with mutinous weed.
Dark, bereaved like the ground, I found him feeble and sick,
And cold, for neither the sticks nor his lamp with a shrunken wick
Would light. He was gone through the wicket. His clock continued to tick,
But it stopped when the new flakes clustered on an empty room below.

The Mare

The mare lies down in the grass where the nest of the skylark is hidden.
Her eyes drink the delicate horizon moving behind the song.
Deep sink the skies, a well of voices. Her sleep is the vessel of Summer.
That climbing music requires the hidden music at rest.

Her body is utterly given to the light, surrendered in perfect abandon
To the heaven above her shadow, still as her first-born day.
Softly the wind runs over her. Circling the meadow, her hooves
Rest in a race of daisies, halted where butterflies stand.

Do not pass her too close. It is easy to break the circle
And lose that indolent fullness rounded under the ray
Falling on light-eared grasses your footstep must not yet wake.
It is easy to darken the sun of her unborn foal at play.

The Scythe

Custom shall not restore
The scythe to its old place,
Not with the selfsame hand,
Nor leave a single trace
Outside the greenhouse door
Of him who owned this land.

Yet when I look I see
A stooping figure pass
With his low-handled barrow
Trundling a load of grass
Where now the abounding tree
Has lost his flashing shadow.

Within that gloom the bough
Inclines Zacchaeus' keys
Not ready yet to fall.
Lift the scythe's edge to please
His testing hand who now
Remains beyond recall,

Leaning above his blade
Near the long-shadowed sheaves,
Guarded by that true stone
Under the Summer leaves
On which an edge is made
When the last light is gone.

Call It All Names, but Do Not Call It Rest

Go, death, give ground, for none of yours is here.
Weep with no sound, figures around a well.
Here gales knock down the chestnuts year on year,

And block with leaves the entry to the temple.
There the inscription no man's eyes can spell,
Archaic, in the forgotten character.
Sleeps near the nymph the font that christened her,
A shell unfastening to the vanished marvel.

Apart, life suffering in a tale of shadows,
Her patience lives, like light on infants' graves.
Rain drowns their names, the ground is full of echoes,
And there are rainbows buried in her naves.
Night cancels debts, the prince's and the slave's,
And one stays true, though quitted by his fellows.
The winter earth forsaken by the swallows
Rocks through blind storms their nest of cloistered waves.

The seasons' ritual offerings, fruit and leaves,
Die at her feet. Hazels in foliage dressed
Fall; but her tomb for men no increase gives.
Here for the thirsty no quick vats are pressed.
Yet her love's dayspring here breaks quietest,
Light for the doomed, and for the lost, reprieves,
The ring-dove's changing light, heaven found through olives;
Call it all names, but do not call it rest.

Here where through trees death's voice, all-severing, blows,
Hung with stone tongues, the language of farewell,
Great doors are opened which no hand can close
And wide heaven flies into the bud's cold cell.
So is her sickness her last oracle
Where from its falling we may seed the rose
And her new joy from her remembered sorrows
Which time, being stony, has no tongue to tell.

The Spring

Dark the words break:
The spring rebounds,
Knocking awake
With earlier sounds
Forests and hills
Enchanted here
Where water spills
From year to year.

Here salmon leap.
The ancestral climb
Matches in sleep
The fall of time.
Pause here sublime
Where moments course,
Your hand through time
May touch the source.

Music enthrals
The listening ear.
Breath on breath falls,
Binding the weir
With passion's oath
That it shall bring
Through sleep and sloth
Unageing Spring.

Time, that is brief
Yet is not true,
Tells from sunk grief
Its beads for you.
Dark, it repeats
Those words again:
Hark how the beats
Renew the chain.

Do not reject
The insistent prayer:
There move the elect;
Their thread is there.
Silence it brings
To you alone
Where water sings
From stone to stone.

Sigh, for the reach
May never say
How close to each
The sunbeams play.
There let conjecture
Lose to love
The silence music
Murmurs of.

Vertical rains
Fall, to deliver
From sterile chains
The abounding river,
Prophetic, blind,
A Titan, born,
Losing to find
His wine, his corn.

Peace in the Welsh Hills

Calm is the landscape when the storm has passed,
Brighter the fields, and fresh with fallen rain.
Where gales beat out new colour from the hills
Rivers fly faster, and upon their banks
Birds preen their wings, and irises revive.
Not so the cities burnt alive with fire
Of man's destruction: when their smoke is spent,
No phoenix rises from the ruined walls.

I ponder now the grief of many rooms.
Was it a dream, that age, when fingers found
A satisfaction sleeping in dumb stone,
When walls were built responding to the touch
In whose high gables, in the lengthening days,
Martins would nest? Though crops, though lives, would fail,
Though friends dispersed, unchanged the walls would stay,
And still those wings return to build in Spring.

Here, where the earth is green, where heaven is true
Opening the windows, touched with earliest dawn,
In the first frost of cool September days,
Chrysanthemum weather, presaging great birth,
Who in his heart could murmur or complain:
'The light we look for is not in this land'?
That light is present, and that distant time
Is always here, continually redeemed.

There is a city we must build with joy
Exactly where the fallen city sleeps.
There is one road through village, town and field,
On whose robust foundation Chaucer dreamed

A ride could wed the opposites in man.
There proud walls may endure, and low walls feed
The imagination if they have a vine
Or shadowy barn made rich with gathered corn.

Great mansions fear from their surrounding trees
The invasion of a wintry desolation
Filling their rooms with leaves. And cottages
Bring the sky down as flickering candles do,
Leaning on their own shadows. I have seen
Vases and polished brass reflect black windows
And draw the ceiling down to their vibrations,
Thick, deep, and white-washed, like a bank of snow.

To live entwined in pastoral loveliness
May rest the eyes, throw pictures on the mind,
But most we need a metaphor of stone
Such as those painters had whose mountain-cities
Cast long, low shadows on the Umbrian hills.
There, in some courtyard on the cobbled stone,
A fountain plays, and through a cherub's mouth
Ages are linked by water in the sunlight.

All of good faith that fountain may recall,
Woman, musician, boy, or else a scholar
Reading a Latin book. They seem distinct,
And yet are one, because tranquillity
Affirms the Judgment. So, in these Welsh hills,
I marvel, waking from a dream of stone,
That such a peace surrounds me, while the city
For which all long has never yet been built.

Hunt's Bay

Hurled, hollow darkness, hungry caves
Where the eye, bending, magnifies
The sea-world, all the imagined graves
Of voices where a tree-log lies:
The centre never is attained;
All is deception, broken-grained.

I have been among broken things,
Picked up the fragile lace

Of a sea-shell through which the wings
Of a gull in a clear blue space
Could be seen, then lost:
By a wave of the sea it was tossed.

Black, tousled weeds,
Bundles of foam, bottles,
Oil, shivering seeds,
Urchins, razorshells, cuttles,
And clouds combed like fleece:
The roar of the sea was peace.

I have walked this beach alone,
I have startled with my praying
The cloven tongue of stone
And seen the white foam straying
Where raven, rock and air
Rock in a dead man's care.

The winds are mad about this time,
Mad the storm's outrageous drum,
Man himself a witless mime
Because the equinoctials come
To snap the needle of his fate,
Tempting his eternal state.

Yet, whether he go or come,
Tossed to the Furies, lost in foam,
Struck by destruction's beak or dumb
Steel, the spirit finds its home.
The raging moon has lost
All conflict with that ghost.

Between the carcase of the tree
And life's imponderable seed,
The mammoth sea-log and the sea
Clutching it with mounting greed,
The creature's truthful husk
Casts out the pagan dusk.

Touch you may and touch you can,
White and strange, the drifting wood,
But never touch the severed man
Torn from history for good,
Nailing to splints and spars
Night, and the turning stars.

A Wreath for Alun Lewis

I

To-night West wind: the riderless waves of the sea
Bring to the stones your voice from the silent land,
Press this message that breaks, that dissolves into sand.
Here thought finds peace. O spirit, rest and be free.

Spindrift, caster of lives, cry that to be
Is the plummet falling through nature, as sea-rocks stand
Accepting change, yet remain a witness to grand
Glory of cloudlight, spray, whirled water and scree.

I mourn, on the edge of your world, the loss to our sailing
Of your wrists and honest eyes. Your skilful words
Were needed now, for you knew men's strength and failing,
Their death by storm who could manage intricate cords;
And you knew their speech, no wave of silence affords
That lacks your picture in time of griefs unavailing.

2

I climb the cliff and I feel my foot on the stair
That leads to music locked in an unknown grave.
I stoop and hear, between a wave and a wave:
'Care this moment for one who has cast off care'.

Never shall death divide them, not by a hair,
Man's shade and the light of his resurrected love,
And those joined hands that could make the mountains move
Are raised by a plummet's fall, by the measure of prayer.

Nothing of man shall pass if his pulse has found
Through grief, through love, a plummet falling to rock,
Itself twice born. Waves' thundering, empty shock
Beating on sand proclaims, while the rocks resound:
Death himself must deliver the souls he bound
Unchanged and true, though the winds and the waters mock.

3

Here, as I walk the cliff's edge at the close of day,
I see vast clouds assembling, white as the moon,
A column of cloud-shapes solemnly moving, soon
Encamped in darkness, high as huge Himalay.

Eastward moving they pass, but the mountains stay.
Rock and waterfall wait, and King Arthur's Stone
Pulls faint, mimicking plovers with rending moan
Whose crippled wings tear darkness, close to the bay.

Remorseless wind, ah landscape of undrawn swords,
Straining rocks, and the stalling white sea-birds!
True as a needle-rock, you knew to divide
The anarchic waters rising against their guards.
Shades on the sea, your pity plumbed their rewards,
For every wave has a voice not the voice of the tide.

Poet and Goldsmith

He was now alone. The lovers had wandered across
The field. About him the air fell sweet with singing.
Very close to his eyes a bird was carrying moss.
It gathered a wisp of straw, pecked, and looked up,
And flew to a secret nest. He watched the bough
Tremble. Now it was still. There was dew on the field.
Petals began to close. The roots of the elms
Held his wonder: 'Be warned: about you are symbols.'

Over sea, gold distance hung in a fiery crucible.
No fingers, however cunning, could sift the grains
Of hurrying sand. Mathematical, yet inscrutable,
Each rose with the rising wave, then slipped through the
hour-glass.
No shore could set a term to the curlew's call.
The voice returned to itself round the sevenfold world
And perched on mystery. Night, like a working goldsmith,
Heard waves beat on the indestructible core.

The poet sang: 'All ages bud like the sycamore.
Brown keys spin down to beginning. There are two natures.
Blest are the lost, packed hidden within life's door
Like seeds in the husk. Yet, since a small man climbed
The crooked trunk, and groped, and sat in the branch,
The minutiae of earth are changed, and the blackbird's praises
Are now twofold: they speak, and they speak beyond knowledge.
Even so, these hands have touched the harp of the dead.'

The dying light moved down to birth in his eyes,
And his eyes experienced music. Night was athletic;

A powerful glory tensed the proportioned skies.
And he murmured again: 'One thought that is dear to love:
True characters do not age in each other's eyes.
Indeed, we die each moment the life of another,
And there is no separation, no spear in the side,
Except in that forgetting of mutual death.'

'Unsearchable distance! The gliding avalanche
Wounds me,' he sang. Sycamore leaves against heaven
Moving, sighed. Then, as he touched one branch,
The force of his fingers entered the roots of the tree.
'Earth, cradle of riches; the speed and grace of the hunter,
Born here; plumes of the pheasant shining with dew:
They speak, singly, of inexhaustible treasure.
Night speaks, the artificer, beating out gold.'

The Sloe

Too like those lineaments
For waking eyes to see,
Yet those the dream presents
Clearly to me.

How much more vivid now
Than when across your tomb
Sunlight projects a bough
In gradual gloom!

Even such a curious taste
I found, seeing Winter blow
Above a leafless waste
The bitter sloe.

It will not yet begin
To act upon the tongue
Till tooth has pierced the skin
And juice has sprung:

A flavour tart and late
Which, when the rest had gone,
Could hide in mist and wait,
Its root in stone.

Trust Darkness

Trust darkness. Dig down
Through earth's crust to no crown.
The surface will moulder
But, tenacious, the root
When you are older
Bring blossom and fruit.

Pull bindweed up first,
That parasite cursed
Which preys on the vision.
From dark root and thorn
In the death of ambition
Let patience be born.

On the spade press your foot.
Dig up by the root
Whatever encumbers
Your thought in the grass.
There the seed slumbers,
Cold as dawn was.

Such dancers are seeds,
Each knows what man needs
As it glides from his fingers,
Absently cast.
In their fall lingers
All that is past.

Learn to lie fallow.
Trees naked or yellow
Endure through long Winter
And ride every storm.
Great rewards enter
Where they are born.

No love that fears night
Is fitting and right.
If you seek resurrection
Take root and grow strong.
No bond of affection
Is less than life long.

Hold fast the fine thread
From such bonds that are dead.

Far though you travel
Or stray from that touch,
No hand may unravel
Or teach you as much.

The dead earn their living
By holy forgiving.
No upland or meadow
Where the light flies
But draws from the shadow
Of death-disturbed eyes.

Time begins and time ends
In the meeting of friends.
To deny the occasion
Or count up its cost
Is to mock at the passion
Where nothing is lost.

The Return

I lay, pulse beating fast,
While the night raider passed
And gave each hovering tick
The speed of dream.
Sleep in the dead of night could make all quick,
Reverse the extreme
Outrider's task on thought's magnetic beam.

What life-uprooting year
Sent him, an envoy, here
To set two states at war?
I'ld rather set
Those just names up both states are honoured for,
Lest time forget
He is a hostage since our eyes last met.

Now from that neighbour state
One who all war did hate
Came as a witness back
From that night raid,
To make a truce, there in the very track
Where wings had made
A single engine stop, two hearts afraid.

Yet we could still converse
Without interpreters,
For, though spade's land is charged
With sudden springs
Whose atoms may be monstrously enlarged,
Earth-rooted things
Remain the identities to which man clings.

It is our common speech
Comforts the ghost in each.
So, when that restless face
Returned last night,
It gave serenity to time and place,
Though beams of light
Crossed and converged to pick out wings in flight.

True recognition broke
Destruction's dust and smoke,
For there, unfeigned I found,
Knowing him dead,
Life, not with laurels nor disturbance crowned,
But calm instead,
Compassion curbed the challenge of his head.

Our two states merged in dream's
Converging, crossing beams,
Recalling a lost time
Of deaths and sighs
When body and soul had shuddered at the crime
Dark guilt descries
In the wronged heaven, against which armies rise.

Strongly they still can merge
Where the long beams converge.
Why let two states at war
Destroy the mind?
These eyes beneath a brutal metaphor
Can substance find
In all time spurns but cannot leave behind.

The Exacting Ghost

I speak of an exacting ghost,
And if the world distrust my theme

I answer: This that moved me most
Was first a vision, then a dream.

By the new year you set great store.
The leaves have turned, and some are shed.
A sacred, moving metaphor
Is living in my mind, though dead.

I would have counted good years more,
But all is changed: your life has set.
I praise that living metaphor
And when I sleep I see it yet.

Why is it, though the conscious mind
Toils, the identity to keep
Forgetful ages leave behind,
No likeness matches that of sleep?

Last night, when sleep gave back the power
To see what nature had withdrawn,
I saw, corrected by that hour,
All likenesses the mind had drawn.

In crowded tavern you I found
Conversing there, yet knew you dead.
This was no ghost. When you turned round,
It was indeed your living head.

Time had returned, and pregnant wit
Lodged in your eyes. What health was this?
Never had context been so fit
To give old words new emphasis.

If hope was then restrained by doubt
Or joy by fear, I cannot tell.
All the disturbances of thought
Hung on my words; yet all seemed well.

You smiled. Your reassurance gave
My doubt its death, my hope its due.
I had always known beyond the grave,
I said, all would be well with you.

You fixed contracted, narrowing eyes
To challenge my instinctive sense.
The uncertainty of my surmise
Their penetration made intense.

'What right had you to know, what right
To arrogate so great a gift?'
I woke, and memory with the light
Brought back a weight I could not lift.

In sleep the dead and living year
Had stood one moment reconciled,
But in the next the accuser's spear
Had sacked the city of the child.

Why is it, though the conscious mind
Toils, the identity to keep
Forgetful years will leave behind,
No likeness matches that of sleep?

Serena

The cradle stirs.
There life, there innocence, there the miracle shines.
Old, he is old:
Life's earliest word, the first. Light has created him
Out of inscrutable deeps.

And the light breathes;
It breathes in darkness, trembles, trembles and wakes.
There is no help,
There is no help in this room. The divining deluge
Thunders. Time is at hand.

Who knows the print
Of feet, Christ's way, reversing the martyrs' steps,
Their counter-joy?
What fingers touch, through time stealthily flowing,
Music under the sandgrains?

What tremulous dove
Has made shoot, sink and scatter, blind and dark,
Ridges of fear,
That all must fall save him great love has lifted
To walk on his own grief?

Whose eyes now break?
Where is that head so young, it has not seen dawn?
What torches gold

Kindle the temples? What foreboding blossoms
Fall through infinite evening?

With discord, death,
Harpies and Sirens sow the furrowed sea.
Their music moves
Across the water, and the vessel whirling
Feels the destroying birds.

What holds him safe,
Lost in a chaos of conflicting waves?
What thread is wound
About him, that no Cyclops eye may triumph
Over the singing hands?

The zenith sighs.
The voyage of Magellan breaks his sleep.
He treads the waves
Haunted by little ships whose daring reaches
Islands of spice and robbers.

He will be calm
When mutinous seas lay hold upon his ship.
When hope seems lost
And the unnameable Furies, loosed, defy him,
He will be calm at heart.

The source of time
Still binds the flying galaxies to rock.
Nothing shall change
The diamond fixed between vine-masted Noah
And the first deluge drop.

He will be calm
In the first calm that glittered before knowledge.
Nothing shall change
The Primum Mobile's effectual music
Planted within the breast.

He will be calm,
Not through a reason known to man, nor favour,
But through that gift
The First Cause left, printing upon his forehead
The word 'Serena'.

Before a Birth

Hear the finger of God, that has fixed the pole of the heavens.
There the Pleiades spin, and Orion, that great hunter.
Stars silver the night, where Hercules moves with Arcturus.
Spawning systems amaze: they respond to an ordered music.
Ultimate distance vibrates, close to that intimate string.

Stoop, for nothing can weigh the inscrutable movement of beech leaves
Silken, of brightest green, which May has transfigured like music
Born of their trumpet-like buds; this movement, ever so little,
Hangs on a leaf-hidden breath, so near to the nest of the greenfinch;
Nothing so secret as this, under the shadows of Spring.

Love, your measure is full: the stars of infinite distance,
Needing the shade of a bird to knit our time to the timeless,
Fell to-night through the dusk. Ear close to the ground-root, I listened,
Feeling the sunlight fall through May's untranslatable evening;
Then, upon earth, my pulse beat with the pulse of the dead.

Guests go into the house. On the floor, attended by shadows,
Late I can hear one walk, a step, and a fruitful silence.
Touch, finger of Wine, this well of crystalline water
And this earthenware jug, that knows the language of silence;
Touch, for darkness is near, that brings your glory to bed.

Birth and Morning

Are you come then, with the first beech leaves, stubborn and frail,
Dragging new brilliance out of the night of the branch
Where apple-trees move under wind, on fire from the wound of the grail,
Stream of wild stars for a fork-stemmed blossom to stanch?

Birth and morning: full night pulled down to the earth
Drenched by the violence of rain where the dawn wind dries
Buds in the trance of sunrise straining to ultimate birth,
Rigid, expecting Easter, released to the skies:

Silken they stand, weaned from the heart of light,
A splendour of water splashed from original green,
Painted with wax of creation, dazzling, hurting the sight
With a touch immaculate, fading before it has been.

I restore to the garden the footprints of one that was near
Whose arms would cradle you now, a magnanimous ghost,

But who sleeps without knowing your name in the turn and the quick of
the year.
My eyes are fixed on the branches, my soul on the lost.

Yet here is beginning, the broken shell of a bird.
These days that will not be remembered are holy, your first;
The finches fly in and out while the apple-tree buds, wind-stirred,
Like sepulchres sleep, where no single blossom has burst.

All the morning the lawn has been filled with a woodpecker's cry
Awake in the shrubbery, diving from tree to tree.
The air is green with his sallies. In the wake of his plumage I
Divine with a leaden plummet the days to be.

I watch you here, and your eyes are closed on the cry
The woodpecker nails to the bark of the fir and the ground.
Wet from the caul of Spring are the blazing beech leaves, dry
The apple-trees' antlered branches where you sleep sound.

Beyond this wall the blue sea: the sap from the root
Ascends where the woodpecker clings to the fir-tree's bark.
And here, out of sight of the sea, I hear his excited shout,
The exuberant, bright-crested bird resurrecting the dark.

And you sleep under sunlight, gone with the wing to the dalliance
Of magical boughs, the pursuit and the pairing of birds
In the shaft of April, that perch, take fire and cavort with the brilliance
Of branches whose shadows interpret the lost and their words.

Larks sing, in the deep, dense blue, above gorse and rocks,
Black specks. Light falls where they mount. A commotion of wings
Rustles the furnace of thorns where blackbirds nest in the thicket.
The shaft the birds fly from, the shade and the phoenix, are Spring's.

Still child, undisturbed by their noise, none asks you to find
The water of life, the stone no philosopher found,
Or the source of that secret river which runs under time and the wind,
Sprung, it may be, from a chalice laid in the ground.

Few are the days gone by since you looked your first
And holy their fingers who laid it, halted in frost
Too early to wake you now to heaven in the apple-tree garden
Near branches knowing nothing of that which is lost.

The Immortal in Nature

I must forget these things, and yet lose none.
Music is light, and shadows all are they.
White is the fountain that begot the sun.
Light on the petal falls; then falls the may.

Sometimes the vulture sees his carrion
A speck on Ganges. White on Himalay
The snows ascend above the light of dawn.
Though distance calls us like a clarion,
How ancient is the voice our souls obey.

I tell my soul: Although they be withdrawn,
Meditate on those lovers. Think of Donne
Who could contract all ages to one day,
Knowing they were but copies of that one:
The first being true, then none can pass away.

Where time is not, all nature is undone,
For nature grows in grandeur of decay.
These royal colours that the leaves put on
Mark the year living in his kingly way;
Yet, when he dies, not he but time is gone.

Beethoven's music nature could not stun.
Light rushed from Milton.
See the Sistine ray.
There burns the form eternally begun.
That soul whose very hand made marble pray,
The untempted, mightiest master, holds in sway
The wrestling sinews death had seemed to own
And might have owned, but that they were not clay.

The Curlew

Sweet-throated cry, by one no longer heard
Who, more than many, loved the wandering bird,
Unchanged through generations and renewed,
Perpetual child of its own solitude,
The same on rocks and over sea I hear
Return now with his unreturning year.
How swiftly now it flies across the sands,

Image of change unchanging, changing lands
From year to year, yet always found near home
Where waves in sunlight break in restless foam.
Old though the cave is, this outlives the cave,
And the grey pool that shuddered when it gave
The landscape life, reveals where time has grown,
Turning green, slowly forming tears to stone.
The quick light of that cry disturbs the gloom.
It passes now, and rising from its tomb,
Carries remorse across the sea where I
Wait on the shore, still listening to that cry
Which bears a ghostly listening to my own;
Such life is hidden in the ringing stone
That rests, unmatched by any natural thing,
And joins, unheard, the wave-crest and the wing.

Kestrel

Kestrel, king of small hawks, moreover
Keenest of sight, blind wings you shake,
Pinned on the sky, and quivering, hover

High over prey. A gloom you make
Hang from one point in changing time
On grass. Below you seawaves break

Rebellious, casting rhyme on rhyme
Vainly against the craggy world
From whose black death the ravens climb.

Stand then in storm; see fragments whirled
And pitched by waters to a place
Where wave on wave in mockery hurled

Shake the great sea-rock to its base.
And still the inviolate wing and claw
Hold chaos in the grip of grace.

High on the rock's grass verge you saw
Your quarry. You above that rock
Hung by inscrutable, patient law,

Motionless. Then you plunged, a block
Between that headland and the sky
Hiding you. Stalling in their flock

The startled herring-gulls gave cry,
Sprung from a sea of beaten flame.
Bird of my wrist, inspired you fly.

Who dares to think the storm untame
Can hurt or master you whom I,
Gathering the doom of all who die,
Uplift, in every age, the same?

Christ and Charon

After more terrors than the sea has waves
Where vultures black beyond redemption stood
Circling that boatman for his tithe of blood
Guiding to Hell his boat's eternal slaves,
I left that nightmare shore, and woke to naves
Of daybreak; there men walked in brotherhood,
Mutual forgiveness, love; their speech was good,
Being governed by the music of their graves.

Then death's rank odour changed to scented balm,
The sweat of horror to a holy gum,
Fierce lamentations to that living psalm;
There stood a cradle where time's waves were dumb
Above which angels sighed; 'Your life is come';
And every sigh a ship destined to calm.

Angel and Man

Angel: Day breaks. All sighs are ended.
The sleep of earth, the long night sleep, is over.
Man: Faint incarnation in the mists ofdawn,
Why do you rouse desires I have laid down
On this sad field where the world tends her wounded
And shrouds their limbs whose eyes are shut for ever?
You are not of this life, but of the days
Of immaturity when, with upturned eyes,
I lay awake, a child, expecting miracles.
I think I waited for a star to fall.
Now it is different, and those early oracles

Have lost that power I in those nights would feel.
Yes, once I thought my dreams had been fulfilled.
I thought I saw, quite early in a field,
The annunciation of the morning star,
And that the world had ended with that light.

Angel: That early moment is come true, though late.
That moment was a prophecy of this.
To me alone was given night's darkest wisdom.
I am the first to learn what is for all.

Man: Do not so look at me, for I am ill.
I would believe you, but I cannot.
Too much is hidden.
I hear your speech, but when your speech has faded
It is the earth that counts, where these men lived.
All these the eyelid buried,
These the rough earth hides,
Where are they, then?

Angel: They are gone to the root of the tree.
Just as the red sun went behind the hill,
They pierced the shadows of imagined rest.

Man: If sighs are ended they should wake now, too.

Angel: They do wake, though your ears are not attuned
To those sunk voices which the ground transfigures.
They are like lightning, or the time in sleep
Circling the earth from which the slow leaf breaks.
They do wake, in the murmur of the leaves.

Man: The leaves made that same sound when they were living
But it was not their voices when they lived,
Nor is it now. Let others be deceived.
I know this for a place where footsteps halted
And where each footstep knocked upon the ground,
Seeking true consolation. Think of this.
Spirits were laid here to whom some were dear,
Who left them, sorrowful. Garments touched the leaves,
And where they passed I understood a language
Breathed in the robe and heard by the dumb ground.
I accept this for my portion. Grief was theirs,
And grief, their lot, is likely to be mine.
Yet in the last, most solitary dark
There lives an equilibrium in the soul
Depending on forgiveness. Grant me this,
And I shall hold truth fast without remorse
Under the turning stars.

Swedenborg's Skull

Note this survivor, bearing the mark of the violator,
Yet still a vessel of uninterrupted calm.
Its converse is ended. They beat on the door of his coffin,
But they could not shake or destroy that interior psalm
Intended for God alone, for his sole Creator.
For gold they broke into his tomb.

The mark of the pick is upon him, that rough intrusion
Upon the threshold and still place of his soul.
With courtesy he received them. They stopped, astonished,
Where the senses had vanished, to see the dignified skull
Discoursing alone, entertaining those guests of his vision
Whose wit made the axe-edge dull.

Here the brain flashed its fugitive lightning, its secret appraising,
Where marble, settled in utmost composure, appears.
Here the heirs of the heavens were disposed in symmetrical
orders
And a flash of perception transfigured the darkness of years.
The mark of a membrane is linked with those traffickers grazing
Its province of princes and spheres.

Where the robbers looked, meditations disputed the legacy
Of the dreaming mind, and the rungs of their commonplace
crime
Gave way to swift places of angels, caught up in division
From the man upon earth; but his patience now played like a
mime,
And they could not break down or interpret the skull in its
privacy
Or take him away from his time.

So I see it today, the inscrutable mask of conception
Arrested in death. Hard, slender and grey, it transcends
The enquiring senses, even as a shell toiling inward,
Caught up from the waters of change by a traveller who bends
His piercing scrutiny, yields but a surface deception,
Still guarding the peace it defends.

Hunter

Naked in woods apart,
A radiance in his eyes,
He crouches to surprise
The breathing hart;
So kneels to aim his dart;
The feathered arrow flies;
The peril he defies
Stands here, revealed by art.

A touch, and time is gone;
The loins their flight fulfil;
Mark the dead hunter's skill
Here where his window shone.

Look, and the limbs are still.
Walk, and the eyes look on.

Erinna and the Waters

Erinna, serene in sunlight, lay on the rock.
The young sea touched her, the gay, the nimble betrayer.
On Earth unrivalled in song, this low flute-player
Could entice, make music and pictures, menace, and mock.

Her eyes were full of the vision her book revealed,
Her head of that secret music. Content was she
To trust for protection against the charming sea
Unforgettable words on the vellum her hand had sealed.

All myths sprang bright in the foam and sparkled with salt.
The forbidden waters flashed to her, beautiful.
In a wave she could see Europa riding her bull.
In the next the god of temptation denied the assault.

Chaste, she unrobed. Her clasp she rose to untwist.
The waters danced, exulting because of her choice.
Old Nereus smiled, and with ceremonious voice
He recalled a nymph and her stripling before they kissed.

And now the waters were left her, innocent
As lambs in darkness dropped in the Winter snow.
Her fingers touched the water like mistletoe.
She caressed the nativity prudence could not prevent.

Prone on the sea the sun, like a great tree felled,
Announced with music of shells a mysterious day
Restoring Mars to the girl born out of the spray,
Unawakened yet by the conch amorini held.

She peered, and the water copied her finger's thread
On tinted cowries, lit the incarnate pearl.
A rainbow dived through the spray, and the marvelling girl
Heard cherubs flying, where petals on air were shed.

And Thetis moved from her shell, and the spiral dark
Kept, unseen, the sound of approaching feet.
Naked her lover stood, and she saw them meet
Where dolphins sported, spun through a perfect arc.

She returned from the rich, voluptuous sea to the cave,
And, gathering her raiment, laid on a ledge near a crock,
She watched in reflection the clouds move over the rock,
And she touched the shadowed water, cold as the grave.

Yet there was her book, her treasure. Quick as a spring
It shone, marrying myth to darkness. Carrying it now,
Climbing the difficult path to the cliff's green brow,
She sighed to recapture the music no sea could sing.

Camelot

She that was a queen stood here
Where the kestrel hovers.
He was resting by the weir:
He and she were lovers.
Praise and passion in her throat
Breathed above her psalter
Long before King Arthur's boat
Moved upon the water.

Though she died in Almesbury
White as any lily,
Laid beneath the darkest tree
Winter cannot sully,
All the colour she had wrought
Stayed in her possession.
Time stood still in Camelot
Till her last confession.

Set your foot upon this land.
Come, for time has vanished.
Part the grasses with your hand.
Here, though he was banished,
Never did the grasses cease
Whispering of their pledges
While the blossoms on the trees
Burst along the hedges.

Far he walked, accompanied
By that lovely creature.
Petals falling from the seed
Told him of her nature.
'Never let your heart deny
Joy that I inherit.
Say above me when I die:
Here all time is buried.'

Wisdom gave her dignity.
Now her crown is fallen.
Light upon the land is she,
And her dust is pollen.
O how hard it is to lose
Passion's reins and ridings,
Yet no better could she choose
To give nature tidings.

Stoop and find the bow unstrung
And the empty quiver.
Limpid now the stones give tongue
In the mountain river.
Silent move the tapestries
Painted in her chamber.
She has gathered all the seas
In a bead of amber.

Leave, as by a mummy's hand,
Ears that none may gather.
She is sleeping in the land
Hidden from the weather.
Look: the kestrel and the weir,
Hunting time, are keeping
Stillness in a point austere
Where her heart is sleeping.

Time in weathercock and stone
Turns and tries to change her.
White as chalk or white as bone
Stands the rocky stranger.
Set her in the saddle now.
Let the water flying
And the kestrel tell you how
All but she is dying.

Knights on horseback from the hill
Move across the meadow.
Like a place where time stood still
Are the trees in shadow.
Still the crest of Launcelot
Shines upon his armour.
Waters rest in Camelot
In the heart of Summer.

She on earth was Guinevere
Where the kestrel hovers,
He a knight beside the weir:
He and she were lovers.
Never has she lost a note
Of the music taught her
Since the hour when Arthur's boat
Moved upon the water.

The Forge of the Solstice

The best are older: with the unrest time brings,
No absolute remains to bind them fast.
One scrawls on rock the names of hallowed things,
Letters and hieroglyphs that yet shall last
When darkness measures with a martyr's eye
The glories shed by life's unchanging tree.

Another, curbing vigour on his page
To movement, makes the abounding life his own
And rhythmic finds in a discordant age,
Singing like living fountains sprung from stone,
Those unifying harmonies of line
Torn from creative nature. Light is born

Under believing fingers. Men refute
By inward protest what their masters teach,
Seeking a deeper meaning. One is mute,
Fearing far more the heresies of speech
Than watchful waiting. Figures move; they pass
Across the cave. Before them flies heaven's glass,

And out of it now falls the winter sun,
Leaving a ceaseless myth of moving waves,
Till darkness quiets all things. Man is one:
The identity survives its many graves.
First was the hunter, then the prophet; last,
The artificer, compounding in one ghost

Hunter and prey, prophet and witness, brought
Into that circle where all riddles end.
Love gives their art a body in which thought
Draws, not from time but wisdom, till it bend
The solstice like a bow, and bring time round
White with young stars, quick from the forge they have found.

The Tributary Seasons

I can discern at last how grew
This tree, so naked and so true.
'Spring was my death; when all is sung,
It was the Autumn made me young.'

Midwinter: packed with ice the butt,
Splitting its sides.
Roots hard as iron; the back door shut.
Heaped wood a ringing axe divides.
Sacks on the pipes. No river flows,
No tap, no spring. A skater goes
Skimming across the pond. A stone
Stays on the ice where it is thrown.
Under a bone a blue-tit swings,
The keen light glancing on his wings.
To robins crusts and crumbs are tossed,
Yellow against the white of frost.
A quilted world. Glazed mistletoe.
Spades glint, and sledges glide, on snow.
Boys scoop it up with tingling hands,

Steadying the snowman where he stands,
Numb into dusk. Then holly boughs
Darken the walls in many a house,
While moth-flakes pile on wood and ground,
Muffling the panes, and hide all sound.
The tree of Winter, Winter's tree:
Winter a dark, a naked tree.

What you have seen you have not known.
Look for it now that Winter's gone.
The Winter stars, the silent king,
The angelic night, give way to Spring.

March into May: the lengthening day
With forward light
Kindles the finches in their play,
Turning their wings in amorous flight.
No star in frost more brightly shines
Than, in white grass, these celandines.
Now sunlight warms and light wind shakes
The unopened blooms. The jonquil breaks
Clean from its sheath. Gold wax and gums
Hold the buds fast. The chestnut comes
First into leaf, its trance-bound hands
Pulled from the shell by silken strands,
Breathless and white. The sap unseen
Climbs the stiff stalk and makes all green.
All timeless coils break through, sublime,
The skins and cerements of time.
What spikenard makes the dark earth sweet?
Life from the hyacinth's winding-sheet
Breathes on the fields, and thrushes sing:
'Earth is our mother. Spring is Spring.'
The tree of Spring, the selfsame tree:
Spring is the green, foretelling tree.

What you have seen you cannot know.
Winter is gone, and Spring will go.
These blossoms falling through long grass
Will fade from swallows' quivering glass.

Now the meridian. Summer glows,
A furnace weighed,
Deep in red rose and burnet rose,
Entranced by its own musk and shade.

Birds sing more softly. Foxgloves keep
Over the hedge a misty sleep.
Gardens are secret in their walls
And mountains feel their waterfalls.
Murmuring among thick blooms, the bees
Plunge, and in silence honey seize,
Then bear it droning to their hive
Of light by labour kept alive.
Yet still the toil, where leaves are dense,
Breathes of the Spring's first frankincense.
Butterflies dance in blazing beams.
Great trees are hushed, and still the streams.
On river banks, where boughs serene
Reflect their every shade of green,
Bathers take rest, and bodies come
Naked to peace, and their first home.
  The tree of Summer, Summer's tree,
  Lost in the sleep of Adam's tree.

Might this indeed have been the prime,
That Eden state of lasting time?
Men reap the grain and tend the vine,
Heaping their tributes, bread and wine.

At last late leaves bright-coloured bring,
Turning time's keys,
Those fruits foreshadowed by the Spring.
Acorns and nuts restore their trees.
As certain jewels have the power
To magnetize and guide the hour,
So seeds before our eyes are strewn
Fast hidden in the pod's cocoon.
These die, yet in themselves they keep
All seasons cradled in their sleep.
Guarding the lost through calms and storms,
These are the year's eternal forms,
An alphabet whose letters all
Mark out a sacred festival.
The birth of vision from these urns
Into whose silence dust returns
Fills the dense wood. Saint Hubert's rein
Stops the swift horse; for there again
A stag between its antlers holds

Heaven's unique glory, and the world's.
  Tree of beginning, Autumn tree:
  Divine imagination's tree.

Moonrise

Dew is falling now: the daylight is spent.
Softly, darkly it gathers: night is at hand.
Our world is changed. Along the remembered land
Each landmark changes, hiding the way we went.
All will be altered soon by the moon's ascent,
Her strangeness melt the dimensions we understand,
Bright waves more loudly break, and bring to the sand
Cold threads of moonlight, shreds of a nomad's tent.

Do not succumb to the lure of strangeness. Trust
Better the scarf you wear than light diffused.
Words that once bound shall bind us when we are dust.
Trust narrow bonds; and when you have refused
The enchanter's dissipation of light and shade,
Tread with my heart that place where worlds are made.

The Mask of Winter

Winter is sparkling. Looms
Wake from the freezing North
The crying snow of lambs
Suffered and shaken forth.

Hard now in iron ground
Waters their song refuse,
Leaving the scattered sound
Of lambs that call their ewes.

A buried spring is born
In darkness, that makes full
Lambs from an ivory horn
Under the warmth of wool.

Crisp windows in their vice
Grip the white sheaves that show

The whispering ferns of ice
And crystal world of snow.

Nothing is now so still
As the white drifts that lie
Reaching the window-sill
To chill the newborn sky.

At Winter's coming I
Test my perceptions, not
By changes in the sky
But by the secret root.

Until the waking bud
Forms on the sleeping tree,
By dictates of the blood
The dead admonish me.

I cannot separate,
So soundlessly they shine,
The windings of past fate,
Nor the lost lives from mine.

Yet nowhere in this waste
Voices from time endure.
No footprint here is traced,
No dying signature.

No rain, no curlew-cry
Calling across the field:
The locked lane under sky
Is blocked with snow and sealed.

Men will complain of Spring's
Late coming, and those gifts
Checked by the weather, things
Lost in the gathered drifts.

The mask of Winter then
Shall not deceive them, known
To those rough-handed men
Like one who has with them grown.

And still the mask will stay.
Earth in their eyes will spread
A quilt as white as may
Quick with her newborn dead.

Touch With Your Fingers

Touch with your fingers
The strings of song.
Love runs deeper
Than all time's wrong.
I have considered
Such things long.

Banishing waters
Bore it once.
D'Orléans looked
Towards the coast of France.
Florence exiled
Her noblest sons.

Under the rising
Spectral moon
Rome, Alexandria,
Babylon,
Athens and Carthage
Rise in stone.

Time that is over
Comes not again;
Yet instinctive
The strings remain.
All is fugitive,
Nothing vain.

Magical foliage
Glittering shone.
There they trembled
Who now are gone.
Dancers perish:
The dance goes on.

What then compelled me
To take on trust
Words of the poets
Laid in dust?
Time cannot answer.
True love must.

Love is compounded
Of all it cast.

Sacred forgiveness
Binds all fast.
Timeless vision
Discerns no Past.

Shade of Calliope,
Guard my days.
Such compassion
From dust I raise,
Nothing is valid
Except that praise.

Bread and the Stars

How clear the stars to-night,
All the bright heaven how still!
Under dense groves of white
This glistening sheet displays
A frost of spellbound streams.
All is at rest. I gaze
Out on the paths and beams
Of night's unresting mill.

So deadly white this frost,
It kills both bird and mouse
Hid where the swedes are tossed
Into an iron barn.
Owls upon vermin feast.
Their solemn hootings warn,
When every sound has ceased,
Man in his mortal house.

Nothing now comes between
The inane and this hard crust
Close to the roots of men
As shrouds are to their dead.
How precious now the loss
Of souls whose printless tread
Where many footprints cross
Takes the whole night on trust.

How full the clustered sky!
Beyond the uncounted crop

Of stars I still descry
Where the white millstream runs
Glittering in ghostly race
New multitudes of suns,
While here galactic space
Hangs, like a frozen drop.

Night with her teeming brood
Unites the faculties
To polarize the blood
Moving, yet fixed and still,
Drawn to her secret North.
The same unerring will
That called conception forth
Now bids the bloodstream freeze.

Yet men to Earth are bound,
To heats from which they grew.
They sift the stars who pound
The corn with leavening yeast
Till the whole bread is made;
And plenty crowns their feast,
Wine from a cellar's shade
Preserving all that's true.

None need look far for proof
That passion bears the sky.
The elect, beneath time's roof
Dropping from steadfast eyes
The plummet of their peace,
Hold to each man that dies
A measure of increase,
A cup to judge life by.

Bread of dear life, and cup
Or glass made dull by breath,
Those spinning worlds far up
Whose fiery swarms recede,
All cannot match the weight
Of your immediate need,
Brought on a man-fired plate
To break his fast to death.

Clear night, great distances,
Faith, like a pestle, drums

Your baffling silences.
Hard though the wintry crust,
What truth has man but loaves?
Bread will compel man's trust,
And not the starry groves:
Wisdom is hid in crumbs.

Buried Light

What are the light and wind to me?
The lamp I love is gone to ground.
There all the thunder of the sea
Becomes by contrast idle sound.

What hammer on the anvil falls?
Who shapes the cyclone to his will?
The moments and the intervals
Gain their estate from what is still.

All hunting opposites I praise.
I praise the falcon and the dove.
Night's intense darkness gives to days
True pictures of regenerate love.

Come, buried light, and honour time
With your dear gift, your constancy,
That the known world be made sublime
Through visions that closed eyelids see.

Come, breath, instruct this angry wind
To listen here where men have prayed,
That the bold landscape of the mind
Fly nobler from its wrist of shade.

Sons of true sacrifice are there.
Rivers and hills are in their hands.
The lightest petal the winds bear
Has mocked the Serpent's swaddling-bands.

And men may find beneath the sun,
Dashed into pieces by old wrong,
A relic, lost to nature, one
Whose passion stops the mouth of song.

For a Christening

The Word shines still
Locked in dumb stone. We approach
The cloistral, chill
Shell that no touch
May take from its own source, its secret rill.

Cupped in this crust
Of crumbling age, light lingers
Liquid in stone. Ah, trust
Your christener's fingers,
Child, and receive our homage, as is just.

Here let him place,
Held in the slanting light,
Your head, touch water, trace
Your name, and write
The effective seal by which men come to grace.

By this one way
They who are dead live more.
This day is still their day
Who went before,
And you their hope, in the sun's moving ray.

Worshippers here,
We are come to see that prism
Take fire, where Christ's own tear
In your baptism
Consecrates, first each drop, then all the sphere.

No future fate
Dismays us where we stand.
The centre is our state
Who hold time's sand
In scales of worship, though it falls by weight.

Of radiant love,
Given starlike without stint
By Father, Son, and Dove,
Take now the print
Which death shall not obliterate, nor time move.

Seeing lives go by
Unlit, the Father chose

That His own Son should die
And His eyes close
On truth, to make a new theology.

Even as He fell
With sabachthani cries
To those three days in hell,
So must your eyes
Close, for three seconds now, to be made well.

Dive, then: receive
This water with our prayer,
That, when the stunned drops leave
Love's image there,
A cloth by pressure may your life reprieve.

For time's old beat
Must change to music when
Fly to His steadfast feet
The souls of men,
And lightning play on every winding-sheet.

So raised, learn this:
To admire a paradox
Is not enough. It is
Lightning that rocks
The shroud itself, if our own loss we kiss.

Then, then alone
We live, when our lives take
That brightness for their own.
So sink; then wake,
Shining, being raised, where holy water shone.

The Replica

Once more the perfect pattern falls asleep,
And in the dark of sleep the replica
Springs to awareness. Light is born of dark
As the young foal beside his mother steps,
Closer than her own shadow. All runs down
To agile youth, born of laborious age.
She feels his presence in the pulse of earth,
Entranced above her pasture, how his eyes

From that new darkness at the end of time
In wonder stare, astonished by her world.
Each pristine, airy venture is prescribed
By weight of the maternal shade he left,
The circle ending where his race began.

The waterfall by falling is renewed
And still is falling. All its countless changes
Accumulate to nothing but itself.
The voice of many mountains or of one,
The dissipation of unnumbered drops
Vanishing in a dark that finds itself
In a perpetual music, and gives light
In fading always from the measuring mind:
Such is the waterfall; and though we watch it
Falling from rock to rock and always changing,
Cast to a whirlpool, pent by rock, pursuing
A reckless path, headlong in radiant mist
Leaping within the roar of its own chains,
We know it lives by being consumed, we know
Its voice is new and ancient, and its force
Flies from a single impulse that believes
Nothing is vain, though all is cast for sorrow.
There hangs the image of our life, there flies
The image of our transience. If you ask
Where may divinity or love find rest
When all moves forward to a new beginning
And each obeys one constant law of change,
I cannot answer.
                    Yet to man alone,
Moving in time, birth gives a timeless movement,
To taste the secret of the honeycomb
And pluck from night that blessing which outweighs
All the calamities and griefs of time.
There shines the one scene worthy of his tears,
For in that dark the greatest light was born
Which, if man sees, then time is overthrown,
And afterwards all acts are qualified
By knowledge of that interval of glory:
Music from heaven, the incomparable gift
Of God to man, in every infant's eyes
That vision which is ichor to the soul
Transmitted there by lightning majesty,
The replica, reborn, of Christian love.

Ruth's Lament for Naomi

I cannot count the times we met.
You clasped me near the field of hay.
I stood when Orpah would not stay.
Now death has brought us closer yet.

O mother, whom no lips have sung,
A seal is laid upon my tongue.
I watch the waters glide away
And guard the image they forget.

I, Centurion

I, centurion out of time,
Re-enact for Cherubim
The living truth which makes them wise
Forever present to my eyes.
I myself was witness then
Of God's love revealed to men
Walking in flesh amongst mankind
Which gave their sight back to the blind.
I can reveal those acts which made
Centuries obey one shade,
For mortal vision ends at length
And there the Cherubs draw their strength.
Their wisdom is direct, but ours
Emerges from a stress of powers.
No mortal man could see as much
As their eyes, opened at a touch;
Yet no Cherub's eyes had shone
But for the detail that is gone,
And their wings would not so beat
But for the pressure of those feet
Set on the world's revolving ball,
Their wisdom being reciprocal.

For me, a witness, it were wrong
To praise the gifts of time in song.
Let others for long years sing praise;
I marvel to have seen two days
Whose likeness shall not be again.

The first recalls that cry of pain
Heard from my servant's bed when I
Despatched one, fearing he would die,
To entreat his life might be restored.
I followed, asking for one word
Of grace. That word I heard Him give
And knew at once my man would live.

All that is true in earth or sky
Begins and ends in music. I,
Truth and obedience being my trade,
Hearing the voice even Death obeyed,
Was smitten then by hidden strings,
Seeing this last of underlings
Healed and made whole. And then again
The next day, by the gate of Nain
I passed, just at the hour when one,
A young man dead, an only son,
Was carried out. Beside his head
A woman, mother of the dead
And she a widow, softly wept
As to the graveyard forth they stepped.
With their committed steps her tears
Took up the burden of lost years
And every step returned her groan,
A stone-like grief given back by stone.

My eyes were fixed upon them when
They left the gateway. It was then
He stopped the bearers, said to her:
'Weep not'; and, stooping, touched the bier.
Hearing the harp-string of the dead,
The young man then upon his bed
Sat up, and He restored him whole
To his mother.

I, in love's control,
Speak of these happenings from which came
The risen light their wings proclaim
Who gaze on God. As from a mould
That neither changes nor grows old,
They with their vision make all fresh.
The ages, to have vigorous flesh,
Must of such moments take account

Which gave life back, as from a fount,
Even at the threshold of despair.
Earth turns, and while the wheels of prayer
Revolve, these lightning spirits move
Forever back to incarnate love,
Even as the galaxies of night
Still seek a single candle's light
Before whose flame I kneel, and praise
The strict dimensions of two days.
That is their need, which I beheld
On Earth, whose words the lightning held,
To me and to that woman said,
Opening the doors that held our dead.

In the Protestant Cemetery, Rome

Where cypress and acacia stand,
Grave upon grave on either hand,
Touching the wall's peculiar bell
I hear the new vibration tell
I entered through this very door
Violent, yet measured, years before,
To stand in shadow from the sky
Where Shelley and Trelawny lie
And find the spot where sunlight eats
The letters on the grave of Keats.
It was a moment when I still
Knew no remedy for time's ill,
Among the many or the few
No power effective to renew
Substance loved and treasured most,
Seeming irreparably lost.
Watching those animated trees
Move above the contraries,
Writing shadows on the dead,
Lifting the shades, their dying shed,
I, like one who was gagged and bound,
Having no words but in the ground,
Defying time and memory,
Sought to resolve their tragedy.

Nothing has changed. No string has gone
This morning from the harp of stone
Above the epitaph which belies
That youth who looked with earnest eyes,
Confident that he would be
Remembered by posterity.
Yet what a monument for tears!
Severn, surviving sixty years
That long day on which he penned
The portrait of his dying friend,
Is laid in death beside him now
Underneath the selfsame bough.
Keats, whose searing, fevered ache
Boyhood's ambition could not slake,
Found that his friend's devotion brought
Anodyne for the pain of thought.
Blossoms falling through the air
Make the very dust aware
By what sad stages he had come,
Leaving great hopes, to die in Rome.
There hangs a darkness, as of waves,
On Shelley's and Trelawny's graves.
The sailor who outlived his friend
Like Severn Keats, and in the end
Moored his boat beside that stone,
Neighbours him now, as time moves on.
In Shelley's coat when he was drowned
Keats' book, with Aeschylus', was found.
He, so unlike Keats, for whom
He brought his poem to the tomb,
Well understood what gifts were hid
Here, by Cestius' pyramid.
He knew *Hyperion*, knew his pall,
But did not know the unfinished *Fall*.
Shelley, who from the first began
His concept of a sinless man,
Inspired by passion's desperate stream
Translating substance into dream,
Yet who transfigured him to thought,
Making of life what it is not,
Ignored that resurrection must
Come of true substance, and of dust.
Byron to his burial came

And saw Trelawny through the flame
Pluck the heart which would not burn
Destined to this unspeaking urn,
When on the funeral pyre he lay,
Carried from Lerici Bay.

How still the graveyard: one at peace
And one so restless. Time must cease
Before they understand each other.
Yet now they do, for now their mother
Casts on them her falling leaves.
No longer the miraculous grieves
For youth cut off, reclaimed by age,
Where history sets a tragic stage.
Character keeps its vesture on
Holding the body, though it's gone;
And the paired friends, a space apart,
Draw the leaves' whisperings, heart to heart.
Yet now once more the gate is closed,
The new life seized, the limbs disposed.
Altered by a gentle breeze,
The cypress and acacia trees
Take root again where first they grew,
The place where contraries are true.

Ode at the Spring Equinox

Gone is the solstice, gone the weaning time
Of lambs. These graze the hard
Ground, and the cliff is charred,
The gorse being burnt where now I climb.
Sparse violets, shivering, break to the low sun.
Life has already, though unseen, begun,
Yet still no sign is given; the shore
Sparkles inanimate in the span
Of headlands. Fossil now and man
Speak of a death which was not here before.
It is man's fault if it is so:
His guilt has brought him low,
And where I climb and cast a shade
I bear the consequence of that,

For the mind's load is great
Which knows what menace hangs on all things made.

Icily keen the wind blows, still from the East
Driving the wrinkled tide.
All's withered on one side.
For twenty days it has not ceased
Thrusting against mankind its edge and hate.
The rock resists, borne on its own dead weight.
There the winged form of a lost age
Is fixed, defying from these rocks
The merciless, cold-eyed equinox,
Set to annihilate life with its blind rage.
I see transposed the living sign
Linking that age to mine,
Words upon obelisk or tree,
Vessels of intricate workmanship
Thrown from a battered ship,
Strewn with the wasteful treasures of the sea.

I mark how savagely the knife-wind blows,
Nailing me to the slope.
Out of this earth what hope
Rises with larks, or what repose
Lives on the sea or moves in seabirds' wings?
The wind starves all things and the seaspray stings
The dried-up grass. How can it serve
The lives of men? Storm bringing wood
For fires and pyres, but never food,
What can it offer but the sea-knife's curve?
And now the incurious goats go past
Crossing this charcoal waste,
Moving from bush to rockhead far below,
Feeding on all that man rejects,
Prophets the hill protects,
Lingering in shade like still unmelted snow.

Ravens return, that pair, sailing in space
Over my head, great wings:
I have watched their foragings;
And now three-quarters up the face
Of vertical rock they have perched upon a ledge
Where, ragged as a bush or blackthorn hedge,
Their nest hangs, out of reach of wave.

And there the raven cliff's burnt gloom
Matches the fiery wing's charred plume
Pitched above strands from many a sandy cave.
Surely the constant that I seek,
Though every hope should break,
Is balanced, hoisted to that rock's
Dangerous height, the uplifted order
Safe from the track of murder,
The streaking, vanishing form of the red fox.

Ruffled with radiance now the black silk wings
Float out, and from this verge
I see them drop, then merge
Wind's desolation, broken things,
With secret life concealed in mottled shells.
I in predicament match them, nothing else.
How could they know as I must know,
These hasards they must overcome
Of whirlwind, thunderstorm and foam,
Are nothing but the shells from which they grow?
All is so hung that harmony,
Though pitched precariously,
Conquers uncertainty, remorse
And every flickering shaft of doubt
When the pure gift flies out
And wonder, like a spring, renews its force.

I watch, and feel the pulse of turning Earth
Now, in the forespring time,
And mark that power sublime
Which makes the passing moment worth
All unformed years lacking this present form.
See, they return, riding both sea and storm.
These they have overcome, but man,
Seizing the blind stone ignorance flings,
Himself can break this chain of wings
And, aiming, maim the loom where life began.
The immediate presence of that fear
Brings distant ages near.
Never let it be said that he,
Despising his own intellect,
Art and his whole Past wrecked,
And cast his planet's faith beneath the sea.

Good Friday

After the winter solstice came
Ice and low flame,
The cockerel step by which the light
Shortened the sleep of earth and night.

And slowly as the days of Lent
Waxed and were spent,
Trees, birds and flowers all increased
In expectation of the feast.

Spring with such promise did abound
That the gemmed ground
Already showed in clustered grass
The printless light of unseen stars.

But now light grows where rays decline.
Now the crushed wine
Transfigures all, leaf, blossom, fruit,
By reference to the sacred root.

Day must die here that day may break.
Time must forsake
Time, and this moment be preferred
To any copy, light or word.

In this a night we apprehend
Which has no end.
Day dies. We make our choice, and say:
'This, this we seek; no second day.'

Not in the speculative skies
Instruction lies,
But in the nails of darkness driven
Into these hands which hold up heaven.

For, as old ages antedate
Love's present weight,
So the pulse falling gives the chain
Momentum to what years remain.

All lives, to flourish, here should stop
Still; and all hope
To live, must die here first, and pull
New ages to this mountain skull.

Now let the geography of lands
Learn from these hands,
And from these feet the unresting seas
Take, from unfathomed grief, their ease.

Our mortal life is composite
Until we knit
All possible days to this, and make
A seal, from which true day must break.

Come, Easter, come: I was afraid
Your star had strayed.
It was behind our darkest fears
Which could not see their God for tears.

Great Nights Returning

Great nights returning, midnight's constellations
Gather from groundfrost that unnatural brilliance.
Night now transfigures, walking in the starred ways,
Tears for the living.

Earth now takes back the secret of her changes.
All the wood's dropped leaves listen to your footfall.
Night has no tears, no sound among the branches;
Stopped is the swift stream.

Spirits were joined when hazel leaves were falling.
Then the stream hurrying told of separation.
This is the fires' world, and the voice of Autumn
Stilled by the death-wand.

Under your heels the icy breath of Winter
Hardens all roots. The Leonids are flying.
Now the crisp stars, the circle of beginning;
Death, birth, united.

Nothing declines here. Energy is fire-born.
Twigs catch like stars or serve for your divining.
Lean down and hear the subterranean water
Crossed by the quick dead.

Now the soul knows the fire that first composed it
Sinks not with time but is renewed hereafter.
Death cannot steal the light which love has kindled
Nor the years change it.

Affinities
1962

Waterfalls

Always in that valley in Wales I hear the noise
Of waters falling.
There is a clump of trees
We climbed for nuts; and high in the trees the boys
Lost in the rookery's cries
Would cross, and branches cracking under their knees

Would break, and make in the winter wood new gaps.
The leafmould covering the ground was almost black,
But speckled and striped were the nuts we threw in our caps,
Milked from split shells and cups,
Secret as chestnuts when they are tipped from a sack,

Glossy and new.
Always in that valley in Wales
I hear that sound, those voices. They keep fresh
What ripens, falls, drops into darkness, fails,
Gone when dawn shines on scales,
And glides from village memory, slips through the mesh,

And is not, when we come again.
I look:
Voices are under the bridge, and that voice calls,
Now late, and answers;
then, as the light twigs break
Back, there is only the brook
Reminding the stones where, under a breath, it falls.

The Precision of the Wheel

to my Son

How like a wheel of prayer
The year returns,
Precision plucked from air;
And the soul learns
The rustling of those trees,
The changing sound,
Music of cypresses
In hallowed ground
And of that younger green

Which drops its blooms
Sudden as swallows, seen
When April comes.

Your birthday; and, that night,
I stopped, to bind
What I had come to write.
That month my mind
Had run upon a coil
Where light newborn
Revealed in weaver's toil
Lady and unicorn.
The sixfold tapestry
In my mind's eye
Held darkness searchingly;
And then your cry.

Twelve years since then have passed,
And to the day
This verse arrives, my last;
And I must pray,
If on the door I knock
That hides so many dead,
That savagery on rock
In vain be shed.
A secret law contrives
To give time symmetry:
There is, within our lives,
An exact mystery.

From this October night
May you be given
Peace, though the trees by blight
Or storms are riven.
And though the abounding spray
Destroy what issues from it,
May time that law obey,
Strict as a comet,
Which gives in gratitude
All we give, back,
By that rich love renewed
Which misers lack.

Child, what would I not give
To change for you

The world in which we live
And make it new,
Not in the paths and towers
Of prayer and praise,
But in the outrageous powers
Their waste displays.
May night's twin mysteries,
Time's equipoise,
Call upon love, and these
Build all your joys.

The Interval

This now being finished and the next unknown,
I must wait long to find the words I need.
Verse tests the very marrow in the bone,
Yet man, being once engaged by song, is freed:
The act itself is prayer, deliberate in its speed.

Nature needs waste; even friendship needs a gap.
Wines love delay and boats a measured stroke.
Distance divides lightning and thunderclap,
Yet time can in a crystal cleared of smoke
Show Earth's arrested lives in mute, transparent cloak.

Now by what current is the swimmer borne
Feeling its pull and subterranean force?
Are the dead parched, or hunger the unborn
For present music, that its certain course
Alone may fill their need and heal them of remorse?

No pressure from this upper ground compels.
It is that dark source which makes all things new
Scoops out, with changing lights, those fragile shells
Whose voice would perish, did I not pursue
Their inmost labyrinth still, to give the god his due.

Rewards of the Fountain

Let the world offer what it will,
Its bargains I refuse.

Those it rewards are greedy still.
I serve a stricter Muse.

She bears no treasure but the sands,
No bounty but the sea's.
The fountain falls on empty hands.
She only gives to these.

The living water sings through her
Whose eyes are fixed on stone.
My strength is from the sepulchre
Where time is overthrown.

If once I labour to possess
A gift that is not hers,
The more I gain in time, the less
I triumph in the verse.

Ironies of the Self

When hostile circumstance
By thunder, sleet or hail
Turns the sun's radiance
Into a coat of mail,
Ironies of the self,
On you I rely
To cut the loss by half
Of that clear sky,
And to restore the place
Of Adam's dream
Where Eve would walk with grace
In the direct beam.
What though the scales are tipped
Darkly the other way,
Humour is near the crypt
Where the saints pray.

And even the mocking birds
Are on your side,
Preening their sudden words
Against the satisfied,
Just as the crow alights
On a sheep's back

To kill the parasites,
Or thrush will crack
A snailshell in the sun
Against a stone;
They show the self undone,
Pick clean the bone.
Still, then, to gain true ends,
All opposition set;
To enemies, not friends,
One owes that debt.

Yet he is blind who mocks
A clear stream flowing,
Nor learns the paradox
Of its grace and going.
Who can have health
And laugh at those who spend
The true, continuous wealth
The mountains send
After a fall of rain
Through many stones?
Again and again
That secrecy intones
Pure bounty which
The heart alone can have,
By penury made rich,
Refreshed by love.

Whatever trinket
The bright-eyed jackdaw choose,
Thought can but link it
To what the heart must lose
If it forsake
The strict, unswerving path
A stream will take,
Making a stone its hearth:
Dancing in the sun
Better than any,
Making all treasures run
From its own penny
That sings, renewed each instant,
Leaps, being displaced,
And keeps, in yielding, constant,
In falling, chaste.

Vine

Deep-rooted vine, delay your fruit
Beyond youth's rashness. I have seen
Rich promise wither to the root
Before its time had been.

Drain all the darkness of the soil
And stand there shrivelled, crisp and dry,
Too lifeless in your parchment coil
To open one green eye.

Some watch the March winds animate
Those early bulbs in Winter's bed.
Envy them not, but keep your state.
Let others think you dead.

Contain in secrecy that balm
Strengthening the sap before it move,
That the broad leaves from wells of calm
One day grow dark with love.

I know a tree as dry as yours.
The patient leaf is put forth late.
Its life is anchored in the hours
For which the heart must wait.

Affinities

I find them in the wings of every age
While fools and rhetoricians hold the stage.

They know instinctively that speculation
Will never reach a single true equation.

There is no theory, however strict,
A work of genius cannot contradict.

Who pulls tradition down and sets up fashion?
Pretence is one thing, and another, passion.

In every smith whose work I come across
Tradition is the ore, fashion the dross.

They who skim ice cannot afford to stumble;
If pausing they went through, they might grow humble.

Pretenders mock the dead to make their mark,
As little children shout who fear the dark.

'His work is new. Why, then, his name encumber
With ancient poets?' He is of their number.

Complain against the dead, but do not sue.
They never read you, much less injured you.

Must it be anarchy to love that nation
Which counts among its assets inspiration?

Demands of the Poet

I set my heart against all lesser toil.
Speak to me now more closely than the birds.
That labour done, on which I spent my oil,
Avails me nothing till you test the words.

How much the beating pulse may hold the years
Yet write the athletic wisdom on the page
You alone say. You bring the authentic tears
Which recognize the moment without age.

No lesser vision gives me consolation.
Wealth is a barren waste, that spring forgot.
Art is the principle of all creation,
And there the desert is, where art is not.

Demands of the Muse

I call up words that he may write them down.
My falling into labour gives him birth.
My sorrows are not sorrows till he weeps.
I learn from him as much as he from me
Who is my chosen and my tool in time.

I am dumb: my burden is not like another.
My lineaments are hid from him who knows me.
Great is my Earth with undelivered words.
It is my dead, my dead, that sing to him
This ancient moment; and their voice is he.

Born into time of love's perceptions, he
Is not of time. The acts of time to him
Are marginal. From the first hour he knows me
Until the last, he shall divine my words.
In his own solitude he hears another.

I make demands of him more than another.
He sets himself a labour built of words
Which, through my lips, brings sudden joy to him.
He has the illusion that at last he knows me.
When the toil ends, my confidant is he.

Vision makes wise at once. Why then must he
Wait through so many years before he knows me?
The bit is tempered to restrain his words
And make laborious all that's dear to him.
So he remains himself and not another.

Why is he slow to praise me when another
Falls at my feet? What conscience moves in him
To make a stubborn stand before he knows me?
It is reluctance that resolves his words.
I have been cursed, indeed, by such as he.

Yet, though a school invoke me, it is he
I choose, for opposition gives those words
Their strength; and there is none more near to him
In thought. It is by conflict that he knows me
And serves me in my way and not another.

Sonnet

TO CERTAIN ANCIENT ANONYMOUS POETS

Poets, like ancient streams which time like sand
Covers, across your lyric utterance thrown,
Found again fresh, emerging from dark stone,
Though dead, through you the leaves of life expand.
Ah, were it possible to understand
The life sung down to men, then each alone
Might fix his eyes where envies are undone,
Nor feel an exile in his native land.

I thought of such a power when first I grew
As might control base passions from those tombs

Where laurels rest and the acacia blooms,
But now I find it where the ground wears rue.
Always it is from joy my music comes
And always it is sorrow keeps it true.

Muse, Poet and Fountain

No living man may compass what I seek.
No eye outside my own may judge these things;
And mine are downcast that my hand may speak.
In me tears end; from me the fountain springs.

Though time still falls from future into past,
Nothing is gone my hand may not restore.
Mine is the pulse that makes your pulse beat fast,
Harmonious joy with stillness at the core.

I am your peace, wherever fortune move you,
Your strength, your birthright and your native ground.
I wait to give, whether men scorn or love you,
Prodigal strength, returning to my sound.
Not while you live, but when grass waves above you,
When you are dead, your labour shall be crowned.

The Crane

The crane, at his wits' end,
Dances behind his mate.
She will not apprehend
His lonely, ecstatic state,
Nor that fine beat of the brain
Which makes the wings unclose,
Unclose, tremble, and close again:
Nothing of this she knows.

He is moving, moving in ecstasy,
The faintly flushed white wings
Gathered as if to fly.
He moves to certain strings
Stretched between earth and sky
That enforce a rigid stance.

Desire has fixed his eye
To execute his dance.

She and the distance are cut off
While he is thus engaged.
Whether spectators scoff
Means nothing. He is enraged,
Being the relict of love,
At her distracted mind,
Nor can he demonstrate enough
To make her look behind.

A bead or trivial thing
Beckons her steps away
From the live, dramatic wing.
She has let her attention stray,
Nor listens to that strict beat
Balanced upon two toes.
He knows the extremes from which they meet:
Nothing of this she knows.

Drawn by the opposite
Of the solitude at her side,
She eludes the startled fit
Delusion has deified,
The exalted, staring eyes
Fixed on remotest space.
Against their abstraction she supplies
A movement in time and place.

He is dancing, he is possessed
By something beyond the dance.
She is held by his unrest,
Controlled, compelled to advance,
As though to define the hour
By a step exactly cut.
She feels the penumbra of his power
In wings that open and shut.

Who separated the pair,
Born of the selfsame feather?
He simulates despair,
But night will bring them together.
It is this that excites his brain
And makes the wings unclose,

Unclose, tremble, and close again:
Nothing of this she knows:

Ode to Swansea

Bright town, tossed by waves of time to a hill,
Leaning Ark of the world, dense-windowed, perched
High on the slope of morning,
Taking fire from the kindling East:

Look where merchants, traders, and builders move
Through your streets, while above your chandlers' walls
Herring gulls wheel, and pigeons,
Mocking man and the wheelwright's art.

Prouder cities rise through the haze of time,
Yet, unenvious, all men have found is here.
Here is the loitering marvel
Feeding artists with all they know.

There, where sunlight catches a passing sail,
Stretch your shell-brittle sands where children play,
Shielded from hammering dockyards
Launching strange, equatorial ships.

Would they know you, could the returning ships
Find the pictured bay of the port they left
Changed by a murmuration,
Stained by ores in a nighthawk's wing?

Yes. Through changes your myth seems anchored here.
Staked in mud, the forsaken oyster beds
Loom; and the Mumbles lighthouse
Turns through gales like a seabird's egg.

Lundy sets the course of the painted ships.
Fishers dropping nets off the Gower coast
Watch them, where shag and cormorant
Perch like shades on the limestone rocks.

You I know, yet who from a different land
Truly finds the town of a native child
Nurtured under a rainbow,
Pitched at last on Mount Pleasant hill?

Stone-runged streets ascending to that crow's nest
Swinging East and West over Swansea Bay
Guard in their walls Cwmdonkin's
Gates of light for a bell to close.

Praise, but do not disturb, heaven's dreaming man
Not awakened yet from his sleep of wine.
Pray, while the starry midnight
Broods on Singleton's elms and swans.

A True Picture Restored

MEMORIES OF DYLAN THOMAS

Nearer the pulse than other themes
His deathborn claims are pressed.
Fired first by Milton, then the dreams
Of Herbert's holy breast,
Out of his days the sunlight streams
And fills the burning West.

I look where soon the frosty Plough
Shall hang above the sill
And see the colours westward flow
To green Carmarthen's hill.
There sinks the sky of changes now
On waters never still.

Praise God, although a time is gone
That shall not come again,
If ever morning rightly shone,
A glass to make all plain,
The man I mourn can make it live,
Every fallen grain.

I see the house where we would meet;
I see my steps return,
Kicking the sparks of the Swansea street,
And still those windows burn,
Struck by the sunrise hour of life
With all men's lives to learn.

My echoing footsteps when they stop
Reconstitute the town,

That working window at the top,
The neophyte and clown
Setting the reel and arc-light up
To pull illusion down.

The various roofs beneath that house,
The crooked roads and straight,
The excess or strictness God allows
In every devious fate,
He honoured these with early vows
And cursed the aloof with late.

The latest dead, the latest dead,
How should he have died,
He in whom Eden's morning
Had left its ancient pride,
Adam, God, and maiden,
Love, and the yearning side?

And Wales, when shall you have again
One so true as he,
Whose hand was on the mountain's heart,
The rising of the sea,
And every praising bird that cries
Above the estuary?

He never let proud nature fall
Out of its pristine state.
The hunchback fed upon a love
That made the crooked straight,
No single promise broken
On which the heart must wait.

The heron poised above the glass
With straight and stabbing bill,
Among the water's moods that pass
Choosing to strike and kill,
Transfixed the sky with holiest eye
When the whole heart was still.

Down to the solstice moves the sun
And through Saint Lucie's night
Under the earth all rivers run
Back to the birth of light.
Among the living he was one
Who felt the world in flight.

Climbing Cwmdonkin's dock-based hill,
I found his lamp-lit room,
The great light in the forehead
Watching the waters' loom,
Compiling there his doomsday book
Or dictionary of doom.

More times than I can call to mind
I heard him reading there.
His eyes with fervour could make blind
All clocks about a stair
On which the assenting foot divined
The void and clustered air.

That was the centre of the world,
That was the hub of time.
The complex vision faded now,
The simple grew sublime.
There seemed no other valid stair
For wondering feet to climb.

That strictest, lie-disrobing act
Testing the poem read
Which, after toil and plumbing,
Left the first cause unsaid,
Showed me his nature then as now,
The life he gave the dead.

There, near Cwmdonkin, first and last,
Witness of lives below,
He held the unrisen wisdom fast
From heaven in overthrow,
Where lamps of hooded meaning cast
Light on the words below.

And later, in that toppling house
Over the village hearse,
Where the Portreeve assembled
His birds and characters,
It was the dying earth he gave
To heaven in living verse.

In London, when the blinds were drawn
Blackening a barbarous sky,
He plucked, beneath the accusing beams,
The mote out of his eye.

In the one death his eye discerned
The death all deaths must die.

'My immortality,' he said,
'Now matters to my soul
Less than the deaths of others.'
And would not fame enrol
Every forgotten character
If Shakespeare held the scroll?

The latest dead, the latest dead,
What power could pull him down
Who on a breath of vision
Could animate a town,
Could plunder every shy retreat
And give the lost renown?

Not by the wars of human minds
Nor by the jealous word
Nor by the black of London's blinds
Or coffin's rattling cord,
But by the stillness of that voice
The picture is restored.

Let each whose soul is in one place
Still to that place be true.
The man I mourn could honour such
With every breath he drew.
I never heard him wish to take
A life from where it grew.

And yet the man I mourn is gone,
He who could give the rest
So much to live for till the grave,
And do it all in jest.
Hard it must be, beyond this day,
For even the grass to rest.

Ode to Nijinsky

That you should die at peace, all would have prayed.
That you should ever die, none would believe
Once, where the dance upheld you,
Winged like a god, and creation's wonder.

Who fostered you? The grace of Mallarmé's Faun
Smiled; you brought to Gautier's perfection life.
Valéry dreamed, and waking
Saw in your dance his divine Narcissus.

Which of the gods did you most resemble? None
Could match your singular art, so lithe on the world
Alighting, not even Orpheus
Could create such pause, such mysterious cadence.

Yet from an earlier myth, young before Greece,
Your fingers learnt the unspoken language of flowers.
Eloquence, gained by silence,
Rose to declare the eternal moment.

Yes, as Diaghilev saw, where your shadow fell
The centuries merged; your hands united the ages.
Taught by a deeper idiom,
Movement you took from the core of stillness.

Both light and shadow crossed your figures prescribed,
Yet you broke, like a fish, all nets of design,
Coiling distance, a dolphin
Doubled in dance, in a fountain leaping.

Glorious form, the fate of the greatly endowed
Embodying, you incomparably we see
Dance, where the moving heavens
Answer Copernicus' pictures, dying.

He whose hands lay crossed on the starry heavens,
Knew his heresy true of the circling Earth:
Strict and true revolutions
Hold us still, like the heavenly bodies.

You, you also, fearing the truth you revealed,
All time's limits held in your rigid clasp,
Pressed by divine renewal,
Acted the rite of your valediction.

In the cell of windows whose secret you alone knew,
Dark as your drawings controlled by shadow, there shines
A statement, cut by a diamond:
'I, when I am not loved, must perish.'

Rhythmic demigod, prince to marvelling eyes,
Presence controlling their myths extended in space,

Dancing you wore, Nijinsky,
And dead you transfigure, the mask of genius.

A Bell Unrung

In those days stone became bright and the dove bright-grey.
Bells in sunlight fell upon births and weddings.
My tongue clove to heaven's roof, where night and morning
Moved as before. Yet it seemed from the East each day
The sun rose more slowly, announcing tidings.
I noticed the page of history my hand was turning,
And looked at it twice before I laid it away.

Sickness struck. Thieves overheard, or Shades,
In the garden of Eden known to me from my birth
Held distance hung on a sensitive needle's trembling.
Had I not seen in a leaf before it fades
The symmetry of the heavens? And touching earth
The round sun dropped, as low as a leaf, assembling
In a heavy drop all places, postures and trades.

A fuller's whiteness filled heaven from the fall of dew.
How still the world! I listened. The bell in the steeple
Did not move. All night the loom of the stars
Was winding, watched by the counting clocks, a new
Sheet for one soul in a city emptied of people.
Precious time! I kept my shade, like a vase,
From the voices of substitution, silent for you.

Three Sonnets for Charles Williams

I

Crystalline scribe of the pure Parousia, chronicling passion's tale
Of Logres, giver of questing knights, deliver from sorcery's hands
The chivalry of the star-plucked heavens; reveal, where Galahad stands
Near the wolf in the forest of Broceliande, Taliesin the nightingale
Soothing Helayne in the night of labour, divining the labouring sail
Of the song-borne ship, and invoking her joy, her infant in
swaddling-bands,

Substitution's fruit, to Blanchefleur carried, foretelling that union of
lands
Which won, through Lancelot's son, the grandeur and grace of the Grail.

You still of that excellent absurdity jealously guard the key
Which maps the just, geometrical heavens for King Arthur's avatars
In a luminous pattern, a network of roads, Jerusalem carried by sea
In a ship, and Byzantium's womanlike Europe pondering above her wars
Those time-consuming acts of identity narrowing to make men free,
Intricate watcher, catcher of men, in a net drawn close to the stars.

2

On Pelles' castle the dove alighting, the wing;
On Orkney's rock the seabird falling, the scream;
In garden and rock the face forming, the dream
Knit with the dream of Empire: these you sing.

Beat on the basin of gold, beat, to unchain
Fettered spirits; strike, till the hammered joy's
Vibration, pierced by the dove, by the seabird's noise,
Makes known immortal healing and mortal pain.

Poets may choose one time. When the choice is made
Time takes root, and the lovers within that time
Begin purgatorial journeys, Shade by Shade.
You did not stretch to the compass of Dante's rhyme
But made a mosaic of history, where sublime
Courtiers tell time's truth, and the penance paid.

3

How early a room in the heart you prepare to receive our King,
Breakfasting on that glory, translator of temporal day
To the ninefold access of heaven, with recoil and interplay
Where every gesture, pause of the heart, achievement or suffering
Is a witness held in check. For you the immediate thing
Has true dimensions; no time is for chance to spirit away,
No space for stars to outspeed. Through strictness the pictures stay,
Caught by the voice, and held: an eternal banqueting.

Christ's Second Coming governs all lives; and the time you chose
Is the dawn of the expectation. Nothing of life can pass
In their meeting and parting from those who lived, revealed in the
window-glass

Of your dazzling verse, like the flight of a sleigh under bells where Libra
shows;
Yet for you the ninth heaven moves where a petal falling on grass
Divides Taliesin from Dindrane, in the fire-forged light of her snows.

Ode

TO T. S. ELIOT

Since the human motive is always fallible
And the design of good
Draws from none but the humble
Such a life as is always new,

May you, sifting truly the power of fantasy
Over the growing child,
Kindling time like a candle,
Marvel, seeing its praise transformed.

Warn mankind, though softly: 'Time remains plausible.
Test the contented man;
Seek within his responses,
And in yours, what must still be found.'

Since the self-corrected alone is innocent
And the impulsive heart
Brings betrayal of glory,
Nor can thrive till it live by prayer,

Who can better teach how little is visible
Save in the eye of God?
Tentatively you struggled,
Mapping slowly the land we know.

Not by wide acclaim you tested accomplishment.
Early fame was deceit;
Failures nourished the honest,
Moulded still by a force unknown.

Rich in time's ambition, you yet chose penury,
Paying a timeless debt,
One intensity binding
Future ages and all the Past.

Next you pruned the English language of luxury
Lest it should waste its strength,

Matching strictness to music,
Incantation to living speech.

Art is various, verse develops unsearchably.
See, from the mid-leaf born,
Growth may copy the cactus,
Yet adhere to its ancient root.

Prayer alone makes all that perishes permanent.
Step by step we are led
Past a moment of terror:
From that moment our works proceed.

These things came to you as you waited patiently
Under the tree of life.
Taking Dante for master,
You descanted on London Bridge.

Many streets and lives we judge by that instrument,
Yet no measurement can
Judge the loss of a person,
So discreet is the dance of life.

Let none doubt the disguise. See how deformity
Under attentive eyes
Bears perfection within it,
Speaking low its athletic style.

Strong is he who knows mankind through infirmity
And who practises love,
Seeing each from the godhead
Living here as an earthly son.

This, then, most, your birthday justly will celebrate,
That the divining mind
Finds regenerate waters
Turning all to effects of grace.

Fountain cities, too, preserve a community
Never entirely lost
Though destruction, though bondage
Leave their mark on the roads and walls.

Vision gives man strength no danger will dominate.
Time is redeemed, while he
Earths in safety the lightning
Shining through the ironic mask.

How best keep the bold example in memory?
Age is potent to show
Youth's impelled emulation
How to feed its exalted will.

Each for all men's hearts is counted responsible.
Therefore that land is waste
Which forgets for a moment
Passion's healer and treasured spring.

Zennor Cottages

ONCE SHELTERING D. H. LAWRENCE

What pledge of honour
Obsessing the whole mind,
Broken near Zennor
Into stone and wind,

Shows one inhabiting
A cottage, who gave wrongs
A name, while he would sing
His German songs?

Who would have thought that here
Where the yellow flower breaks stone
His presence should appear,
And those years gone?

Two wars, two cottages,
Where famished the hawk falls;
The heart's imprisoned seas
In granite walls

Revive with a sigh
The man's peculiar load
When before Italy
He trod this road.

Here is the landscape he
Knew bitterly; but now,
Where breaks the exterior sea,
I notice how

The fields he knew, though bleak,
Still nourish for their own
A strength which cannot speak
Till life is gone.

The Ballad of the Mermaid of Zennor

Where grey Land's End repels the sky
The granite boulders stand
Reared in a column. There they lie
Laid by a giant's hand,
And there the ascending seabirds fly
Beyond the last of land.

The shallow hills reflect that grey,
The walled-in fields are bleak.
The road from Zennor winds its way
West, in a barren streak,
Shunning the softer forms of day,
Forgetting what men speak.

Who stands upon that farthest ledge
And sees the Atlantic break,
Back through the fields with stones for hedge
His Eastward way will take
To Zennor's valley and its pledge,
A legend cut in teak.

The tale in teak has worn away
These last five hundred years
But still the church of granite grey
Its haunting music hears
While fields are singing or obey
The silence winter wears.

The black teak near the chancel stands
And shines there like a shell.
The boy above her dripping hands
Had sung too well, too well.
The mermaid dragged him to her sands
And bound him with her spell.

He: 'Why break, why break, unending waves?
O take me, lead me home!

The stones I long for are your naves
Where Cornish folk would come,
But here black wood, in secret caves
The darkness of the foam!'

She: 'Come down, come down from that high chair,
That hook with hassock hung;
Climb from the sailors' swinging stair,
Leap from the bottom rung.
Now throw your life into my care
And be forever young.

For you and I as one must be,
A mermaid and a boy,
Joined in the always moving sea
Where dolphins leap for joy.
Forget the stones, the starry tree;
The thought of graves put by.

This music hovered round your soul
Before you first drew breath,
And those its caul has covered whole
Shall never come to death,
Long though the murderous seawaves roll
With many and many a wreath.'

A thousand tides, a thousand tides,
And bridals on the hill.
The sunken ships with broken sides
Lean over and are still.
A granite church the seaweed hides;
Its aisles the fishes fill.

He: 'Why break, why break, unending waves?
O take me, take me home!
Down to your stones, along your naves
The worshippers have come.
But mine the night, the secret caves,
The darkness of the foam!'

She: 'Bend down, bend down, and hear my wood:
None was more sweetly strung.
The tenor boy who fell was good.
I heard his golden tongue.
He raised my spirit from the flood
And on his voice I hung.

His music pierced my heart, and then
I called him from the sea.
He left the church, he left the men,
He stood upon the quay.
The long rope ladder held him then,
And then the rope went free.'

But was it he who heard her sing
Or did she first hear him?
Black as bright teak the cormorants fling
Up from the waves they skim
The silver fish, and mussels cling
And close above the hymn.

The mermaid knows what no man knows,
The secrets of a shell,
The pearl on fire, the breaking rose,
The murmuring, foundered bell
Whose sound through singing chambers goes
Crossed by the tingling swell.

And every adolescent knows
How searching is that song
And how mysteriously it flows
Plucked from a death so young
When unborn years with passion close
The casket of the strong.

He: 'However long the waters roll
Longer my love shall be,
Nor shall you leave my burning soul
Torn by the moving sea,
Though all the bells of Zennor toll
And say you died for me.'

Héloïse

Stay, stay, of silence best example,
Making that distant moment mine,
You to whom love assigned a temple,
You in whom love preserved a shrine.

Day after day you took young pleasure,
Caught by your tutor, clasped and held,

Served by his love in double measure,
Chastened by wit, by will compelled.

You, then, he taught, your neighbours cheating,
Hiding the joy which made you wise.
Abelard's rebuke, the noise of beating,
Guarded the pledge in your two eyes.

Still did your married body, grieving,
Cherish, though banished, his warm breath,
Chilled by his words, no promise leaving
To count the embraces after death.

Twenty-one years, twice borne, are ending.
Shock, then bereavement, come of age.
Your body falls. His arms ascending
Take down your constancy for wage.

Now the grave creaks beneath your lover.
Nightingales sing for bride and groom.
Seeing you cut off, yet bound for ever,
Are not all dumb before your tomb?

To Hölderlin

Poet of godlike stillness, anchorite,
Son of the world God made before man sinned,
Outcast of Hellas, aether's lonely friend,
Worshipper wounded at the shrine of light:
Children were no less glorious in your sight
Than those blest genii whom you saw descend;
The sea held riches from the same first mind:
Love was to you as to the birds their flight.

You looked for constancy. Heroic power
Greece gave you. Deep was every breath you drew,
Deeper the sacrifice which overthrew
All with divinity; but then love's hour
Had broken Rousseau's consecrated flower,
The tragic splendour of the entirely true.

*

Harmonious Nature named you her happiest child,
Singer of Patmos and the golden islands.

Godlike, reborn of light's aethereal silence,
The Christian and the Greek were reconciled.
Your senses prayed, and on that happy field
Heaven's light, all-healing, bathed the enamoured lands.
You heard the stillness under which Christ stands.
In Diotima's eyes stood love revealed.

Over the castle hung with a kestrel's power
Her memory, rivers, mountains peaked with snow
Descending sheer, for shadows to devour.
Smooth on the flowering lake, swans plunged their eyes
Into a walled, a wintry world below,
Where light was cloistered, and became unwise.

To Heinrich Heine

ON THE CENTENARY OF HIS DEATH

Heine, they do not know you.
Your footstep crossed the sun,
And where you stepped the world was changed:
You and the world were one.

You used the range of fancy.
Your colours were the Spring's.
There was no leaf in all the wood
But listened to your strings.

Softly the Muse had told you,
Cradled above the Rhine,
To tell both France and Germany:
'This that you claim is mine'.

In truth that secret cadence
Remained through exile strong.
No other could recall his land
In such elusive song.

Since love endured oppression
You painted with your hand
A subtle, mediaeval mask
To hide your native land.

There you concealed your wisdom.
Little the mask betrayed
How long the lightness of your line
Had struggled with the shade.

To you earth's crust was crystal.
You saw through it like glass.
The grief of lovers under ground
Beckoned the constant stars.

Out of the grave you raised them,
The nightingale and rose.
To you death's pillow was a stone
Where running water flows.

No, none has understood you
Since the last words you gave
While Paris overheard you sing
Upon your mattress-grave.

Hatred and wit engaged you;
Your language was your sword.
Yet you despised all words save one,
And candour was that word.

How well that sculptor showed you
Lifted above the dead,
Spirit with deathward gliding arms
And backward glancing head.

So slight a faunlike spirit
A prostrate figure clung,
It showed your inarticulate love,
The coin beneath your tongue.

The statue stood in Frankfurt
On a rose-planted lawn
Embodying there a double dream,
Fliegender Geist, yet Faun.

That dream which formed your vision
Still with deceptive art
Retraces passion's bas-relief
Back to your secret heart.

Wordsworth

The barren mountains were his theme,
Nature the force that made him strong.
This day died one who, like a stone,
Altered the course of English song.

A hundred years! The waters still
Murmur the truth he bent to glean
Where bird and sunset, copse and hill
Composed the grave, harmonious scene.

The humble and unknown became
His oracles. Infirm old age
Matching obscurity to fame
Taught, like a child, the listening sage.

About his melancholy mind
Thundered the waterfalls. How few
Have left on water, light and wind
So calm a print of all he knew.

How cold the waters, yet how clear:
How grave the voice, how fine the thread
That quickening the returning year
Restores his landscape and his dead!

The Death of Keats

Try as you may to banish from your mind
The fact of his arrival, here he came.
Say that another age is not the same;
But still the Past, with Future intertwined,
Confronts you. On this page the name he signed
Brings back the time, as embers bring the flame.
The achievement does not matter, nor the fame;
The death-mask does: for here his head reclined
In death on its last pillow. Love's low cloud
Whose intimate language he had overheard
Sheathing a lightning-stroke too bright to bear
Controls his death-bed, while the pilgrim crowd,
Thinking of one whom Genius had preferred,
Wait in the realm of homage, not of prayer.

Browning in Venice

I am lucky to come here, though late, to encounter his shade
With the splendours displayed
In these galleries bounded by walls
Where the wave-ripple falls,
And the book about Browning in Venice with poems he built
To analyse guilt.
Do the pictures throw back the grave scrutiny he gave them once?
There is nothing to show
That their eyes in the dark-shuttered house that was later his son's
Met his own long ago.

At that time he would not be disturbed by so distant a ghost
Walking here with that host
Of his characters beckoned from tombs
To evocative rooms,
Men and women alive in their past where the lives he had drawn
Sauntered up with the dawn.
The spectral chimaera of absence he knew was controlled
By the presence and gaze
Of the pulse that looked forward to age as a book that would hold
The beginning of days.

Very gently the ripple glides out from the gondola's track
Expecting him back
From the flaming Giudecca, or else
At the sound of dark bells
From Torcello, Murano, where glass or a gold-beater's shop
Compelled him to stop.
It was here, as the wake became still, that his forehead was caught,
Unaffrighted by time
When the doors of San Marco flew open and laid upon thought
Their Moor-stricken chime.

Yet how close would he be to our access if gone were the grace
Of this magical place
Tintoretto and Titian supplied,
Nor Bellini denied,
Where time is suspended in light, in a hive that contains
All its opulent gains?
Here in Venice his voice murmurs back like the wash of a boat
From the water-struck print
That could capture the prow of the past with its confident note
And serene aquatint.

How the wrist is impelled by desire when the shadow Earth flings
Gives the moment dark wings?
So last night I saw thoughts go like ships
Through the path of eclipse,
And the race of that darkness returns to my foot on the stair
From inscrutable air.
Here the walls and Tiepolo's ceiling are shuttered in gloom
Where no sunlight can break,
And a secret, unsatisfied ripple returns to the room
From the gondola's wake.

What controlled expectation was here, what delight and what wit
When the waters were lit
By that intricate thread of the mind
He would slowly unwind
Binding nature to art as he brought to the poems he made
The tools of his trade!
They are gone, and a speed-boat goes past them white-winged in its grace
While the hand that is free
Holds the tiller and leaps the gold surface to gratify space
On its path to the sea.

The Childhood of Hölderlin

'Only one Summer grant, you Powerful Ones,
And one Autumn to my full-ripened song,
That my heart willingly by the tender
Harp-strings be satisfied; let me die, then.

The soul to which its godlike right when alive
Came not, down in Orcus shall find no rest;
But once the holy one that against
My heart lies close, the poem, is uttered,

Welcome, then, O peace of the world of Shades!
Content am I, even if the play of strings
Has not down-guided my footsteps; once
Lived I as gods live, and more I crave not.'

'To the Fates'—Hölderlin

I

Surely the racing foal has discerned through darkness
The light out of which man came, and the violet-root

Has sucked the fountain over which Dante bent
And found the river of light. Yet dust is dust.
Who could rebuild from this the childhood of Hölderlin?

Who dare look twice, who dare look once, into heaven?
He looked, his eyes upheld, and the aether loved him.
In that pure instant he knew the workings of nature.
He had found stillness, the calm of beautiful bodies.
When he looked down, his eyes were blinded to shadows.

Refusing change, he fashioned the shafts of the Odes,
A quiver of joy. Where faith from the single eye
Travelled, the light was immortally true; yet he
Suffered. A wound was in the nature of man.
He grieved, while Spring restored green life to the tree.

He thought of that ancient error, returning home.
Sophocles' music changed him; the chorus-endings
Pierced his marrow: joy had a tragic base.
Nothing but grief could match the joy in his heart.
The wound of love was his, the unhealing wound.

In tragic suffering he touched the heart of the god.
Pindar taught him majesty, Sophocles, beauty.
Under creation moved the myth of Empedocles.
Harmonious nature differed from exiled man.
Yet man knew God: for him the universe mourned.

2

He came, like love, to beseeching strings. Before birth
He had experienced death. He sang in the cradle.
He knew the tenderest fire in eyes declined
Where his mother leaned. Then, racing out in the fields,
True friends he found: the mountains were his companions.
At dusk the rivers returned to the edge of the eyes.
He touched the stars, the wind, the crowns of the reeds.

If he lingered late, he felt the sigh of the dew
Like souls found late upon Lethe. In purest darkness
His eyes shone with tears. He thought of the underworld.
He grew in stature. He felt the arms of the gods
About him. When people spoke, he remained confused.
If he touched a bud, he knew the secrets of nature.
The Rhine, the demi-god, thundered, a Titan in chains.

At evening he would return by a wooded path
To his mother's house where myths of the Greeks were stored.
His eyes marvelled, reading the deeds of heroes.
At night, when his book was closed, the curtain stirred,
Pure gold in the rising moon; and he saw the valleys
Transformed with unearthly light. He acclaimed his kindred.
Quite still, he smiled, caught up to the plains of heaven.

'Holy dawn, the man who is not a hero
Does not see you; therefore you are not honoured,
Beautiful sun-god; therefore your lyre is silent,
Except where pious peoples watch you ascend.
You are too still for the eyes of men; your music
Rises solemn, not knowing trouble or care,
In perfect praise, much brighter than any dream.

I have known and loved you, Aether, better than men.
Late, when moonlight bathed the enchanted fields,
When the last notes of the sun-youth's lyre had faded
Leaving the listening mountains lost in music,
I have seen them walk, in airs of the gods, those genii,
Patient as stars. My tongue is the tomb of angels.
My words are silence. Orpheus plays to the Shades.'

Yet nearer the bone were his words on the master of tragedy,
After the sun-god's music, this upon Sophocles:
'Many attempted in vain, through joy, the most joyful to utter;
Here, at last, I am held: here, in the tragic, it speaks.'

3

Once he saw the two halves of life in a lake,
Swans on the lake, and above it, falling blossoms
Touching the surface dividing youth from age.
Then, where they dipped through the surface, all was shadow.
Had he seen the future, by walls of Winter entombed,

Discoursing, when Waiblinger saw him, of Zimmer's kindness,
A mask of deference hiding the features of youth
Of one the world had rejected? Who could have heard,
In that breath of suspended magic, the weather-vane clatter
Of the castle to which he was doomed?

4

Early, taught by Greece,
He sought the heroic in man. Apollo

Played to him. That gold fleece
Moved on the water; and the host
Of Homer's heroes moved. A lost
Age compelled him. He must follow,

Source of Promethean fire,
Source of the Danube's waterfall,
The godlike: great desire,
Glorious Heracles' feet,
With tiger and vine in thrall
Where the West and Asia meet.

There sprang from ancient silence
Music of gods, the clash on rocks of seas.
He saw those silver islands,
And he heard Mnemosyne's
Lament for Achilles and Ajax, Ajax dead
In the grotto by the sea-bed.

His eyes beyond Greece beheld
At the end of the poem 'Bread and Wine'
The torch the Syrian held
Awakening through the divine
Love, that ancient keep
Where the old gods fell asleep.

Late, caught up by a genius,
Borne over streams and dawn's strange lands,
Their peaks flowering in Asia's flame,
Seeking John, the witness,
To Patmos, the last island,
He in a vision came.

The lightning held him.
He thought to have seen God's face in youth
As John beheld Him,
But saw, where ages converged, the sign
Single and forever,
Poured to the dust like wine.

This was the bridal feast
Where Greece, by Christus' lightning stripped,
With Asia and the East
Met in love's utmost wish.
And the Baptist's head in the dish
Shone like unfading script.

All stood at the bridal feast
Changed by the downward-pointing sign.
The deepest joy was released
By the deepest shadow in death.
'Since Christ, like morning mist
Are the names of the souls of breath.'

5

The pine moves. Like an instrument it responds
To the music of Earth. It drinks the life of the underworld.
The pine-cone falls, rolls, rain-sodden, at rest.
Under the rock thunders, remorseless, the waterfall,
And trampled, year upon year, by confused horses,
The violet-root secretes the breath of the century.

Poet of rivers and supernatural love,
His crime was tenderness. Goethe was reigning in Weimar,
Holding, majestic, his court, like a classical sun.
For Hölderlin Schiller surpassed him, the last of the Hellenes,
An unapproachable star. Yet neither accepted
Their eccentric visitor, pledged to a loftier myth.

Acclaiming creation hung on the word of God,
His was the hardest task, his lot to be spurned;
And yet his fragments outshine their accomplished works.
The living universe moves in the final hymns.
The measure, there, is the deepest measure of thought,
Sprung from the purest love, for love is the measure.

'The beginning of riches is truly', he said, 'in the sea',
Springing from dissolution, the dazzling one
Casting up shells, out of its boisterous movement
Casting up Greece, the light of perfect meanings,
The shape of perfect statues, that are still:
How soon the tumultuous waters make all nothing.

Terrible destinies sleep in the shadow of calm.
The prophets of order suffer on harmony's wheel
The tension between their vision and that which exists.
Involved in the sun, the language of petals and leaves
His mother tongue, he saw, as one blind, by miracle
Given true sight, divinity's earth-born day.

And late, remembering the mountains and the Dordogne,
His eyes fixed in thought on the tumbling river,

He wrote, at the end of the Andenken:
'Great as a sea,
The river goes out. The sea, though,
Takes and gives recollection,
And love, too, fastens the eyes intently.
What endures, however, poets create.'

6

He saw Dionysus clear from the forge of Vulcan,
Birthplace of wonders, flash of the deathless moment.
For who could train down with such grace the intuitive lightning
To the thunderous chains of his cloud? The courses of rivers
Remained a compelling mystery; yet when he wrote
Of these, he no longer watched, he *became* the river.
So swift his thought, so close to the life he saw,
He knew the rose as the rose is known to herself,
Fell with the cataract's fall, or became that eagle
Of piercing sight, or learnt the time of the fig-tree,
Not by time, but by breast-feather and leaf.

7

Dawn breaks; the sunlight moves like a spirit.
Faint breezes play through arresting leaves. The morning
Moves through the sky. The divine, far-reaching blueness
Yields to the flight of birds.

Now he should come, the serene, transfiguring hero
Rocked in light's cradle, bearing the snake he has killed.
Too dark without him were Earth, and the cloistered greyness
Walled from sunlight and flowers.

What might the gift not bring to their holy light
Who ask love only? Sacrifice willed by the heavenly ones
Raises our god-pierced eyes. Our selves are nothing;
That which we seek is all.

Earth is green, is gay, but is fair no longer.
Wild is the sea, and white: the ships are glorious.
The running river looks for a vanished picture.
Who is at peace, what mortal?

Surely, below, the goddess lives, Diotima.
Did she not lift me, blinded, carried to godhead,
Resting with genius in clouds? The cataract thunders;
But, for the lovers, stillness.

Truth, I have seen her live, here, in the body
  Moving; not a far country. No medallion
    Of Hellas matched her. Death has fastened her eyelids.
      Orphaned is night, is morning.

8

But now it was late.
The sands were chill, no comfort in earth, and in air
The bird of night which hovered before his eyes
In premonition of exile, herald of fate,
Left him now, to return when the hour of death
Closed his lips on an incomprehensible prayer.
In the room where he passed his days his book lay open,
But the verses he made in age were formal and simple;
He scattered some on the stream from the tree of his tower,
Like leaves of acceptance, tranquil in thought and rhyme.
Long he lived there, a stranger to his own name,
Entranced with landscape, smiling over the Neckar,
Dying beyond his time.

9

If there could be
A second genesis of the first Adam,
His mind fixed on the all-creating God,
A child to the mother raised, his eyes remaining
Full of that first pure concord, light with light,
Adam redeemed, both Heaven and Earth at once
Mirrored in eyes, proportioning the limbs,
The mountains moving in their primal shape
In dew and worship, cities and their rivers
Moving in harmony with that first music,
Hölderlin's dream would live.
                                        But now he speaks
In fragmentary language
Of castles built by the heavenly ones; man as demi-god,
And a world huger, torn in fragments, glory
Accessible only to faith, miraculous bridges,
Visions too great for man without the cadence
And broken utterance of our elected guide.

And still, through darkness, Nazareth, Capernaum;
The hymn to the Madonna;

Holy vibrations of unbounded joy
Still sounding from the deepest hour of man,
Grief keeping pace with joy.
Still, since the great wrong and the wrong redeemed,
To live would be to suffer, from that hour.

Because his song was pure false tongues are silent.
Through him the dead speak, and the quick are changed.

Angelo's Adam

Design upon this image holds the vast
Will of the sculptor no desire could speak.
There the strict outline overcame the weak
Before the face could hold the radiance cast
And let that finger gather all the Past,
Revealing at a stroke in light oblique
In muscular strength of neck and curve of cheek
The harmony of line for which all fast.

Exuberantly the kestrel rides the storm
Motionless, carved in air. It is the form
Speaking against the false forms it cast out
Whose fixed proportions still return with grace.
Athletic genius has no room for doubt
And laughs at all designs to take its place.

The Fossil

Rest in your bed, yet ask that bed:
What if,
Unseen by man, the fossil also moves
Where stone,
Hammered by centuries of sun and wind
Deep in the cliff,
Will not lie still in darkness, but instead
Repeats the bivalve's track, its winding grooves,
The nerve still gripping though the limb is gone?
Wedged in rock strata, all is still defined
By streaks of bone.

Touch now, this rock, but while you touch,
See, see
Light's colours dancing where the long waves bring
A shell
Tossed by the tide that wafts it in, to spin,
Dandled and free,
Clinging the nest of form, the mother clutch,
With all its colours beating like a wing
Harbouring the secret heaven from which it fell,
Rolling to sand, yet guarding far within
The wild sea swell.

Frail, fresh, dry, ancient, day and night,
Who may
Unite these two, on this or any shore?
Rock's grave
Holding life's pattern, steals the vital lustres,
Drains them away.
Makes that lose colour which the sea made bright,
Locks, till their music can be heard no more,
These vessels which, when taken from the wave,
Throbbed with mysterious wonder. Dry, their clusters
Hide what life gave.

All that we are binds both, I say.
If, then,
Seeing this fossil, all men lack the wit
To match
This to the thing like blossom, who shall know
Women and men
Who still may have the power to build our day
After such transformation? For each bit
Curbs, and the keen spur kindles, when they snatch
Disciplined glory, swift in heaven, and slow
On earth to catch.

If man brings honour to nature, then,
Cold earth,
Give back to man his detail. Let none write
Vague sound
To separate his truth from living words.
Their shape is worth
More than pretence, the false nest of the wren.
Keep strict that idiom printed on the night.

Even where life's magic vanishes through your mound,
Frail though the blossom seem, it is the Lord's,
Cast inward, crowned.

Expectation of Life

This rocky headland now picks me,
Watching once more the ancestral tides,
To reconcile what death divides
And knock the breath out of the sea.
Here, where a cavern holds the key
To all tempestuous nature hides,
I bind the changing seasons fast,
While the wave breaks whose voice disowns
All shipwrecked lives for whom, being past,
Nothing is left but earth and stones.

Now the low sun, life's wake, when lambs
Add to dead snows the snow of birth:
No flower upon the cliff breaks forth
Through the black gorse-boughs' perished flames.
I pick my way where the goat climbs;
Then, as I dig my heel in earth,
Into the teeth of wind I say:
This has no memory of men's groans.
When Winter takes our life away
Nothing is left but earth and stones.

Hands from necessity began
Shaping the earliest tools of life,
The flint, the javelin, and the knife,
Against the wind's destructive dawn.
Into this cave where waters yawn
Under the prehistoric cliff
Again, again, the plunging sea
Gropes for a trace of human bones.
Empty again the foam goes free:
Nothing is left but earth and stones.

A keen wind lashed the first of March.
Two ravens flew about these rocks
Building and foraging. White sticks,

Dropped by their beaks in cleft and arch,
Three-quarters up the sheer rock hitch
Their straggling nest. Beneath, a fox
Flashed on its errand to strike dead
The young of less exalted thrones.
The quartz is sparkling where they bled:
Nothing is left but earth and stones.

Into this slope I wedge my feet
Fast against wind. Fly past, vain days.
I am pledged to one you cannot raise,
Lost in the waters' winding-sheet.
Winds cannot foster nor repeat
My prayer, nor guess what downcast praise
Anchors all time. Let doubt waylay
The living. Each true dead intones:
'For men inconstant when they pray
Nothing is left but earth and stones.'

What sudden whiteness drifts between
The bright and dark side of the slope?
The sun now lets a curtain drop;
I see the headland intervene.
Surely beneath it snow is seen
Preserved in shadow? Ravens swoop.
Under their wings a goat flock moves.
They dip and rise like galleons,
Feeding on thorns; beneath their hooves
Nothing is left but earth and stones.

Return, return, you black proud wings,
That I may see you cross the verge
Of cliff, and perch above your charge,
Guardians of true and threatened things.
Fast in the rock you guard those springs
Where looms and energies emerge
Kindling the vision breath has made,
Without which, though the patriarch owns
The apportioned lands of light and shade,
Nothing is left but earth and stones.

The Smoke of Cities Passed

The smoke of cities passed, and in its place
I saw one city and one street grow clear,
Remembered now from childhood's endless year,
And there I looked for one expected face.
As one may see, where many waters race,
A single moment held, so it was here.
I recognized the Present as austere:
Time has the line no other time can trace.

Yet this late meeting earlier years had sown.
Wind gathered light and passed it through the trees
Indifferent to the face I came to greet.
The power to reperceive was mine alone,
Something distinct from time, as life with ease
Put on another skin and shed the street.

Bishopston Stream

River last seen in Spring, you race in the light of Autumn.
Now, as you run through hazels, their leaves are already falling.
Out of the wood I come, astonished again to find you
Younger and swifter.

There were two voices then, moving about in foliage.
One called the other voice, then a great bird made silence.
This was their meeting-place, here where the heron paddling
Stepped on the square stone.

Crossing an open space, haunted in June by mayflies,
Into the gloom of trees you wind through Bishopston Valley,
Darting, kingfisher-blue, carrying a streak of silver
Fished from oblivion.

Over your tunnelled song, pulled in the year's declining,
Lies an uprooted elm, struck by a gale or lightning.
Trout in the shadows hide; black is the hurrying water,
Thronged once with Spring stars.

May not the two I saw be in this hour united
Who are gone different ways? Water, that young Rebecca,
Naomi, Ruth, once heard, voices above a pitcher,
Late let me stoop here.

Yet if I listen closely, singing of separation,
Singing of night you go, through a continual darkness,
River of exile's voice, harps that were hung heard plainly
Now, in the clear dusk.

Even by day you run through a continual darkness.
Could we interpret time, we should be like the angels.
Always against your sound there is a second river
Speaks, by its silence.

The Present

Strange, is it not, that he for whom
The living moment stood in flesh,
Should bring the future to this room
Held at arm's length, and always fresh.

Strange, that his echoing words can spell
New meanings though the die is cast,
And tell us more than time can tell,
Immediate in a timeless Past;

And stranger still, for us who knew
The living face and now return
Its pictured gaze, so quick, so new,
Love's vital fire being its concern,

To think, though years should gallop now
Or lag behind, he will not care,
So calm the eyes beneath the brow,
Held in a breath by angels there.

Taliesin's Voyage

The coracle carried me.
The seawave tossed me.
Hawk, hound harried me.
Caridwen lost me.

Hid in the hollow
Of a rounded bark,

I heard swift, swallow,
Fly through the dark.

Raved, nor remembered
Earthly things,
But wide-ribbed, slumbered
Under those wings.

Past day and night,
Past night and day,
Under the flight
Of the stars I lay.

At last emerging
With dawn I woke
Where rough seas surging
On shingle broke.

Caridwen's prey,
Child of the sea,
I was cast that day
On wild Pwlldu.

The days of my voyage
When numbered are
As a glacier's age
Or a shooting star.

Swift and slow
In one rope twined
A sail did throw
On my dreaming mind.

Time I pursued
And saw the kill.
Life was renewed
Where time lay still.

Sand and the year
That seemed deranged
Are filled with grandeur,
For all is changed.

O raven, kestrel,
Wheeling round,
Teach your minstrel
The heart of sound!

I, Taliesin,
Know the cords
Between that pin
And the turning birds.

But the wind's hound
And the mussel's sting
Between the drowned
And the seabird's wing.

Where have they left
Destruction's key,
Hid in what cleft
Of the crying sea?

Taliesin and the Mockers

Before men walked
I was in these places.
I was here
When the mountains were laid.

I am as light
To eyes long blind,
I, the stone
Upon every grave.

I saw black night
Flung wide like a curtain.
I looked up
At the making of stars.

I stood erect
At the birth of rivers.
I observed
The designing of flowers.

Who has discerned
The voice of lightning,
Or traced the music
Behind the eyes?

My Lord prescribed
The paths of the planets.

His fingers scattered
The distant stars.

He shaped the grave shore's
Ringing stones
And gave to the rocks
An echoing core.

He bound great mountains
With snow and ice
And bathed in glory
The lesser hills.

He made the sun
Of sulphurous fire.
From secret darkness
He called the moon.

Under her voice
And moving light
He chained the tides
Of the great seas rolling.

Still upon Earth
Was no live creature.
Barren still
Was the womb of the sea.

Mute the features
Slept in the rock,
Limbs and the soul
Inert, unbeckoned.

Marrowed with air
He made the birds.
Fish He sowed
In the restless wave.

Antelope, horse
And bull He made.
From caves of ice
He released the stormwinds.

He numbered the meadow's
Drops of rain
Caught in the cloud
And the teeming rose-bush.

Lions He made
Like fallen suns,
Fiery sand
And the beasts of burden.

He gave to the trees
Mysterious fruits
And twined in the husk
Miraculous corn.

Where lizards breathed
On the pathless desert
He gave each atom
A hidden sun.

Last, all labour
He bent on dust.
Out of the red dust
Made He Man.

Ancient music
Of silence born:
All things born
At the touch of God.

He built for him
His eternal garden,
Timeless, moving,
And yet in time.

He cast on him
Dark veils of sleep.
Out of his side
He took the Female.

Ask my age:
You shall have no answer.
I saw the building
Of Babel's Tower.

I was a lamp
In Solomon's temple;
I, the reed
Of an auguring wind.

What do you seek
In the salmon river,

Caught in the net,
What living gold?

What do you seek
In the weir, O Elphin?
You must know
That the sun is mine.

I have a gift
For I have nothing.
I have love
Which excels all treasures.

Certain there were
Who touched, who knew Him.
Blind men knew
On the road their God.

Mock me they will,
Those hired musicians,
They at Court
Who command the schools.

Mock though they do,
My music stands
Before and after
Accusing silence.

Words to Artemis

Virginal Artemis, rising late,
Round above the falling dew,
Violence made Alcmena mate;
Got with child, with child grown great,
Violently I envy you.

Ecstasy beyond the tomb
And the boughs of Adam's tree,
Brilliance never known to groom,
Let me touch your secret loom.
I am bound, but you are free.

You that never felt this weight
Nor the strength of life unborn

Kick against the bonds of fate,
Aid me now to cast this great
Burden aching to be borne.

Bright beyond my days are you,
Yet within my toll and fee.
Do what none but you can do.
Bound to none, these bonds undo
Holding back the prisoned sea.

Let that circle be fulfilled
Ancient as the loom of man.
Not by peace the heavens are stilled
But by all the strength we willed,
Now to comfort girl or man.

Shine above me, cool this fever;
Lift to you the newborn eyes.
Set your bow against their quiver
That in darkness they discover
Eyes of love, unsetting eyes.

Music of Colours: Dragonfoil and the Furnace of Colours

I

Bright petal, dragonfoil, springing from the hot grass,
Dazzling profusion continually fading,
Sprung from the white fire, tiger-lily, snake-fang
Basking in brilliance; deep in fume of poppies
Sleep the black stamens.

Where were these born then, nurtured of the white light?
Dragonfly, kingfisher breaking from the white bones,
Snows never seen, nor blackthorn boughs in winter,
Lit by what brand of a perpetual summer,
These and the field flowers?

All is entranced here, mazed amid the wheatfield
Mustardseed, chicory, sky of the cornflower
Deepening in sunlight, singing of the reapers,
Music of colours swaying in the light breeze,
Flame wind of poppies.

Lizards on dry stone; gipsy-bright nasturtiums
Burning through round leaves, twining out in torch-buds;
Even the stream's tongue alters where the rose-blaze
Hangs in forgetfulness. Who beneath the water
Plucks at the dark strings?

Where is the young Spring, clustered myosotis?
Have you forgotten, drugged beneath the heat haze,
White stems of bluebells hidden in the dark wood,
Swan of the lily, purple-throated iris,
Lost in your silence?

Speak: what Ophelia lies among your shadows?
Is it her music, or is it Eurydice
Gone from your bank, for there a spirit's absence
Wakens the music that was heard by Orpheus,
Lost, where the stream glides.

Far off, continually, I can hear the breakers
Falling, destroying, secret, while the rainbow,
Flying in spray, perpetuates the white light,
Ocean, kindler of us, mover and mother,
Constantly changing.

2

Brand lit in foliage, in the heart of summer,
Breaking from the live coals, torn from the seed-pod,
Flaunting its brilliance, petals of the burnet-rose
Stirred by a slow wind, under gold antennae
Wasp-gold, simmering, hovering in heat haze,
Red silk of poppies:

June wakes the music that was known to Orpheus,
Breathed by the fire-god, muted for enchantment,
Fire-misted marigold, clustered myosotis
Sprung to remember the river's lamentation,
June flowers hiding the footprints of Eurydice
Seized by the dark king.

Yet the turf tells me: she it is, no other,
Touches the rose-blaze, gathers what became her
Music. Forgetfulness holds her like a girdle
Silent. Only by absence is the song made
Audible. Orpheus, leaning above Lethe,
Knows every note there.

There the stream flies on to its own beginning,
Slips through the fresh banks, woods of their escaping,
Leaving in glory patterns of a lost world,
Leaves that are shadows of a different order,
Light, born of white light, broken by the wave's plunge
Here into colours.

Ocean, kindler of us, mover and mother,
Assailing the rock with variety of music,
Inconstancy of pattern, eternally renewing
Through mother-of-pearl the colours of destruction
Dissolving, lost in the whisper of the sea-cave,
Sigh of a gull's wings!

Here now is summer, this perennial wonder
Of fireborn blossoms, the sudden incarnation
True for this moment, therefore never dying,
Never transfigured by the net of sunbeams,
Being of the spray, the rainbow from the breakers,
Born, like the white girl.

3

Who half asleep, or waking, does not hear it,
Drone where the bees swarm, sky of the cornflower,
Blaze of a water-lily, music of the reapers,
Lithe bodies moving continually forward
Under the heat haze?

Dust drops from campions where the hedge is hottest.
Foxgloves and grasses tremble where a snake basks,
Coiled under brilliance. Petals of the burnet-rose
Flash there, pulsating: do the gold antennae
Feel for the white light?

All that is made here hides another making;
Even this water shows a magic surface.
Sky is translated; dragonfly and iris
Rise from the grey sheath; unremembered shadows
Cling, where the bloom breaks.

Yet, not that bloom, nor any kind of foliage,
Cup, sheath or daystar, bright above the water,
Clustered forgetmenots tufted on the stream's bank,
Not one recalls the virginals of April
Heard, when the wood grieved.

Waking entranced, we cannot see that other
Order of colours moving in the white light.
Time is for us transfigured into colours
Known and remembered from an earlier summer,
Or into breakers

Falling on gold sand, bringing all to nothing.
Fire of the struck brand hides beneath the white spray.
All life begins there, scattered by the rainbow;
Yes, and the field flowers, these deceptive blossoms,
Break from the furnace.

Quem Quaeritis?

POEM FOR VOICES

Whom do you seek? No life is in this ground.
The napkin stained and linen clothes lie round.
Here is no fountain but a land of dearth
Where thorns forget the forehead they had crowned.
Whom do you seek?

'What is pure gold or what are diamonds worth
To that first vision, men like trees on earth
Walking? For so He showed them first, and then
Opened my eyelids, who was blind from birth.'
Whom do you seek?

'In that clear stream I also was made clean.
Going from the priest, I turned, the last of ten,
To give God praise, being healed of leprosy,
Though He had warned me: Hide your praise from men.'
Whom do you seek?

'I was so hidden, my hand He could not see
When, in that press of people, on my knee
I touched His garment; yet my life was known.
That moment from affliction I went free.'
Whom do you seek?

'When, among graves, despairing I was thrown
By devils to the ground, I heard each stone
Echo His words, until the walls cried out:
Come out of him, and leave My son alone.'
Whom do you seek?

'He loosed my tongue. That power how could I doubt?
Though all denied Him, each would stay devout,
Had he been bound like me, both deaf and dumb,
Until those sudden fingers made me shout.'
Whom do you seek?

'They look for glory in day, and we in gloom.
We look for Him who has overcome the tomb.
By Him, by His first promise we are bound,
Whose narrow dwelling gives us greatest room.'
Whom do you seek?

Five Poems of Magdalenian Darkness

1. TOUCH

Never such rest I had
As before I drew breath.
Here I lie on the bed
At the point of death,
I, the Magdalen, dead
In all but faith.

Now the sorrow I lived
Is taken away.
Death now calls for the gift
And I must obey.
Joy is the certainty left:
Do not delay.

Many shall murmur of me:
'I have known such,
Fickle and bright as the sea,
Gave herself much.'
Broken at last though I be,
Truth is in touch.

2. THE STAIR

Bitter my life has been, not sweet,
Yet grief has made me strong.
Was ever vision more complete
Or hope more plainly hung

Than when with tears I washed His feet
Whose body paid for wrong?

Darkness, compel that hour to stay
Whose pledge is in the tomb.
The leper's praises die away.
How silent is the room.
All is remembered from the day,
And still death will not come.

These seconds wait upon the crime
None but the dead can bear,
But I renounce unholy time
And that sweet morning air.
Down through derision He did climb:
I choose the bitter stair.

3. THE MUSIC OF JUSTICE

Death, I know you already: you come to take what I have.
Poor though you think me and frail, in this darkness by which I am
blest,
Never so rich was I yet as now at the edge of the grave.
Of all the sweet joys I have looked for, this is the dearest and best.
I, that was love's anointer, am ready to die as a slave.
Make me whole with the music of justice, and hide what has robbed
me of rest.

4. THE KNOCKERS

Older in sorrows and years
Than the girl I was then,
I remember in darkness the spears,
Low voices of men.
That knocking that fell on my ears,
I hear it again.

Run, spirits, and find in your track
All the days that I spent.
Take the joy I would willingly lack.
Leave me broken or bent,
But inspire me to drive the mob back
Or curb their intent.

In starlight the legions are come.
Northward they move,

Leaving one dead in each home,
As when there drove
Spears from that Herod, now Rome
Fearing His love.

5. THE ANOINTING

Hour of anointing, dear life, how near you are now it is late.
My heart beats: it is stronger than death that takes it away.
There are footsteps again in the courtyard: I can hear the conspirators
wait.
How still the room; and the stars of midnight stay.

Where now are the many companions I met in the field or the road?
When reaping was done, or the treading of grapes, they came for delight.
Yet beyond the grave One drew them. To whom is my last breath owed?
I touched, I anointed His feet, on the threshold of night.

And where are the many He cleansed, the lepers, the lame and the blind?
A new generation has risen. They are come who did not know Him.
Tell them that this is the room the strong must infallibly find,
Their vigour kindled and fed by the love they owe Him.

Revisited Waters

for the Quatercentenary
of Repton School, founded in 1557

1. THE CONSTANT STREAM

How patiently the stream
Renews the archaic song,
Giving to lives though long
The transience of a dream:
A thread, a slender theme
Flying to break, though strong,
Being gathered from that grave
Where what men lose they have.

In the stream's watery glass
We pass, and do not pass.

Arches and walls of stone
Unpatterned by the flow,
With scarce a print to show

Four hundred years have gone,
Forget what time has known,
A press of lives below
Arches and walls of stone
Unpatterned by the flow.

These that were fugitive,
They died: in death they live.

The generations rise
To seek their destinies.
They move between the trees.
Time is before their eyes.
The tragic heroes' cries
Come to them on the breeze.
They dramatize their death
And birth with every breath.

In the stream's watery glass
We pass, and do not pass.

And often by that stream
I felt a secret power
Making the passing hour
A gift of small esteem.
Verse could for me redeem
What nature would devour,
And often by that stream
I felt a secret power.

These that were fugitive,
They died: in death they live.

Four hundred years ago
Who would have guessed, in seven
More years, that sacred heaven
Would teach a child to know
Wisdom against time's flow
Alone to Shakespeare given?
Lay then a hint concealed
In hedge, or path, or field?

In the stream's watery glass
We pass, and do not pass.

And lives of speechless fame,
Spirits at beck and call,

Massed in a panelled hall:
Their flesh I now reclaim.
Near many a gold-leafed name
Their eager voices fall,
And lives of speechless fame,
Spirits at beck and call.

> These that were fugitive,
> They died: in death they live.

Yet I distinguish most
Certain whose genius, come
Rustling in walls long dumb,
Disturb the moving host.
I had not thought one ghost
Could break so young a tomb,
Yet it was wit that made
Peace between breath and shade.

> In the stream's watery glass
> We pass, and do not pass.

Timeless the souls remain,
Distinct in memory,
Unique through history,
Born once and not again.
While earthquakes crack the plain
And storms uproot the tree,
Timeless the souls remain,
Distinct in memory.

> These that were fugitive,
> They died: in death they live.

Bodies by sense are bound
As souls are bound by grace.
Likeness may bring a face
Back, which the years have drowned.
I have seen such, then found
Those features giving place
To another in the street:
In thought all creatures meet.

> In the stream's watery glass
> We pass, and do not pass.

All are within my prayers
On whom time's burden falls.
Fingers that touch these walls
And feet that climb these stairs
Know not what scream declares
Blind war, whose waste appals.
All are within my prayers
On whom time's burden falls.

These that were fugitive,
They died: in death they live.

How could the young conceive
A tragic mask serene?
Yet it is this makes green
The lives these waters weave.
To praise where men most grieve,
To love where hate had been:
This I would wish on each;
No less the prophets teach.

In the stream's watery glass
We pass, and do not pass.

And secretly the stream
Renews the archaic song,
Giving to lives though long
The quickness of a dream.
Most men mistake the theme
Flying to break, yet strong;
And secretly the stream
Renews the archaic song.

These that were fugitive,
They died: in death they live.

In the stream's watery glass
We pass, and do not pass.

2. DEDICATION

I'll not be servant,
No, neither pursuivant,
To that inconstant
Bird that takes wing,
Never remaining,

Leaving this raining
Land of complaining
  Spring after Spring.

Though I see shiver
Signs on the river
Where swan and diver
  Calmly alight,
All that I treasure
Trusts in a measure
Folding its pleasure
  Fast against night.

Here in this breaking
Dusk of my waking
Never forsaking
  Earth it has known,
Dawn brings before me
Like a lost army
Lives that were stormy
  Linked with my own.

Some that knew hunger,
Some that grew stronger,
Some that lived longer,
  Looked for time gone.
Youth made them tougher;
Yet, to discover
All the young suffer,
  We must live on.

When the wings starting,
Bulrushes parting,
Migrant, departing,
  Rise from the stream,
From the four quarters
Come to these waters
Memory's daughters,
  Torn from their dream.

Like the Earth spinning
Into beginning,
Innocence winning
  Time to its use
Makes the past present,

Sacredly crescent:
All obsolescent
  Time it renews.

Make me, then, servant,
Yes, stubborn pursuivant
To the stream's fervent
  Spring that remains,
Naked in bounty,
Stripped to give plenty,
Strength of this county,
  Mountains and plains.

3. PRAISE

I have no tongue but to praise
Certain whose hands
Silenced the clockwork of days
Mining the lands.

Cherish illusions and die:
So the cry went.
Scorning the signs of the sky,
These were intent,

Not upon rumour's blind word
Haunting a town.
Doctrine more secret they heard,
Then took it down.

These beheld night as a threat,
Yet in the shroud
Masterful features they met,
Humble and proud.

Earth could explode in their span
While the debate
Swung from the courage of man
Over to fate.

Call the example they drew
Christlike at length:
It was the just and the true
Gave them their strength.

Instantly each would impart
All he could give.

Death, as it aimed at the heart,
Taught men to live.

Terror could detonate near,
Murder unmake
All that was loved on the sphere;
Yet at the stake

Some on the surface of sleep
Still would perform
Works that were destined to keep
Lives from the storm,

All the potential of time
Saved from the blast,
Healers of vision and limb,
Honoured at last.

4. ORIGINS

Spirits united today and tomorrow dispersed
To places forgetting one place where the wind and the cloud
Conspired with the waterfall's thunder and found it accursed
If the peak of its bondage was proud:

May you speak with a tongue that learns only from love what it knows.
May your strength be the strength of wild eagles, and may the blind shock
Of the elements warring create in you joy and repose.
May you honour the heart of the rock.

For we came out of silence and back into silence return.
We were stripped for the elements' fury; by them we were dressed.
First they mocked us, but then we grew stronger and mocked them
in turn,
In the heart of the whirlwind found rest.

We took refuge in caves of our daybreak. The flint and the knife
Preserved us from want and from peril. A mountainous sea,
Ice, famine, or battle, predicted the end of all life;
But from horror we shook ourselves free.

As the night of those ages gave birth to a desolate day
We protected our flocks; where the tiger, the wolf and the boar
Besieged our survival, we killed them, and killed birds of prey:
So we nourished our life at death's door.

Yet nothing we knew in that rock of a soul that would climb,
Of a Christ that would save us, contracting all heaven in a span.

Compassion was silent. The reticent forces of rhyme
Lay still on the slumber of man.

What numberless ages of anguish were sifted like sand!
What yearning and ache of the loins, while an offspring of hate
Flung babes to the furnace, until the true veins of the hand
Through the prophets transfigured the state:

Then at last man encountered himself, his Accuser and end.
He saw his own Hell and the labouring lusts that destroy;
And Jerusalem showed him the pastures where friend dies for friend,
And the end of all labour is joy.

Returning from Harvest

It is always so: the declining
Daylight touching the edge
Of a window quickens knowledge,
Whets the invisible wing

Of thought, as the mist-hazed hummer
Michaelmas patterns weaves.
The stream understands the leaves
Better than in high summer.

And however the intellect
Predict the pattern of days,
It is never repeated. Always
A change we did not expect

Interprets the sickle gleaning
High sheaves for a sheltered place.
A young moon hangs in space
But shines with a different meaning.

Evening never deceives
Man, as the waggon swings
Back from migrating wings
To his mud-encrusted eaves.

They are gone before the stoat
In the iron track dawn-fires smelt
Changes his chestnut pelt
For the white of the ermine's coat.

O freshness of the precise
Season, frost-clear sky,
Full harvest tilted high
In the ruts of tomorrow's ice.

Fidelities
1968

Two Sources of Life

The time we measure and the time we know
Move in the branches drinking life, the giver.
Being young, we bathed here, and shook off the river,
Then stood above the stream and watched it flow.
An image in the water shone below,
Armed with a secret we could not deliver.
Those beams were like the arrows in a quiver
For which our expectation was the bow.

But ask: when was it that the current took us
So deeply into life that time forsook us,
Leaving us nothing but the need to give?
We were transfigured by the deaths of others.
That was the spring, when first we knew our brothers
And died into the truth which made us live.

Earth and Fire

All do not seek the exalted fire;
All do not let the moment bless.
And yet, what so rewards desire,
So nourishes? Confess:
He's wrong who toils for less.

Measure the ground and weigh its yield,
Changing the crops while seasons turn.
Yet who can say a barren field
Where the dry brambles burn
Brings not the best return?

Then the fine breath of wintry air
Answers the crisp and stubborn earth.
Without the exaltation there
Uniting death and birth,
What is a man's song worth?

Earth's natural order brings a wealth
Of promise, bounty, and regret.
Through changes he alone has health
And writes off all the debt
Whose heart on heaven is set.

The Sibyl

While kings rode forth to conquest I stayed here.
The shadows of their laurels crossed my wall.
While heroes came to terms with their own fear,
They did not know I should outlast them all.
Whether men called me wanton or austere,
My cave became their common port of call:
How many left me, chastened by the tear
Which knew their destiny, but would not fall.

And still my vision knows behind the bone
To separate their lives and set them free.
I hold from heaven the power to see what's gone
So clearly, that what is or is to be
Hinders no whit the noblest I have known,
His passion rooted, singing like a tree.

The Parthenon

The Parthenon, the pride of man,
The Muse of Homer and the Fates,
The marbles of Athenian dawn;
Reject them: they return in Yeats.

The impassive heroes match the force
And calm of his daemonic verse.
Into the stone he drives his horse
That neither time nor death deters.

He swears, the Muses most exult
In the hard clash of steel on steel.
When conflict ends the words are dulled,
No pleasure in the song they feel.

And rightly from the grave he draws
The athletic pulse of deathless art.
Why, then, must passion break those laws,
The martyr and the hero part?

Forever, when those horsemen move,
In souls of Earth's divided sons
The cadence of enduring love
Is destined to subdue the bronze.

Though strong men laugh at human kind,
Though bronze endure and iron ring,
The metaphysics of the mind
Are secret, and a harder thing.

And bones of unregenerate souls
Laid by the sword in their cold vault
Fast for a prince whose love controls
Time's error, and the primal fault.

Still, where those ancient heroes fought,
Proud horses rear their heads in stone;
And still the bridles horsemen caught
Move in the marble, and are gone.

Phaedra

Absence divided us.
Now it is meeting
Tears us apart:
O heart, stop beating.

I have a right to anger.
I was preceded.
The bridebed I shared
Had served another.

She was the mother
Of my undoing.
Without her Hippolytus
Had not been seeded.

Theseus took her
To bed when younger.
Had their embraces
Raised a girl,

I had been spared
This present ruin:
The thread of perdition
Had not been spun.

My lord, my guest,
At your suspicion

He had confessed
The breakers over us.

He has not come.
It is the wall
Draws with vermilions
The charging bull.

Why must the stallions
Kick their traces?
I and his son
Undone before him.

Hippolytus: what made
These eyes adore him?
She is the guilty one,
She who bore him.

Theseus the Shade,
Dead, yet living,
Strength coupled
With pitiless anger.

So long in mortal danger,
Then, one day,
Killing the Minotaur,
While I forgot him.

Where is my refuge
From the unforgiving?
Had she not known him
I had not been troubled.

Where is Hippolytus?
Had I obeyed,
My guilt had spoken;
The son had stayed.

How shall I gainsay
His noble lying,
Looking on Hades?
Thunders begot him.

The Minotaur's shadow
Travels the wall.
Sea-wrack and refuse
On us shall fall.

I hear him coming.
His footfall stays.
What way but dying
Out of this maze?

Semele

I saw you come in a swan's shape,
But when you covered my escape,
Closing my shade in that white down
Which cast no shadow of its own,
I rose, seeing earth and heaven join,
Until the glory from your loin
Leapt in my body, and leaping, made
The whole sky pure.
I sank, afraid
Of such pure terror. Then I knew
What a god could, swan could not, do.
How long before that hour had I
Loved as a virgin, doomed to die?
Kisses were dear, time short, but now
Time can but last as you allow;
And still the hour-glass runs. I pray:
If you come back, come after day.
Let sunset vanish from the wall,
The colours, deepening, fade and fall.
Then, in clear darkness, in cold state,
Let birth on revelation wait.

How quick love's infant moves in me,
How the child kicks, to be set free!
The leaves are darkening like a storm.
Come down, but come in your true form!
No masks or copies now suffice:
Show me the face that none sees twice.
I hardly see beneath the shapes
Of clouds, the black, full-ripened grapes,
But hear the first drops fall, and now
Your thunders reinforce my vow.

Now show, though I be struck stone dead,
All radiance in one instant shed.

Put temperate meanings from my mind:
If truth be blinding, make me blind.
Purge all but your own power away
With brightness more intense than day,
And all my nature now prepare
To bear what none but I must bear.

I hear my pulse beat fast, I hear
The quickening drops, like steps, come near
Another second must reveal
The last irrevocable seal
Flashed by the god.
So here I stand,
Parting the curtain with my hand
To reach the unbridled element
Entirely at each moment spent.
Time is translated; I am dumb
Because the unrivalled hour is come.
I, killed by lightning, loved the vine.
My unborn child, being half divine,
Mingling a twofold fire, shall make
The crushed wine glitter for my sake
Who never saw him. May he know
The soil of Greece where vine-leaves grow,
And may my shade in this true place
Protect him from his father's face.
Infant of one he cannot see,
May he be saved from following me.

Eyes of an Eagle

Eyes of an eagle, strong enough to stare
Into the sun's heart, wings
Mounting, no longer care
What sun has passed or what sun is to be.
They see where sunrise brings
A new sun always, and ascend once more,
Plumaged with beams, not blinded by their play:
The glory lingers; glory is like day.
Beautiful heaven, renewed continually
By light, by love, beating to quicker golds

The waters where they flash about the rock:
There where the talons lock,
Where rock is seized, an inner heaven unfolds;
That grip transfigures all that went before.

Fined by Copernicus, the sacred rings
Give mortals keener sight.
So in their marvellings
Norwegian children see the sun return,
Rising from Arctic night
Out of the winter months, the buried store
Of gold made richer by those months of dark.
So squirrels spring to the tree where light, a spark,
Touches the treetops and begins to burn
The valleys with white mist and fill the fjords
Where ships lie anchored fast in packs of ice,
All ventures in the vice
Of total stillness held, arrested cords,
A sea whose voice the sun-god must restore.

Before night's veils, patterned by myth, were drawn
From navigators' eyes,
What bridles held the dawn,
What birds of omen crossed the unknown sea?
Who now can see it rise,
The sun, as first it rose above the shore?
Only the last and first make vision true.
Their lives are richer for the breath they drew
Who saw as children or as eagles see.
Slowly to watch will not deceive the heart.
Music and mathematics both are right,
Yet Blake would say of sight:
'Systems beget, but vision governs art:
No fruit can die if holy be the core.'

Falaise

Gold is not the only metal. It may be the oldest, but
Iron has another brightness.
Gold speaks, but then iron acts. There is no witness
On Earth so eloquent as silent gold,
Speaking of those lost hands that touched the lipped

Vase, trinket, the brooch. Gold is the speech
In the square tomb. It is the letters' flame,
Gold in mute ash. And yet gold dies; gold is not
Partner of winds and of the flying shade.
Here stop: these massive walls are dumb, where looked
The Conqueror down, and saw the cobble-stones,
His mother's eyes, the well; and lived here hidden.
Iron borrows gold from darkness, borrows rust,
Bringing its goldcoat like a ransom from the dust of battle.
Shut it under earth, then dig it up; the crooked wreck
Will twisted shine, as after its long sleep
It cries for the edge of the air; and how it slipped
Keen through live winds (now less than a memory) it alone
knows.
Nor what dark shames it carved in the world, jabbed deep,
Thirsting for that wild blood, cast to the crypt,
Can it quite hide, though it disguises these.
Gold is patient; it can wait always; iron cannot wait.
Iron is birdlike. Look, in a flash it passes,
Light in black wings,
Jackdaws above Falaise.

Poem for Conrad

My brothers are just out of eyeshot, conspiring against me.
Let me crawl and surprise them.
What's for me, in this house of their gains?
My sister lies out on the lawn, a pattern of patience.
She lies on a rug, a rug I intend to cross.
But my brothers are plotting, plotting. Their gain is my loss.
They are quick to count chocolate money, and then to eat it,
And they quarrel over their trains.
They are never content to hold nothing, or to divide
Their spoils. They do not lie down; or not for long.
They deal in extreme situations:
The door must be dangerous, bushes are places to hide.

One of them dresses up in feathers
And the other crouches,
Endlessly running wheels over floorboards and carpet
And chanting to make them go.

The third comes in, in his hands a fledgling.
He is gone again, and they are gone after him
To watch it. Now there is nothing
But clumsy furniture.

Is it enough,
Enough, with extended arms, to master this floor?
I can, and will stand up.
I, too, can walk,
Unsteadily, but in one direction,
Between the wall and the door,
Towards the shouts in the garden.

I saw nothing, but a crane has carried me in.
I am here again, and Dylan is jumping before me.
I laugh, and the louder I laugh, the higher he jumps,
First from the chair, then, in a crash, from the table,
His feet disappearing, the table's legs giving way.
I bang my cymbals, and one rolls away. He is rushing
At the wall. Chairs are behind him,
And now he is under the chairs, and he throws them up
With balls, dominoes, toys, and the tower of bricks
Falls. The crash and laughter have made me fall over.
It is wonderful here, but suddenly comes the word *No,*
And it all comes to rest, the see-saw in dancing walls,
And the feathers fallen.

I brush against dark cloth, caught up by a hand.
Snatched up to a shoulder's height,
I am told we are going to the sea.
Now, on the prickly path,
I remember something unpleasant,
The sea interfering with my enjoyment of sand.
They are talking under me, someone banging the gate
Behind us. All is blue in the air I am riding.

There are my brothers, laughing and running ahead,
And a voice behind
Saying: 'Whales have the sea,
And sea-lions, balancing balls, have perfect control;
But that house, those walls were not built to contain the exuberance
Of the performer. Let him loose
And if he continued long enough
His triumph would be complete. This would be said:
"He believed, not in walls but trumpets.
In amusing his brother he destroyed the house".'

The Guest

All day, all night, wind and wild rain had blown;
Then the gale dropped, and in September weather
Where sunlight lingered on the pulse of stone
Red thistle and wild harebell shone together.

The cliff's crossed paths lay silvered with slug tracks
Where webs of hanging raindrops caught the sun.
A thrush with snail cocked sideways like an axe
Knocked with quick beak to crack it on a stone.

Stumbling, a blue-black beetle groped its way
Where crickets perched and dropped like jewelry.
Dawn's pestle mixed fresh colours for the day,
And, far beneath, a cormorant crossed the sea.

There was no guest to watch the landscape change.
All day slow, silken threads gold spiders spun.
Towards evening then I broke them, seeing a strange
Fleece in low heather catch the western sun.

There, halfway down the cliff, in fallen flight
I came on plumage, tufted claws, wide wings,
A white owl dead, feeding fritillary light
Into those roots from which the heather springs.

No wound appeared, though death had shrunk the eyes.
The bright wings held no marking but their own.
How close it lay no mouse dared recognize,
Lest it should pounce, and tear it to the bone.

The Razor Shell

I am the long lean razor shell:
Do not interpret me too soon.
Streak of the wind with tawny stains,
The sky's quill-feather marked my grooves,
The sea is hidden in my veins.
I am a part of all that moves,
And more than this, of what remains.
Here on the sand in burning noon
I lie, forgotten by the swell.

I hear the breakers and the oars
Falling along the level shores
And beating down the golden grains.
Let Solomon consider well
And take me cool into his hand,
Then ask, before he count the sand:
What is that labour to the moon?

The Crinoid

This lily wind and waves have grown
Lies here embedded, white in grey,
A crinoid, set in patient stone
Three hundred million years away
From where it rooted in the sea
Close to a stone with coral ring,
So dark an architect was he
Who cannot know, as I know, Spring.

Out of what silence it has sprung:
Half it reveals and half it hides.
Let the stone echoing hold its tongue,
Having outgrown so many tides.
How late it nestles in the hand,
Cold as a fruit, compact, serene,
Turned on the lathe of sea and sand
By breakers where they lose their green.

Lost creatures still preserve the power
To mime a nature not their own,
By imitating stalk and flower
To darken and deceive the stone.
Alive, this could not yet attain
The transformation death achieves.
Not wind or sea but stony rain
Made the sea-lily put on leaves.

Smoother it is than corm or root
Knotting the brilliant weeds in brine,
While from an earthpot leaps a shoot
Keeping the bud's ancestral line,
Out of the matrix of that ghost

Seizing the lustre locked in grey,
Revealing what the mind had lost,
The fragile colours of the spray.

Fisherman

I learn, as my fingers mend the net, what none without nets can know.
The sun of that knowledge flickers within. It is not the knotting of cords;
It is not the silent pull on the net, the pull of the sea, when the flow
Carries the weight of an unknown tide, when the heart is laden with words.

How many tides have ebbed and flowed where pebble and broken shell
Shine in a tumbled spangle of weed: O little weights of the mind,
O little floats to carry me up in a moment none can foretell,
We are taken, each, by the task we choose, by the net our hands designed.

There are silver fish that flash before day, in the fragile moment of dawn.
I have seen them shiver before my eyes, then vanish before light shone.
I know the weight of unspoken words, of speech that cannot be drawn.
I crouch, and my life returns to the sea. It trembles, then it is gone.

Fingernail Sunrise

The salt wave sings
Before, beyond, and under time, and along the long sand falls,
Dinted with brilliant things
Coiled or broken, deaf to the wild birds' calls.

Pause, and look down.
The flash we saw in the distance now becomes for us a shell,
Spun from the loom of waters to its own
Stillness, and inward music: mark it, where it fell.

Stilled at the core
Of sky and water, skimmed by shag and oystercatchers flown,
Leaving the print of talons on the shore
Of daylight, and the shore of all that's known:

Thought ends in this.
A hundred footprints now arrive at this fine skin of horn
Divining daybreak here by artifice,
Fingernail sunrise, rifted sky reborn.

Should a man die,
Leaving a fingered skein, though never of this workmanship,
Certain and cold, and be outlasted by
Such art, who then might hear the speaking lip,

Unseen, confess:
*'Here, in the heart of colour, in the tidewrack of the sea,
This mask of mine, for winds to dry and waters to caress,
Shuts history out, till turned by its own key'*?

The half is written,
Split like a shell, silvered with pearl, now death has overlaid it,
Secret, beautiful, and forgotten,
Mute, remembered alone by him who made it.

Hurdy-Gurdy Man in Winter

He touches, and the wheel of time goes round.
Oh, listen—nothing's in the world so strong.
The larks of ragtime lovers come to ground.
This carrion moment makes men feel they're wrong.

And see the children crowding round the cart,
The sordid cart, where love in memory's lap
Sucks at the bubbling spring designed to start
Remorseful coins to fill the beggar's cap.

He leans on sound as on a ramp of air,
Floating his tunes through doors and window tops,
Tipping up pomp, upsetting habit's chair,
Catching the silver penny where it drops.

What cities feel his battering ram of tune
Break their defences with nostalgic ease,
Breaching the walls of day that seemed immune,
Painting the dark with sunset poverties.

Rattling a cup, he saunters to waylay
The rich, whose conscience he makes insecure.
Down the long, captivated street he'll play.
The starlike snowflakes lend him strange allure.

His monkey, chained and dressed in exile's cloak,
Leaps up and, crouching on the organ's rim,

Frowns at the shapes that pass, whose breath is smoke;
The sun may turn its wheel, but not for him.

Here comes his master, croupier of the town,
Counting his coins like snowflakes on a bag.
He rakes their mysteries in and puts them down,
The missing bridegroom and the midnight hag.

The Sure Aimer

to Marianne Moore

Time falls,
Falls into place
And into stones, turned, ferned,
Combed by continual waterfalls
In a thunderdown burlying race,
A music earned
By luck, as one said of Verlaine: 'He falters with grace.'

The will,
Watching that force
And seeking how it may best wrest
Life's ring from hammer and anvil,
Leaps the precipitous course,
A salmon at rest
In the trance, like a swallow suspended, of purposeful torse,

That ease
Turning the whole
Starred bestiary of heaven, even
Past power of Hercules,
A thirteenth labour of soul,
To you is given,
Your needle uniting all mind's meandering scroll.

What proves
To the hypocrite
Most hostile? Vision reveals seals
Struck and bequeathed by love's
Authority. But wit
Reconciles planets' wheels
To plants, creatures and shells, and makes all fit.

You take
Both these, and free
Time with stern details, logic the world threw, true
And of archaic make,
Which you restore and make us see
In a flash, as through
Precision you humble strength, a David for accuracy.

Taliesin at Pwlldu

Through leaning boughs I see the veil of heaven,
Through leaf-ears fluted from ancestral playing
To inward darkness, to the windblown tree,
Marvel of time, caught in a living cell,
Daphne enshrined, in this pure moment given
To air, all leaves!
I look, and hear them saying:
'In boundless light only the bound are free';
And music flows through me as through a shell.

Clear is the shell upon these watery sands
And, washed with light, leaves break in these dark woods.
Streams dance and glitter, and the rocks have veins.
My Master from the rainbow on the sea
Launched my round bark. Through darkness, trailing hands,
I drifted. Wave-gnarled images of gods
Floated upon the whale-backed water-plains.
I looked; creation rose, upheld by Three.

And there are three about me where I stand.
Ah secret place within the source of tears
Caught by stream's light, uniting all that's gone:
Pure stream, by pebbles masked and changing skies,
I touch you; then I know my native land.
Pride cast the pattern from primaeval years,
The avenger's knives in glacier-driven stone
Changed by God's peace, transfixed where morning flies.

Sea Chant

TALIESIN TO VENUS

Venus, Loreley-breasted,
Ceaseless mother of change,
Born where the rainbow shivers
Bright from the breaking wave,
Rocked where the seabird rested,
Did you not charm the strange
Boats from the various rivers
Into a single grave?

Sprung from merciless weathers
Hard and hostile to man,
You that have launched and shaken
Ships, and destroyed so much,
Why should a crest and feathers
Which in wild air began,
Wheeling, dive and awaken
All that you dare not touch?

Patterning sunbeams serve you,
Doves, and pinks in the rock,
Drenched where the spray of breakers
Flies to the ravens' nest.
Who but I can preserve you
Chaste, from shudder and shock?
See: all others forsake us;
Only the dead have rest.

Yet that golden-eyed egret
Still as a hawk shall stay,
While you proclaim to islands
Nothing dark shall endure.
I have discerned a secret
Hid from the arc of day,
Locked in the heart of silence,
Stronger than death, and pure.

Lacework pattern of fingers
Spun and cast by the wave,
Brilliance a rainbow scatters,
Bride-veils falling away:
I, the last of your singers,

See how the shells you gave
Shine where the breaker shatters
All that we know of day.

Just as Semele's wonder
Looked for the thunder's truth,
So, as the breakers whitening
Crash on the brittle shore,
Out of a clap of thunder
Springs an immortal youth:
He who is born of lightning
Lives under time no more.

I, with strength from the giver,
Kindling coral and horn,
Taught by the tides of ages,
Take you, at last subdued.
I am come to deliver
You, of the white spray born.
Do not all faiths and sages
End in a child their feud?

Dialogue

Earth, I would learn of you
What the sea holds fast.
Waves inside shells renew:
I can hear the vast
Prodigious waters proclaim what never is past.

'What slow truth would you learn? I teach
Moments, not years.
My dawn brings wonder to each;
My night brings tears.
All ends in dissolution, confusion and fears.'

Tell how they sailed through time
And did not return.
Constant the stars would climb
And, speechless, spurn
Fixed, purposeful eyes, fixed hands, with a wheel to turn.

'Do they haunt and trouble your sleep?
Though stormwaves mount

And tracks disappear, I keep
An exact account.
Time flings wide circles, but still they obey one fount.'

Honour transforms their dust:
One course they follow,
One point of departure trust,
True as the swallow,
Bending all distance back to one home, one hollow.

'They have gone their way. Be content.
All share one fire.
The explorer, pitching his tent
When the dog-team tire,
Drags into darkness the sledge of your own desire.'

Yet, as he leaves the land,
The disturbing sea
Changes the rock-caves, sand,
Crunch of the scree,
Till he breathes: 'The rope that restrained me has now
gone free.'

'All his travels one truth shall bring,
New dawn restore
The garden he left in spring,
The remembered shore,
The rock-rooted tree, the stone with its ringing core.'

The Life Thread

With what reluctance,
What misgiving,
Torn from the substance
Of timeless living,

Parted from night,
At last you fall
From the secret waters'
Circling ball.

After long waiting
Starfish-wise,
Transfixed, creating
To praise the skies

No mystery more
To marvel at
Than her laboured-for
Magnificat;

Plucked from the womb
But strange to breath,
You enter this room
So near to death.

And who shall unravel
From spire and shell
The coil of marvel
From which you fell?

Wonder unmet:
Beneath that sea,
Unsundered yet,
Though dropped, not free

From the swaying cord
By which you fed,
Green infant lord
Of the dark sea bed,

Your instincts probe
For what is not there,
A watery globe
That has not known air;

Then at once life races
To fill your veins;
Night's shell unfastens:
The pearl remains.

I saw blood travel
Along your veins,
And breath unravel
From ancient skeins

Life, as the shivered
Hour-glass ran,
That cry delivered
Which made you man.

Swan Narcissus

Snared in the rustling sheath of winter,
Neck high in March, not yet remembering
Water-notes near the nape attentive,
How like a swan the narcissus opens.

Slow the ascent, compact the statement,
Patient the shell, still shut forever,
Stubborn against the beat of sunlight
Falling in waves of its own divining.

This, as the star knows night, knows earthspring.
Torn from the husk and coil of seasons,
Sprung from dark earth, in the air it rises,
Printing on time its eternal pattern.

How like a wing that single petal
Breaks from the gold eye fixed on darkness,
Born like the solitary to stillness,
Praising alone what surpasses nature.

The Compost Heap

Think from how many trees
Dead leaves are brought
To earth on seed or wing,
How many traceries
Their silence wrought
Before the stubborn spring.
The stuff of life made these:
It was not thought.

Then Earth, where spirits tread,
Turns in her sleep
And keeps a magic round.
Children of the dead
Run, run and leap
Where all is common ground,
And the cunning thread
Of time they keep.

All that is fit to praise
Where twined limbs cross

Grows from such a bed.
Fear no dearth of days,
For life will toss
As many as are sped;
Only in other ways
We count our loss.

Think, where the dancers tread
And mourners weep:
All is common ground.
Where life and leaf are shed,
The rose will keep
Both light and substance sound,
That holy fire being fed
By the compost heap.

For a Wine Festival

Now the late fruits are in.
Now moves the leaf-starred year
Down, in the sun's decline.
Stoop. Have no fear.
Glance at the burdened tree:
Dark is the grape's wild skin.
Dance, limbs, be free.
Bring the bright clusters here
And crush them into wine.

Acorns from yellow boughs
Drop to the listening ground.
Spirits who never tire,
Dance, dance your round.
Old roots, old thoughts and dry,
Catch, as your footprints rouse
Flames where they fly,
Knowing the year has found
Its own more secret fire.

Nothing supreme shall pass.
Earth to an ember gone
Wears but the death it feigns
And still burns on.
One note more true than time

And shattered falls his glass.
Steal, steal from rhyme:
Take from the glass that shone
The vintage that remains.

Cornfields

Corn waves in the wind:
A sigh, early and late.
The eye of the barley is blind
When the stalk is stiff and straight.

Ears, ripening, rise,
Then gold, heavily fall;
The breath of nativity sighs:
The star is laid in the stall.

Learn, learn of the corn
Of things coming to pass,
Of wings, and a foal unborn
To the mare asleep in the grass.

Crest follows on crest;
A sigh moving in air,
A rustling of wings in the nest
Ascends from the dreaming mare.

Birth's tremor within
The fruit earth has concealed,
Does it summon life to begin
And the sun to reap the field,

Joy weighing at dusk
The scales, heavy and light,
The balance of ear and husk,
Daybreak dreaming of night?

Movement of Autumn

Dusk, and the swallows flown,
So late in going.

Secret, from stone to stone,
Water sings, flowing.

Under the year it ran;
Now it is clearer.
Gone are the pipes of Pan.
Winter is nearer.

Symbols are circling you,
Leaf-patterns flying,
All that in spring was new
Drifting and dying.

Dumb roots are cherishing
In a fresh language
All the leaves perishing,
Sunk into age.

Where the stone dial-figure
Stretches the shade,
Winter the gravedigger
Thrusts with his spade.

Stone will stay proving;
Light goes advancing.
Leaves teach by moving,
Waters by dancing.

What sings the running brook?
Vain without tears were verse.
He who first made the book
Used dying characters.

Who then has profited
By the year's stream?
He who was buffeted
Out of his dream.

Narrow the water slips
Gently away.
Sealed are Zacchaeus' lips
While the notes play.

Sycamore, sycamore,
Drop your winged keys.
Open the hidden door
None living sees.

When shall the spring of the year
Break from these dolours?
Ask the tree fading here
Under bright colours.

Exegesis

So many voices
Instead of one.
Light, that is the driving force
Of song alone:
Give me this or darkness,
The man or his bone.

None shall replace him,
Only falsify
Light broken into colours,
The altered sky.
Hold back the bridle,
Or the truth will lie.

Englyn

Bitter it is to see the noble cast down,
Breath broken, truth taken, while wit, brother to fame,
Hostage stands in each letter,
Witness, still, to his calm, till death overcame him.

A Neglected Grave

for Heine

Those others take the mountain path
And these possess the plain.
You, you alone your mother Earth
Held back, as by a chain.

You knew the bitter taste of salt,
You sang the exile's wave.

Your love, forgiving every fault,
Could not forgive the grave.

Your spirit saw what was denied
More clearly than the rest.
If wit and courage calm supplied,
How calmly you would rest.

Trees in a Town

Why must they fell two chestnuts on the road?
I did not see the lorry and its load
Before a wall had grown where they had stood.
I wish I thought that sphinxlike block was good
Builders have raised, to brood upon the loss
Of those two chestnuts where the two roads cross.
In spite of all the gain some say has been,
How can my eyes accept the altered scene?
How often, checked here on my way to work
By the instant luck of life, I saw themes fork
Into the boughs, where thought could learn as much
As sight will learn, till it is taught by touch.
In March abounding sunlight drenched the tree,
But still those sticky buds would not set free
Their secret fledgling silk of crumpled fronds
Held in the icy trance of winter's bonds.
Summer's wide green brought gloom where eyes could range
Up the dark foliage of attentive change;
But soon that gloom was battered by a squall,
Then the long, yellow leaves were first to fall.

After, in a frost, when all the boughs were bare,
What sudden grace the trees would print on air.
Call either tree a book for men to read
In any season; and then ask what need
A foursquare building had to pull them down.
I can forgive the traffic of this town
Its noise and brutal speed, but only just.
Metal and brick and glass above the dust
Smile on the road and on the lawn between.
What else is there the planners have not seen?
A fig-tree, thick with fruit which never grows

Ripe in our sun. When June is here it throws
Young, yellow fruit to the pavement while, unspent,
The broad leaves thrive and spread a fertile scent,
Warm memory of abundant nature's loins.
The shrivelled figs grow hard as ringing coins,
Seeming to prove the toll-gate has been paid
Out of that garden to the builder's trade.
How patient is the shadow those leaves cast:
They rob the Present who despoil the Past;
In all Utility's cold eye has seen
Beauty's profusion yields to what is mean,
And yet a fallen leaf can still express
Man's exile, his lost innocence, his dress.

Trees in a town, how long will they survive
The merchant's axe for all that looks alive?
How shall miraculous blossom, leaf and seed
Breathe life into the body lulled by speed,
Racing to nothing in an asphalt place?
Something is lost. The trees' obstructive grace
Seems to slick progress wasteful and obscene,
Whose highway must be useful and be clean.

Sonnet

The prose purveyors of doubt, the dismantlers of
Ecstasy, who traffic without a god
In broken metre, would have their Pegasus shod
With discord, not strict numbers. At love they scoff,
And then, in the revolution of anti-love,
Unsheathe chaos, the death of the period,
While a new Sibyl, shrieking above her tripod,
Proclaims transformation, treachery, trough.

Yet even the disenchanted, disordered, fret
For lost order. Breakers recall rhyme,
Anchors weighed, and divine proportions set.
As hawk hovers, as compass needle in time
Flies unswerving, steadied, where the stars climb,
Fixed laws hallow what none can forget.

Rebirth

Just as the will to power
From youth exhausted spins
To earth, it sees a flower
Rooted in ruins.
From that remaking hour
Perception begins.

This for which I care,
By the crowd denied,
Holds a truth so clear,
By none identified.
I would expound it here,
But my tongue is tied.

Dearest things are so:
Neglected, they stay;
Applauded, they go.
The river runs away
And we check its flow
Only when we play.

Strange, that in all we make
A solemn purpose can,
More than most things, break,
While some lesser plan
By accident will wake
The deepest roots in man.

The Stubborn and the Ornate

The stubborn and the ornate
Compose the work of a man.
Test what his hands create:
The two underlie the plan.
All time, all space I relate
To toil, and the fingers' span.

Why should I make and adorn,
Why with profusion shade?
What I resist is born
And what I protect will fade.

I think of rose and thorn,
Then thrust, with foot on the spade.

The pattern of time runs out,
And then I correct its pace.
I give the weight of thought
To all that my hand would trace.
But what, at last, have I wrought?
Nothing, except by grace.

She That Is Memory's Daughter

She that is memory's daughter,
Looking at running water,
Pauses, aware of other
Words that the water teaches.
Time lets the stream soon falling
Stray among reeds where gather,
One to another calling,
Birds in the upper reaches.

Silence is there renewing,
Losing and still pursuing
Songs of an age forgotten,
So it compels her wonder.
Rain from an ancient mountain
Writes what is unbegotten,
Seen in the playing fountain,
Heard in the cataract's thunder.

Under the river racing
Bridegroom and bride embracing
Fall from the girl whose vision
Plunging divines a constant.
Circle on circle spinning
Fly from her hand's impression
Seeking her true beginning
Fixed in the tranquil instant.

The Snow Curlew

Snow has fallen all night
Over the cliff. There are no paths.
All is even and white.
The leaden sea ebbs back, the sky is not yet light.
Hidden from dawn's grey patch
Behind frosted windows, ash ticks out faded hearths.

How quickly time passes. There is no mark
Yet upon this manuscript of snow.
Where water dripped, ice glitters, sheaved and stark.
The pen has fallen from the hand of dark.
White are lintel and latch.
Earth has forgotten where her dead go.

Silence. Then a curlew flutes with its cry
The low distance, that throbbing Spring call,
Swifter than thought. It is good-bye
To all things not beginning, and I must try,
Making the driftwood catch,
To coax, where the cry fades, fires which cannot fall.

Means of Protection

As plovers trail their wings
To hide a nest from men's concern,
Right lovers turn
Talk that nears treasured things.

The best of judgment says
No case is won by what speech proves,
Least of all love's.
We live by silences.

All that is fair courts danger.
When wit with daring lights a face
Of candid grace,
I, the protecting stranger,

Must turn my gaze, for fear
I lose that vision, for the mind
Needs shade, to find
The full light of the sphere.

Such means will fortify
The true from uncouth trespassers
And keep, in verse,
All hushed, till they pass by.

I must, seeing I have fought
Error, both in myself and men,
Build, like the wren,
To understand my thought,

A number of small nests
In branches that may catch the sun,
To guard that one
In which the interest rests.

Vultures

Fling bones to vultures, who dissect
Thoughts of a living man when dead.
Trust the wide wings to spread his shade
And win what he hates most, respect.

The Stayers

When the trees drop their leaves in frost,
Old Earth, deep-rooted, knows her own;
Poets, who loved her, are the last
To leave her, when the rest have flown.

Swallows

Artists are swallows
Building a nesting-place of earth.
The far each follows,
Returning always to his place of birth.

Welsh ambassadors,
Stubborn of instinct, mould in clay

The travelled shores,
And break down colours from an earlier day.

Vision lifts the mind,
Turning their swallows' flight to grace.
In eaves they find,
But nowhere on the ground, a settled place.

Linked in heart and cry,
They weave a lost age. Devious wings
Traced in crossed sky
A timeless writing, strict as tightened strings.

Bow and harpstring both
Sound where a seawave hits the sand.
Eager and loth,
The two vibrations answer the one hand.

Savage history throws
Chance to the winds and cuts the thread.
Iron and rose
Point recollection, trim the arrowhead.

Here Aneirin drew
Anguish from stone for youth cut down.
Here Llywarch threw
Remorse at Death, who took his every son.

Thought and arrow once
Flew from the rockhead's ambush. Now
Those fallen sons
Haunt the bleak furrows, interrupt the plough.

Still Taliesin stays,
Touching, more near than all we know,
The pulse of praise,
Deeper, more strong, than string of harp or bow.

Sword and rattling shield
Tell, in plucked verse, how sharp-edged war
Struck, in the field.
Without Christ's birth how vain Earth's mornings are.

These, whose flight is toil,
Live but to praise the elusive mark;
Whether in oil,
Sculpture, verse, music, keen wings cut through dark.

Storm will but restore
The wings' true balance. Faith can make
Love's metaphor
Strong, to give time more truth, the more time take.

Against Controversy

Why does discussion take away
From what a single man conceived?
If that was right which he believed,
He knew already more than they.

Where shadow teaches more than sun
The hedge is knowledge to the wren.
Is logic in a thousand men
Exacter than the thoughts of one?

They crowd so thick upon the mind
With branching thoughts, and yet the way
Through these, where many a false nest lay,
A little bird will always find.

Even gathering swallows move as one
And swerve on that unerring race
Whose pivot, time's magnetic place,
Rewinds the distances it spun.

Where many speakers all take part,
No single truth emerges clean.
Style from the living none can glean.
Against the dead we test our art.

The hawk hangs motionless in air,
Its plumage gathered in the breeze,
And when it drops on what it sees,
The beak consumes, the talons tear.

Fixed or migrating, birds obey
Directives alien to despair.
So man, who knows what all men share,
Yet learns from what no two can say.

The Colosseum

Winged walls, ah majesty! sailing, gathering above me
Dust of ages, heaven's huge antagonist, boulders
Tier above tier, commemorating, forgetting
Nothing, and one thing:

The walls have no echo; here root in crannies of darkness
Appian violets; the deepest sockets look farthest.
The arena is blind, commemorating, forgetting
Nothing, and one thing.

Thunders now the applause of a vanished multitude,
But the walls have no echo, the grille, the network of passages
No tread, no tongue, commemorating, forgetting
Nothing, and one thing,

The walls are moving: only our footsteps are still.
This husk is a fountain, a vision, a test of conscience
Arrested in stone, commemorating, forgetting
Nothing, and one thing.

To die there would be to see it, not now but then.
Now the thronged arches are empty, invaded by azure.
It is the cry of man I hear, and the stones of Stephen
Fallen about him.

The Catacombs

Under winged walls binding a sea of blood
Within whose theatre the sun displays
Sunk alleys, rooms, dungeons and passage-ways
Emptied of souls, where wild beasts roared for food,
Great blocks bear witness: there the arena stood,
And there one waited, in that thundering blaze,
That sea of thirsting eyes, and kept his gaze
Fixed on man's heart beneath the bestial flood.

Keep also your eyes down, for here he lay.
His soul found rest through vestures it had cast.
Through dust no morning breaks except the last.
This is his tomb beneath the Appian Way,
An urn of roars, more absolute than they,
Still trembling from the hands which held it fast.

Stone Circle

LA BOCCA DELLA VERITA
for Roberto Sanesi

If that circle were a face,
If that eye could shed a tear,
See, not distance but one place,
Were there music in that ear
Made particular and true
By a woman or a man,
I should say perfection grew
In the sphere from which it ran,
Like a stream, like a stream,
Keeping always what it drew
At the source where it began.

But, since it was cast in stone,
Nor can know how man behaves
More than that reflected moon
Carried by the moving waves,
I should say perfection dies
Of its likeness and grows less,
Lacking what the quick supplies,
Mirth, movement, tenderness,
Like a stream, like a stream,
Till the mouthing water cries:
He who is at fault can bless.

Resting Places

The rose divines her night:
White, thrusting roots grasp earth, where light began.

The seashell grinds its mark,
Dark in the cold miles of the naked beach.

Soul in a sculptor's hand
Spanned more desire than schools will ever teach.

Adam lies fast in Rome:
The moment's magnitude brought near to man.

He drew that body's praise,
Gazing on God. What centuries have since

Turned from those eyes to wage
Ageless, destructive war, all worth made cheap.

Hushed in a single nave,
Grave Angelo and Galileo sleep.

From hands of one were born
Morning and Night, who rest beneath their Prince,

While the next hand explored
Orders of stars no naked eye could reach.

There Santa Croce climbs
Time's holy scaffolding where planets spin.

Time turns; and in death camps
Lamps light the way to lampshades made of skin,

Whose dread contracts the brow.
How can we bring the ransom they beseech

Where, as one prisoner falls,
Walls paint in sleep the murder of his kin?

Such blood on Lethe's stream
Dreams cannot purge. Yet ask: what tongue ruled sin?

What put to shame that strumpet?
The trumpet which accompanied brave speech.

Strictness of Speech

Lord, defend us from the peroration.
Silence all that politicians say.
They who plough us in to make a nation
Have not known the vision we obey.

Wits that learn from mother-wit are keenest,
Nor is there nobility of style
Till the proud man kneels to help the meanest.
They who justify themselves are vile.

Postscript

for J.F.K.

Consistently his courage fought
Contempt of colour, creed or race.
The single faith his youth had brought
Was written on his face.

What better plan could meet his task
Than pick the wisest in the State
To solve the questions he might ask,
But now it is too late.

As politicians rise to play
The popularity they seek,
When eloquence has won the day,
Let the dead profile speak.

Unity of the Stream

Take this into account:
Like water from a fount
Until it reach the sea,
Song is unique delight;
You cannot snap its flight
Like wood across your knee.

You cannot tear apart
The single jet of art
That glitters there entire.
The innocent is bound
To wisdom in the ground
Of that revealing fire.

Song is all mastery
And first virginity;
Without it time were vain.
It lives to make love fly
Through nuptials of the sky
And feed the earth like rain.

Fidelities

The fountain gathers, in a single jet,
Fidelities where beams together run,
Thrives upon loss, enriches us with debt.

Nothing will match the day's full unison.
I love to see light break; and yet, and yet,
The final arbiter is not the sun.

Bounteous that brother, but he will forget
Others whose eyes the hand of death has closed,
Nor touch, nor seek them, when their light has set.

Seeing of what compound splendour life's composed,
Who could believe it now a part once played,
With so much owing to so many a ghost?

Of love's stern language noblest lives are made.
The shell of speech by many a voice is shot
Whose light, once kindled, cannot be betrayed.

A certain cadence underlies the plot;
However fatally the thread is spun,
The dying man can rise above his lot.

For me neglect and world-wide fame were one.
I was concerned with those the world forgot,
In the tale's ending saw its life begun;

And I was with them still when time was not.

Deposition

ON THE PAINTING BY CERI RICHARDS

No longer the gamblers
With dice entreat
These giant, dilated
Hands and feet.
Love has for triumph
Its own defeat.

Take down the litter
Of night and air.
The letters of life

Are written there
In the last constriction
Made fast by prayer.

Those letters of life
To the white sheet toss
In the moment of Godhead's
Utmost loss.
Swift, clasped fingers
Complete the Cross.

The will of the hand
Like an anchor weighs
All time's succession
In terms of praise.
The face transfigured
Imprinted stays.

In the eye of the world
Resurrection fails.
On the curve of the world
Speculation sails.
One reaches the clasp
For the bag of nails.

Belief and Praise

Who but a fool believes
Despair gives strength?
Look at that wall:
The hanging light of leaves
Knows better than they all
Who cry against the length
Of life, or mock its fall.

A tree will testify
Whose ripeness gives
The fruit life raised
Through storm-disfigured sky.
Belief is not erased.
The man who praises lives,
Although he die unpraised.

Herod the king enquired
Of three wise men
What time the star
Appeared. So he conspired
In terror to make war
On all the firstborn, then
Darken with blood each door.

The path those wise men went
With gold and myrrh
As on they moved
Perfected their intent.
Hard though the journey proved,
They saw their maker stir
In darkness, oxen-hooved.

Instruments with strings,
Proclaim the glance
Of him whose law
Makes commoners of kings.
To Jesus they in straw
Knelt, and all bodies dance
From the joy they saw.

Injustice and Praise

When the unjust, uncivil
Or brutal act wrongs
A man, and he can call
No judge to answer the throng's
Bestial hatred, then
Not to retaliate
Against wicked men
Becomes him and his fate.

If in the ritual
Of vengeance he live,
He makes perpetual
His failure to forgive.
No; to those arbiters
Of true behaviour
There is no strength but stirs
To honour its saviour.

A tyrant's victory
Even in the old tales
Left with the dead the glory
Dropped from unequal scales.
When power on every side
Spelt ruin, defeat,
Never was theme for pride
More certain, more sweet.

Plagues, with hostile weather
Driving from chance or hate
When evils come together
In Job could consecrate
A strictness, a trust
Inviolable. To sing
When taunted by the unjust
Is a most sacred thing.

But what if pride of race
That enemy prove,
How shall a man efface
The inhuman scar on love?
How suffer, not pay back
With sworn antipathy
That scar's degrading lack
Where divine love should be?

Though worst injustice came,
He would be right
Not to sully that name
Which gave him light,
Scourged Christ, by whom the devil
Finds himself outwitted,
Whose breast encounters evil
But cannot commit it.

At Cwmrhydyceirw Quarry

I

Let the fused boulder crack, the inert weight
In this gigantic theatre pluck new groans
From lithic silence; tongues issue forth from stones

Sullen, rebellious, or reconciled to fate.
How like that circle where Dante's words relate
How spirits noticed the shadow he alone
Cast; here stones rain down, and the rock intones
Tablets from tombs, tomes for none to translate.

Yet grooves unwind voices; and he who engraves
This stone, soon in his childhood's park to lie,
Shall cut lines incised like a breathing cry,
And give to stone that undulant line of waves.
But who had guessed, in the hush of many graves
Riven by love, it was Roethke's turn to die?

2

Life seems unquarried before the small stones' hail
And electric storm of rock hurled to the pit,
Silent before the blast, showing after it
Tablets fallen in a mass of stones and shale.
So thunders break man; great undertakings fail
In a flash, and broken lie; then only wit
And a rope held, will harness what here was split:
Through rock facets tenacious secrets prevail.

Between this torrent of boulders and the last
In the valley of giants, knowing no weight can stay
The force of roots, we trample the red clay,
Seeking a stillborn offspring of the blast
From silence freed, by glory of diction paid,
Now needed for his own gigantic glade.

(NOTE: A stone taken from this Quarry, pronounced 'Coom-rhee-der-Kyroo', inscribed by the sculptor Ronald Cour, was donated by Caedmon Recording Company, New York, as a memorial to Dylan Thomas in Cwmdonkin Park.)

To a Shell

At last, beautiful shell,
Lie there crushed; but the sea
Cannot obliterate yet
Faith I remember well:
A house facing the sea.

Hard and bitterly
Though waves beat on that wall
From the swirling quicksands of debt,
I swear that it cannot fall.

Nor can you drag those words,
Confident in their day,
Down to the unknown deep.
I have a net whose cords
Gather the fallen day
And make the forgotten stay
In all but the detail death
Moves to the realm of sleep,
So strong is the pledge of breath.

And though the magical dice,
Loaded for nothing, toss
All to perdition, left
In darkness, held in a vice,
No white breaker can toss
All to a total loss.
Still the relic will hold,
Caught in a secret cleft,
Tenderer light than gold.

All I remember, all
Of the locked, unfolding days
Where to-morrow's treasure shines.
Fragile nautilus caul,
Tell the fingers of days:
'Find me. Enter the praise
Of Eden's morning, inlaid
With dazzling, intimate lines.
Touch, and the world will fade.'

Cwmrhydyceirw Elegiacs

Go, swallow, and tell, now that the summer is dying,
Spirits who loved him in time, where in the earth he is laid.
Dumb secrets are here, hard as the elm-roots in winter;
We who are left here confront words of inscrutable calm.
Life cuts into stone this that on earth is remembered,
How for the needs of the dead loving provision was made.

Strong words remain true, under the hammer of Babel:
Sleeps in the heart of the rock all that a god would restore.

Never shall time be stilled in the quarry of Cwmrhydyceirw,
Not while the boulder recoils under the force of the fuse.
Tablets imprisoned by rock, inert in the sleeping arena,
Quake in the shudder of air, knowing the swallow has passed.
One grief is enough, one tongue, to transfigure the ages:
Let our tears for the dead earn the forgiveness of dust.

Digging the Past

I

Here, then,
Where waters spin
Fleeing from men
Round quartz and spar,
The rock shelves in,
Opening the cave mouth, far
Above the waves' morass of seaweed, sticks and tar.

Gulls crying
Pure anguish now,
This, that way flying,
Swoop, stall, proclaim
In trespass how
Under their nests we came
To read such hieroglyphs as give the void a name.

Foot-crossed
The limestone bridge
Lets fall the tossed
Waves with a roar.
From ridge to ridge
Of rock we go before;
Then the receding tide behind us locks the door.

We crouch,
As though a hand
Of kindred touch
Almost in reach,
Knowing our planned
Spadework, laid hold on each,
Or finger signed us dumb, to hear forgotten speech.

Fires fling
Shades on the wall,
Flicker and cling
To earth, being made
By man. Birds call.
White wings on water fade,
And seething waves rush up, swift to consume the shade.

2

Too deep inside ourselves
Lies Elsinore.
Where weapons shone,
Stubborn ore,
Danegeld of our attention
Leaps to the muscles' tension
As the spade delves.

While the gymnastic shade
Compasses effort
To track pierced veins,
Rock's retort
Answers the shoulder's strains.
Fossil of mole remains;
The ghost is laid.

Still we persist, to extract
Bone or ceramic,
Glazed by unseeing
Cataract, then quick
With vision's vital spring.
We stoop to break time's ring
And show clear fact.

Without this toil no city
Finds equilibrium;
No foil discovers
Quick and dumb,
Nor forty thousand brothers
Time's truth, where one grave smothers
Identity.

Still the rock's reticence
Pulls our awareness
Downward, to ease

The forbears' stress
Of soul, till mindstrength frees
Those inmost rarities,
True and intense.

3

Impulsive invader, the wave from the gully now fills the whole seacave,
feeling
Nothing of mind in the sleek black walls, no singular touch or caress.
One wave racing back calls another that hurls the white spray to the
ceiling,
Subduing with trumpets of sea all that lived in the cavern's recess.

So the light-headed spray thrown back from the breakers reports what is
not for man's knowing;
Yet I, who enter above them, ignored by their deafening crash,
In the thunder and conflict of waves, and of waters endlessly flowing,
Find peace in man's counter-wave music, rejecting their turmoil as trash.

4

In the cave's mouth, not far from the headland, breaking
Red clay stacked near stalagmites built by tears,
A dome darkened, unentered thousands of years,
Our fingers grope and sift,
While pick strikes, to break rock they cannot lift,
To ease the rift
Of forms embedded too fast to expect this waking.

And yet how fresh in shadow, under the pressure
Of shredding fingers, white in friable mould
As primrose under dark leaf, emerges cold
This that reveals its own
Fragile form, a clay-stemmed antelope's bone
Fluting to stone
A vanishing note as hunters enter the fissure.

Far under, that breathing monster nuzzles the shady
Steep cliff at the height of summer's tide.
Look up. Forget the youth mistaken for bride
In ochre. Salute the strong
Tang of seaweed, driftwood, spangle and thong:
Never so long
A wake sighed, as for Paviland's Red Lady.

Life returns to the mother; and she, the daughter,
Knows in the desert what gentler touch is here,
Crumbling, close to that pendant worn in the ear
Found in yesterday's stint.
Bone whitens, quickly distinguished from flint,
Like flesh, the print
Of all that eludes and is different, thirsting for water.

(NOTE: The Red Lady of Paviland, the name given to the earliest skeleton unearthed in Britain, because of red ochre rock deposits mistaken for ritual dyes was first thought to be the skeleton of a girl, but was later identified as that of a youth of about eighteen.)

The Red Lady

They found red ochre in the cave
Of Paviland. The salt sea wave
Had left so many buried there,
But when one day the picks laid bare
Bones with the same red ochre dyed
It seemed they'd hit upon a bride
Whose burial rites had stained the mould.
Never was skeleton so old
In Britain found; but bones perplex
Their finders: they mistook her sex.
The rock deposits washed by springs
Had made those ancient colourings;
So the Red Lady's myth began
Before they found she was a man.
His bed the pollen's god waylaid,
But left a bed more safely made.
The moon's Red Lady sleeps the same,
True to her dark as when they came,
While he who took her image on
Now in the upper daylight shone,
Step by step, to be rebuilt
From antlered, prehistoric silt.
His coffin-bearers, halting, heard
The cry of many a wild seabird
Rise from a nest they could not hide.
Their shadows danced upon the tide

Protecting still, unknown to air,
The slender tissue in their care.

Napkin and Stone

Fire-kindled satellite,
Passing the bounds
Of the cold moon in flight
From the pool's hounds,
Midwife to ecstasy
Silver and thrilling free,
Where is your place of rest
Ending an aeon's quest,
Shot from the catalyst
Of the world's wounds?

Fast from this rock of earth
Spring waters run.
Here, till I bring to birth
Daughter or son,
How should I emulate
You in your loss of weight?
All those encircling rings
Fire into distance flings,
Touch not the hour that brings
Labour begun.

Darkness encloses light;
Light pushes free.
Brilliant, abounding night,
Think of this tree.
Swathed in the swaddling silk
Under galactic milk,
You that ascending fly
Through the transfigured sky,
When shall the infant lie
Safe on my knee?

Ponder the secret hearth,
Manger and cow,
You whose dynamic path
Crosses the Plough.

Sucked by unconscious night
Into the speed of light,
What can you know of this
Falling from Genesis
Into the pulse of bliss
Near to me now?

Wheel upon wheel in flight,
Whines the far sound.
Napkin and stone are white
In the moon's round.
Midwife to ecstasy
Silver and thrilling free,
While they conspire to break
Silence for wonder's sake,
Wonder itself I make;
Here it is found.

Orbits

I. THE COLOSSEUM AND THE OUTER SPACES

The Colosseum and the outer spaces are one:
The barter of heaven is done.

Rome's ruined doorways and temples overgrown
Speak to the heart through stone.
Bodies of marble speak; forms of Praxiteles
Breathe. In the Vatican these
Arrest the beholder. After long sojourn in earth
They display an earlier birth.
Who wholly returns their scrutiny, far, yet near
In time? But the martyrs here,
All memory now of sacrifice effaced
In the city long laid waste,
Killed in the Colosseum, with scorn for wreath:
What part have these in the stones' continued resting?
They have purchased heaven through the bonds of their
own attesting:
It is theirs, the air we breathe.

The Colosseum and the outer spaces are one:
The barter of heaven is done.

Races perish, languages die. Yet in this
Place, belief and death kiss.
Still valid in the articulation of dust,
Justice reclaims the just.
They made their choice, and above them, all is majestic,
All in movement, drastic.
Within the gigantic walls boulders like dice
Fall, and the foot falls twice,
Walking, and is challenged at every step
By walls that talk in their sleep.
Consider the tongue of heaven, and stop, where stood
Attentive souls, nor lose, faint echoing, the last
Who willing ran to join them, Saint Additus, cast
To be lions' prey and food.

The Colosseum and the outer spaces are one:
The barter of heaven is done.

At the heart of the Colosseum lives overthrown
Bear witness always in stone.
The air is strewn with bonds, with the strings of breath
Muted in dust and death;
For the dead are near you, and their quarrel is shared
In this place where none is spared.
Your very steps are prescribed like the steps of a dancer,
And at each a voice makes answer:
'Seek no further. I was myself here led
Inward to die, my dead
Near me. We chose to die here, by Tiber's flood,
Nor stayed captive; for joy, that sacred leaper,
Poured, like a fountain, light in the eyes of the sleeper,
In the issue of faith and blood.'

The Colosseum and the outer spaces are one:
The barter of heaven is done.

2. THE REVOLUTION OF THE HEART

Is there a heart in space? Is heaven's wide span
Kindly disposed to man,
Massing new satellites on the dynamic slope
Of his far-travelling hope,
Who sees their return, like planets, vouchsafed by
Orbits in star-sown sky?
This that encircles the Earth, that is his own

Workmanship, returning when it has flown
Through fabulous space, what is it but a dart
Seeking always the orbit of his own heart?
Though pushed by an impulse beyond this atmosphere
Whose heat and pressure might make it disappear,
Re-entering this, it dives, that travelling done,
And drops on water its outcast prodigal son.

Orbits: the spiral marking of shell or urn
Speaks of the heart's return.

Yet thought is pitched by the dignity of a shroud
Beyond orbit or cloud,
And still the most distantly exiled heart must come
Back to this centre in Rome,
Making the circle of stones with prophecy scream,
Struck by its echoing beam.
In the night of the catacombs these the chariot forgets,
On whose inmost, intricate circles no sun sets,
Who evokes them now, laid where the violet blooms,
Propitiating the dark in nameless tombs?
Come closer. Cast doubt's garment. Do you suppose
That over their eyes oblivion's flood can close?
These are the atoms of that most travelled thing,
And the simultaneous light of the angel's wing.

Orbits: the spiral marking of shell or urn
Speaks of the heart's return.

At the heart of the Colosseum reared by man
This wheel of stones began
Its endless whirling. A voice inhabits the air,
Separated from prayer
By contrary mass, the momentous opposite
Of the taper's stillness, lit
In catacomb darkness. However distant it fly,
That outer circle itself must magnify
This inmost loss. What may the wandering mind
Of true substance in outer darkness find?
In Christ is the orbit of love. Where a candle throws
Light on woman or man, or a babe's repose,
True man re-enters his path, where monuments quiver,
Back through his ancient bonds, for bonds to deliver.

Orbits: the spiral marking of shell or urn
Speaks of the heart's return.

The Measure Moves

The measure moves, the grain is never weighed.
Light is redeemed through eyes which cannot see.
A breath in darkness alters dynasty:
The eclipsing mite makes larger talents fade.

Those Philistines who bound the man God made,
When feasting, did not hear his muted cry:
'Put my hands near the pillars. Let me try
My strength once more, by lesser hands betrayed.

Time ends in me, yet shall my life continue
Through prayer whose thunders all who hear must dread.
Come, death, now rear your triumph on my head.

Let me kneel down but once, and I shall win you.
Pour light through me, God, through the rivers of my sinew,
And stay me to gather the columns, alive and dead.'

The Beaver

The violent praise the destructive rites of the hawk;
A kingly deceit has the snake,
Vigilant, sinuous in leaves,
Coiled in a pattern of envy,
With a tongue of venom.

Deep forests protect the weak and provoke the strong.
Like a tree, antlers spring
From the velvet head of the elk.
Wolves hunt in a pack.
Ferocious bears have their cave in rock,

I would impose a form on the barbarous wilderness.
I do not trust the trees.
I trust my own teeth
To move them to my design
Away from this carpentry of death.

Flying out of the sunset, stiff, petalled lilies to pluck,
Flamingoes alight on the lake.
I study their stilted reflection.
At dawn they are gone.
In the reeds, the industrious moorhen,

So early building a nest where those fires were banked,
Knows already by instinct
How high, when the long rains come,
The water will flood, whose calm
Shall make the unwary succumb.

This benevolent water deceives who will not use it.
It speaks in my language, tacit.
In a climate of fear and conflict,
A secret architect,
I carry the plans of the city.

I construct where hostile conditions hold others in bondage.
I fell, and measure to usage,
Turning the course of the river,
Dragging logs of my labour
To uphold the measure of life.

Against wild nature I set the cool and Athenian;
A metrical city is mine:
Lanes in harmony laid
From the central beat of the blood.
I do not sprawl. I saw to the level of need.

The Bloodhound

Dark submission in my eye
Disobeys the spur of speed
In favour of the wounded cry.
Though my impulse wakes, aware
Of truant fox and bounding hare,
In my master's true employ
Fault and tragedy I heed.
How should I judge or yet enjoy
The instincts of another breed?

Why, in sleep, do I carry the prints of a journey,
Do I track, then spring to my feet with unshed tears?
With every beat of the blood an evil is born;
But the sombre shines. It is not the bringing to justice,
Hindered by time, across the network of pathways,
Gives me the jowls of a judge, where anguish appears.
Little they know of joy who neglect the forlorn.
Without knowing guilt, who knows the conditions of pardon?

The retriever will answer the shot and return unbidden,
The greyhound triumphs in overtaking the hare,
But I have further to go and a longer task.
My slow concern is the hare's intermittent burden.
My bloodshot eyes, in closing, divine a fellow-
Sufferer. Since first I was given the scent, I'm aware
Of the vigil of the pursued, and villainy's mask.
And whoever holds me back on the leash must follow

My steps, then halt, concerned with a destination,
Then resume my circuitous course, where the scent prevails.
Do not relinquish your hold, but always, as now,
Trust me. Delay may reward me, even evasion
Bring me at last to truth, to the martyr's posture,
By many paths to a tree transfixed by nails,
Or on to a field of remorse, to a fallen bough,
To footprints under the bridge, and a folded vesture.

A fox, pursued by the hounds, has faith in water.
Where others doubt, where the scent goes down in a ship,
I sniff the edge of the jetty, and still persist.
Distance waits. The rope in the sea does not matter.
I know the delinquent crowd, the vindictive anger
Of the mob. They share the deceit of water. The grip
Of the hovering bird they fear, that drops on the wrist.
Truth? It falls, like the long thread holding the anchor,

Sealed by the dying preacher. A scroll I render,
Born to track down injustice. I lick the wound;
And then it is footpad, footpad, nose to the ground,
Ear and eye to the trail. I detect a centre
The rest might pass, for a moment marks the abridgement
Of many untravelled miles, and the end is soon
Reached, and the end is exultant, whenever found,
So close, so true appears the pattern of judgment.

And true to judgment, I make my erratic journey,
Much though the longing comes to return unbidden,
Trusting the scent to discover my destination.
However devious the path through inconstant water,
I keep the log: my account of the trail I render,
Bringing to light what ferns or the scrub had hidden,
Had I gone the direct way. But, as filings quiver,
I turn, as needle to star, with insistent feet.

Unresting I follow the trail, a lugubrious attorney
To joy's keeper, the sleepless giver of rest,
Great judge of the unforgiving. To find his word
An exuberant calm lends meaning to every journey.
And how should the knight, where sorrow and worship meet,
Carved in stone, his fingers closed on his breast,
Tell his lady he has no need of his sword,
Traced I no path, to watch and lie at his feet?

None pursues his task in vain.
Judgment sent me out. These eyes
Are pledged to make the hidden plain.
By the living or the dead
I was shown a single thread,
And upon that thread a stain.
Love and sorrow made me wise,
Drawn from darkness to explain
The errors none can exorcise.

Triads

Who am I to load the year with continual misunderstanding?
I will not accuse winter of a protracted hardness,
Nor spring of callousness, nor summer of regret.

The oak-leaf changes: green gloss cups the acorn.
First hidden, then emerging from resistance to statement,
The fruit holds nothing in its fullness but the tree.

To have held through hail, stormwinds, and black frost in darkness
Through the long months, gives meaning to the bud when it opens.
Song loses nothing of moments that are past.

So my labour is still: it is still determination
To resolve itself slowly in the weathers of knowledge.
By virtue of the hidden the poem is revealed.

Remember Earth's triads: the faith of a dumb animal,
The mountain stream falling, music to the wheat-ears;
The salt wave echoing the grieving of the bones.

The lamb leaps: it is stubborn in its innocence.
The hawk drops, in the energy of instinct.
Dawn fires kindle perfection like a sword.

Fires: the hawk's talons, the tongue of the chameleon,
In a peacock's wings' lightning the contraction of glory,
In death the last miracle, the unconditional gift.

What do I need but patience before the unpredictable,
The endurance of the stepping-stone before the footprint,
Cadence that reconciles wisdom and the dance?

I need more, I need more. In the moment of perception
Fit me, prayer, to lose everything, that nothing may be lost.
The stone that accumulates history is falling.

History is a pageant, and all men belong to it.
We die into each other: remember how many
Confided their love, not in vain, to the same earth.

Uncollected Poems
1969

Air

If a man have but one string,
One, on which to play,
Or in all the world one thing
He alone can say,

Let him turn to other kinds,
Lose and find himself,
Find the peace another finds,
Never for himself.

Music is of music wrought,
Silent though it stay.
Stretch the string away from thought
And the string will play.

Second Air

After all is said,
Then the words alone
Keep a single thread,
Yes, one tone.

Perfect music is
What it had to be:
Wit, the gift of grace,
Bound, yet free.

Everything is caught,
Singular and glad;
Then the after-thought,
Though not sad,

Leads us to a plain
Where the stream is dry,
And we hear again
That low sigh

Earth has breathed who hears
After all is said,
One with many tears
Still unshed.

The Sea Wake

Thundering, falling
Waves on the shore,
What, in your calling,
Echoed before?

The seawake, the seawake, the seawake is flying

Troughs of white sorrows,
Crosswinds and waves,
All of your furrows
Once have been graves.

The seagulls, the seagulls, the seagulls are crying

Pick but a single
Story: you find
Light on the shingle
Cast by the mind.

The tumult, the tumult, the tumult of waters

Ocean had hidden
Shells where they lay.
Now on a sudden
They shine on the bay.

The darkness and sorrows of Oedipus' daughters

Strike, campanology,
Ring the tale free:
Is not mythology
Wide as the sea?

The spray that gave birth to the white Cytherean

Sighing and dolour:
What do shells sing?
Why has all colour
Gone from the king?

Scatters a savage and terrible paean:

'Fly, horses, faster,
Bridled with spray.
Who is your master?
Dare you not say?'

'He, the young paragon
Cast from a throne,
Innocent, arrogant,
But his wits gone.'

'Theseus, Theseus,
Blind in your rage,
Blinder than Oedipus,
Bent on your wage!'

Seagulls are hidden
White in the storm.
Where moves Poseidon?
Black flies his form.

Look, look, the racing shells!
Dark the sea's face.
Hark how the chariot-bells
Ride the tide-race.

How can that hero hope
Now for the shore?
Sorrow remembers
Sorrow once more.

Deafened by heliotrope,
How can the shells
Hear in their chambers
What the wind tells?

White light that follows
Gold light of guilt,
Lacework of colours
In the sea's quilt:

Who, unforgiving, ran
Thread into thread,
Losing a living man,
Finding a dead?

Theseus, Theseus,
Drowning the bells:
Pound them to pieces,
Crush the white shells!

Swift as death, dark as death,
Pawing the air,

Rises the Minotaur
Undestroyed there.

Swift as death, dark as death,
Towering to gore:
All wrecks are shadows
Of him on the shore.

Whose is the body
Strung to a beam
High in the hollow cave
Where the gulls scream?

Whose is the body
Breathless and white,
Hanged, while Hippolytus
Plunges in flight?

Horses, wild horses,
Why do you break
Axle and traces,
And leave a white wake?

Shells from the stallion
Flash under foam.
Drawn by vermilion,
The bull charges home.

White horses breaking,
Centuries gone,
Fly then, forsaking
All that is done.

Creamy-maned horses
Grazing the wrack,
Stopped by a shadow now,
What turns you back?

All seems forgotten
Where the wheels raced,
All turned to driftwood,
All a white waste.

What is stampeding you
Back through the sea?
Is not the chariot gone?
Are you not free?'

'It was Poseidon
Urging again:
Make death his burden
And his yoke pain.'

Why Do Words in My Ears

Why do words in my ears
Ring, as though they were said
Scarcely a moment past?
Why does the echo last
Sudden, after long years,
Of one so alive, though dead?

Surely there is a place
Which, though abandoned, stays,
Letting the landscape made
By chance or circumstance fade
So that feature and face
May stem the current of days.

Tradition

for Kathleen Raine

The artist's patient hammering
Labours for a sudden thing.

Out of all the massing storm's
Clash of intellectual forms,

Intuition's lightning reads
That confusion in the clouds.

Unity is always more
Than all the different parts it wore:

None so intellectual
As the simplest truth of all.

Labour measures out the gap
From lightning to the thunderclap.

Less than this, too quick for tears,
Equals Blake's six thousand years.

Lightning and the City

He looked at Plato's city and his wall.
He knew the laws which made that city stand,
And saw within them what would make it fall,
Another city, greater than he planned.

Goodness was not enough. Though Socrates
Pulled all to irony's heroic ground
And put the question Kierkegaard would seize,
The perfect answer had not yet been found.

Though harmony, through logic used restraint
To inscribe the stones with letters all could spell,
They neither knew the beggar nor the saint.
These walls were raised for justice, but they fell.

Why should not fingers, in a time of dust
When temples lay in ruins, sift the days
To found a city all mankind would trust?
Till faith, the eyes but measure. Then they praise.

A flash of lightning from the Parthenon
Flies to Jerusalem and the walls of Rome.
Lightning reveals the city, stone by stone,
And lips acknowledge late what struck them dumb.

However slow the city we erect,
However patiently we toil, at last
Justice confronts forgiveness. Intellect
Sees a wronged love, the lessons of the Past.

Yet lightning showed to Kierkegaard the Dane
God in each place, and each like Nazareth;
And made all others mercilessly plain,
Forms of despair, the sickness unto death.

Roots

Roots locked in the ground,
Linking weather and skull,
Hold, as the wheels go round
Of a waggon heavy to pull,
So much life to a track

Where the clustered voices climb,
No sapphire playing back
Will ever recall their time.

Iron follows the horse,
Knives of the tractor hooves,
Yet the ploughman knows his course,
That needle fixed in the grooves.
Those men are bound to their load,
Caught in the track of sound,
Fading back down the road
From tenacious roots in the ground.

Under the heavy tread
Of boot and tractor, strayed
Oak and crab-apple spread
To the girth of their summer shade,
No single taproot lost
Of the thorntree's clutching hold,
Gripping the coat of frost
With a strength that fears no cold.

Who but they can revive
The shadow of leaf and bloom,
Keeping the sap alive
In a dark and icy room,
Deaf to the noise of the harrow
Breaking the winter clay,
Guarding, deep in the marrow,
The reluctant soul of day?

Ode at the Autumn Equinox

Before the darkness of diminished days
Bring the bright wonder of the winter sun
Breaking and entering the rooms of leaves,
Before that music plays
And the rich earth reveals her dying wounds,
I see the clash of waves
Beneath the cliff where run
Ceaseless waters like pursuing hounds,
As though the jaws of water must decide

What is to drift and lie
Demolished and laid by,
Where nothing mortal shall outlast the tide.

How secret lies the spindle of the will.
Men's thoughts, their happiness, their very lives
Turn on belief and on their sense of time.
Nothing is ever still:
Each breath's a lifetime and each hour an age.
Deeper than seawave's rhyme,
Divine perception drives
Diverging forces, harnessing their rage,
Till there is nothing they are envious of;
All objects unattained,
Prizes they might have gained,
Are changed by worship, qualified by love.

There is no sabbath printed on the sea,
No pattern of the seasons marked on stones.
I am here now and I was here before.
The spring again runs free
Out of the rock, the rocky wall is dumb.
The breakers on the shore
Forget what time intones;
Lost years are mixed with years that are to come.
Only where holy sources are obeyed
The spirit knows its home
And binds the drifting foam
Back to the matrix from which life was made.

Resisting the East Wind

Dearth and annihilation come from the East,
The East wind scenting to kill
All that exhibits lithe vigour, and leave it still.
Hard now it blows, and until this wind has ceased,
Man will need fire, and a byre for fodder and beast.

It yearns for wolves that none may survive on earth,
Through skeleton branches praying:
'Rocks, remain grey, nor delude yourselves with playing,
As children do with red kites and snows from the North':
And fiercely it snarls on whatever creature goes forth.

It crisps and shrinks any trace of food or surviving
Charity on this cliff.
Its passage leaves grasses withered and white pools stiff,
Cramping the sources of life with its hard-thrust kniving
And crippling the rust-broken harrow past all driving.

It whets on the quivering waves its knives of steel,
Sweeps across dune and sedge
To blacken what signs of creation remain in the hedge
Where motionless horses shelter, or cattle kneel,
Then whistles where twigs no weight in a wren's legs feel.

Reaching the spinney, it falls with a deadly gust
On green spines, sparkling and brilliant,
And is there lassooed by a body, braced and resilient,
Roping down, like one whom it cannot trust,
Its enemy, ready to parry the strongest thrust.

Claim your dead, but the fire in the fists we clench
Will turn your attacks to folly.
Our sons are intent, and brighter than winter holly
Races live blood in the faces you thought to blench,
As out of your grasp these branches for Christ they wrench.

The Coin

Taste the coin beneath your tongue;
Then the song is rightly sung.

Never shall the fountain leap
Till you come to terms with sleep.

For who knows the worth of breath
Till he measures it by Death?

Then the athletic body is
Made aware of witnesses.

Every ripple on the sea
Has a secret voice and key.

Think how many went before
Then you understand the shore.

Then your cadence will be true,
Balanced by the jet it threw.

Vision, where the fountain fell,
Masters more than time can tell.

Not by reason or by sense
Alone, can words be made intense,

But by this, alive and dead,
Breaking from the fountain-head.

Sage or lover cannot say
Truth in any other way.

Dead and living cannot join
Till your tongue has touched the coin.

Excess Luggage

Luck after labour made the poem tick.
Time was at last no hindrance: it came through.
No other could expound why it was true
And he himself could not explain the trick.

A certain ease beyond the reach of skill,
Taught by the will, yet teaching it, remained.
With less contrivance something more was gained:
The planet circled when the top looked still.

How patiently the journey had been made.
The weight of terror built up that excess.
To travel lightly was to carry less.
Unerring movement: this could never fade.

A single nut reconstitutes the tree.
Dead leaves were worthless, now that one survived.
It was by luck the last of all arrived,
And more athletic now to travel free.

The Revolutionary

I was that youth. Now, from myself estranged,
After the revolution I was seeking,
I stop stone dead, to hear another speaking:
'Change nothing: you yourself must first be changed.'

I travelled seas and learnt to read a chart,
Knew how to navigate through dispossession
The hardest straits, yet wrote in my confession:
'All triumph was resisted by the heart.'

Much evil and much good remain, and yet
The heart has no immaculate remedy.
Life, to be won, is won less easily;
The stars remind us: 'Your own eyes are set.'

Say of this patience that impatience gained:
'When others left their station, he remained.'

Blossom of the Apple

Apple-tree of ages, first and last,
You alone transfigure and remember
Light that flowed from Eve to Adam mating,
Burning secret red in blossom cast,
Tender blossom springing, recreating
April light ascending from December,
Apple-tree of ages, first and last.

Blossom of the apple, you must know
Secrets hiding at the source of rivers.
In the root the second sap was planted
Sprung of love, by which the world was altered.
Tarnished in the grass, you fade like snow.
Over you the hand of time has faltered.
And the fruit which all the ages wanted,
Blossom of the apple, you must know.

Apple-Tree

Apple-tree ancient and fresh,
Carnal and fair,
Changing to colours of flesh
Water and air,
Branching, teeming above
The dreaming thorn,

Born of the error of love,
Into truth reborn:

How much you hide in your bark
Now and hereafter,
Wonder, the stir in the dark
Of excited laughter.
All is transfigured; yet
Children who climb
Move where sunlight has met
The beginning of time.

Light running up through the leaves
Is born of the root.
Fruit of young loins, not Eve's,
Are still her fruit.
Here it is springtime: may
Seals in their eyes
Wax of an earlier day,
The incarnate skies.

Here from the birth of day
The sunlight brims
Through all the magical play
Of exuberant limbs,
Foliage hiding the sprawl
Of girl and boy,
Light redeeming from gall
Their juice, their joy.

Tree, which the hands outstretched
Themselves forgave,
Clear as well-water fetched
From an icy grave,
How secret flows to completeness
From the interdict,
The tart, the stinging sweetness,
By true love picked.

Mozart at Zell-am-See

Who finds for Figaro's sake
Harmony sprung from storm?

Out of nothing the brain
Gathers unerring form
Over the Zeller lake,
And the miracle stirs again.

So may the ripples drift,
Playing their facile song.
And as a salmon leaps to the fly
Out of the current, strong
Into its arc the gift
Ascends, and alters the sky.

Whether foolish or wise,
Cutting the course of time,
Music leaves the unknown.
Wherever delight would climb
In the light of a young girl's eyes,
That light in the scales is shown.

How does Mozart transpose
What is unknown to man
Except in innocent joy?
This that from nothing ran
Leaps from its very close
To enchant the dreaming boy.

Sonnet

Lay the true charge, if I come late to bed,
Which made me toil, groping in blindfold guise,
To take that gift for which the Muse has eyes
And make a lighter pillow for your head.
Though all remained, and still remains, unsaid,
At least I know that nothing satisfies
Born of ambition, which I used to prize;
Nor could I grip with strength till that was dead.

And I remember well what overthrew
That impulse, and invented a new reign.
I know a truth no volumes can explain.
Man is transformed, since priceless treasure drew
His dreaming will, the products of whose brain
Break his intention, and return more true.

Hymn

THE LEPER'S HEALING

Fountain of life whose face we love,
The leper, healed, gives thanks to Thee.
His eyes are fixed, and will not move
From that clear spring which makes him see.

He heard Thy words, he turned his feet;
He passed the impulsive, pressing crowd.
His fingers touched the watery sheet.
He found Thee there, and cried aloud.

Life, the reward, was not denied
To one for whom no men gave place.
They who pressed nearest in their pride
Were not the first to see Thy face.

Our lives run counter to the wheel,
Nor may the soul find peace, unless
It wait on God, whose words reveal
Clear waters which alone can bless.

Those merchants trading doves for gold
Turned from the leper's gift aside.
Life was the bargain which they sold,
But he found life where most he died.

Lead us to grace; let stream and dove
Alter our lives, by shock revealed.
Shine, risen Christ: perfect our love.
Raise us from death, and find us healed.

The Instant

Instant of truth that killed remorse,
Strength beyond all things strong,
Secret of force renewing force,
Your spring I have not sung,
Unwearied through a lifetime's course,
Though found on earth when young.

Who might have guessed that such a gift
Would come his youthful way

Where nothing led him but the drift
Of creatures towards decay?
A weight the ages could not lift
Lay dark upon my day.

That word of buried light was true
And set my feet above
The cobbled flames the sunrise threw
Reflected in the dove:
There was no creature, none that grew,
Excluded from His love.

Restitution

To-day this thought ran through my head:
Is not remorse alone
The bedfellow of each when dead
Under the lettered stone,

If he remembers by what pledge
Of action or of word
He might have spared the sacrilege
And wounding of his Lord?

On such a thought I fell asleep
And in my sleep I lay
Where sunlight with a red more deep
Flushed the thorned boughs of may.

These were the last to break of spring
When many blooms were shed.
I had forgotten time would bring
So deep and late a red.

Whence was the fire which made them shine
Above the mouldering wall?
Their lot was mortal, yet divine:
They gloried in their fall.

'Cast the desire of youth,' I prayed;
'Make fast the truth in age.
Yet, if its words be here inlaid,
Let me not turn the page.'

Till I surrendered what I sought,
I did not know the tree.
The substance and the fire of thought
Were then reborn in me.

For justice heals the suffered act
Where joy's late tears had sprung.
Without it, how could love exact
The tribute of the young?

Candle Constant

This man perceived that time could never catch
The candle, where it flickered and declined.
Each flying thought a second thought would snatch,
Leaving the outline of the first behind;
A certain aura from a blown-out match
Was lost, then re-established in the mind.
What, then, was constant? Still, beyond all doubt,
All flames were gathered where the last burnt out.

True for him also, certain notes would stay,
The meaning of their own supreme desire
Established perfect where they died away.
Such music, not unlike that constant fire,
Made Earth, as though a fountain were to play,
Fresh for a thousand seasons, night and day.

The Debt

River whose secret day
Stays constant where it flies,
No treasure can repay
The tribute of these eyes.

You can remake the weirs
By fathering their fall.
There are no traffickers
Your gift does not forestall.

There though my gaze is set,
I yet can never know

Why, of so great a debt,
So much is left to owe.

Tell me, cup and thorn,
Who can provide enough
To lighten what was borne
In that foresuffered love?

Though all day I toiled
I never could supply
This that no fault has spoiled
Where naked it flows by.

Vision bequeaths a sum
Increased by spending it.
Poor if I first become,
My gain is infinite.

But when did I divine
That what was fugitive,
Like water in a mine,
Alone could make it live?

In other elements
Progress is made, not this.
True poverty prevents
Its own antithesis.

Quarrying the hardest flint,
Marble, slate or granite,
I should have halved my stint
By now, since I began it.

This is a subtler case,
More magical in kind,
Where sacrifices race
And leave a fuller mind.

If I lean down to slake
My thirst at this pure jet
Whose recompenses make
Both lips and eyelids wet.

The very source I touch
Restores what runs away,
Richer than daylight much,
And all we know of day.

The Prairies

The prairies are, and were, since time began,
A treeless distance moving without shade,
Silent, a virgin country not yet laid
By the strong arms of city-building man.
There must be wells, there must be music. Scan
The outer limits till those limits fade.
I think of Sandburg, the guitar he played:
Chicago rising. Dust. The forehead's tan.

Far from the city's energies the plain
Ripens to harvest. All the garner holds
Is fed by absent and by distant golds.
Lost in the city's desert there is grain.
The face of man a distant sculptor moulds
Whose wells supply the seasons without rain.

First Sight of the North-West

A course through the North-West passage: who but a fool would take it?
Muttering mussels, hear me: what should a man decide?
Yeats was willing in age to go upon stilts or naked;
The hermit interprets all waters, shut in a shell of the tide.

Yes, he in the priesthood's calling could hold his thunderbolts fast,
From the cloven retreat of his cloisters unleash a transfiguring storm,
Guide the *Deutschland* from Bremen, battered to grace by the blast,
And keep all ages at bay with his faith's invincible form.

Ice-bound Canada, come: let plumes of the white whales play.
Shades of explorers return, where a candle shadows them forth.
Was not Nansen reproached, and why did Columbus not stay?
Against all valid objections, the needle points to the North.

Icicles change into leaves, with a turning of hands to the West.
An elk in the snow looks indignant; reindeer bound off with a start.
The Rockies were made before man, so am I a premature guest?
Grizzlies, a girl was before you: it is she knows the ages by heart.

Red Indians are fishing the rapids, in the moment of thaw letting fly
First brilliant colours of life; then a totem: I think of Seattle,

Small people descending a needle that turns in the top of the sky
And a station a hundred years old, a young Waterloo with no battle.

Bewildered by lakes and by prairies, I step from the train, prepared
To grasp an expectant hand, like a helmsman trusting a star.
How little I know navigation! Far out in the West I am spared
All but the knowledge of one who knows he has come so far.

After the bilious Atlantic, with luggage tossed in the hold,
What excuse could there be? Either the train is late
Or a man was arriving to meet me, and somebody knocked him cold.
Shame, shame, Seattle, unworthy of Washington State.

My watch is a hundred years out, or am I a century late?
The little tents of the settlers, how far away they are now;
That long iambic line, pioneering a snowbound state,
The mark of heroic writers, before the mechanical plough.

Verse, an eternal freshness, all but fools will agree,
Leaps out of darkness, and stays. Long swimmers, carry your guest,
Canoe cut out like a family in the bark of a Redskin tree,
Skim like a swallow the water, to find where a phoenix will nest.

Beautiful, unknown blossom, uplifted plates of a fountain
Holding daylight, dogwood: has nothing here given ground
Since old Alaska's bears and a white-faced, Chinese mountain
Stared across to Vancouver, as he sailed up Puget Sound?

The Ballad of the Outer Dark

and other poems

1979

The Pledge

True to a single vow,
I bade time take the rest.
Love would make me whole.

What is there left me now?
Body first to divest,
And then lay bare the soul.

Secrecy

Who has shed in this shade
Light where the Lord of light is laid?

I have come where the calm
Shadows seem a muted psalm.

All I love, all I have,
Green one, from the grave you give.

Ever green, though men groan:
They lose stain who touch your stone.

Grant me grace on this grass,
Taught by shades, at peace to pass

Where you laugh through each leaf,
Lending life the calm of grief.

Let me praise what I prize
Though none sees you with his eyes,

You whose dawn was laid down
To obtain a perfect town.

Let me swim in the stream,
Race through water's balm and beam,

Through the leaves daylight loves
Where it dives with song of doves.

Laughing joy like a jay
Shouts and gives reply to play

And the skill learnt at school
All seems pale beside the pool.

When the dusk on my desk
Greets me with a task grotesque,

All the fair starry fire
Fills my desert with desire.

Holy yew, holy yew,
Keeping troth and always true,

Lord of grand, simple ground,
Lending earth your sainted sound,

On this slope where I sleep,
Might I copy all you keep,

You who know all things now
Where the shades obey your bough.

Yet your stone is my own,
Gives again what's never gone.

All I love, all I have,
Green one, from the grave you give.

Matrix of Morning

Say what you will, the matrix of morning is true:
Leafmould masking skeleton leaves from the spring,
Beechleaves opening, white, the light breaking through,
Leafsap shining, green from a forager's wing.
And
Glory is given: wide as the woodpecker dips,
Dives, recovers in air for a loop of his flight,
Gorse-yellow cables are flung to the stanchion he grips,
Taut, crested, a beacon, beaming and bright.
Spanned
Swallow's flight falls from a centre: swiftness is pure;
Each dip or ascent from the ground is the arc of a ring,
True to the lark or the woodpecker. Joy must endure
Weight, the recoil of earth's jettison, straining to sing.
Leaf, fountain and wing,
breaks from the hand,
Lost, found, unforgettable, great where it grew.

Yes; but all that in daylight turns on a mind,
Stirring, wakes to a beam forever begun,

Splashed with the milk of earth's morning, babbles her tongue;
Each is ancestrally copied, true to its kind.
Numberless blossoms break, yet the blossom is one.
Age-furrows darken in man, but the seedlings are young.
Air, weir-water vanishing, never divined,
Nuts, buried, unknown to the beams of the sun,
Rinsed, radiant and wrung,
Plunge to the matrix of morning from which they have sprung;
Splendour in ground descending, grandly designed.

The Dancer in the Leaves

Wisdom is faithful; thought can never fade,
But life will not stay prisoned in that school.
O fetch a dancer, dancing is the trade
To bring the wise man nearer to the fool.

What thought a thoughtless moment will express;
The unconscious glory brings its undertone.
Or how can thought be magnified, unless
The unknown god begets upon the known?

I cannot tell what shadows from the bough
Are truthful, nor what light among the leaves
Is deathless. Where the pattern races now
A wise man scatters what a fool believes;

For life is gathered upward on the gust
Of pagan wonder, and the sinewy joy
Sucks the sweet water to the thirsty dust
The sun, that pitiless phoenix, would destroy.

Sonnet

Muscular man shall guard
The integrity of love
Against the travesty
Of fashion's trivial pose.
The steadfast man in love
Knows the true socket hard

And vision's majesty
Near to the bone he knows.
Let it be said this house
Was strong to entertain
The god while he was here,
For these are sacred vows
And destined to remain
When treasons disappear.

The Fountain of Apollo

Was it Apollo taught men first to sing?
I marvel now that he remains forgiven,
His gold, winged horses flying through high heaven,
So dark a music fills the leaves of Spring.

Was it Apollo taught men to die young?
Those limbs are deathless while the torso strains
Back from the flying light to hold the reins.
He laughs to see them; then the stone gives tongue:

O living stream, O fountain of the day,
Break from these burning lips once more and say:
All is translated since that morning shone.

The tree is light, and light is passed away.
Why should I praise the laurel-leaves that stay,
When music sees the likeness that has gone?

True and False Art

Complexion stirs: desire is quick and soft.
Art is an image of life, a hard, bright doll,
Or mummied shape of that which walked aloft,
Preserved for ages by the craftsman's tool.

Yet look: those rigid features guard a spirit
Quick as a heart-beat. Dreaming Adam brings
His inmost rib, no robot to inherit
Of red lips worked by automatic strings.

Seeing this, I cannot love the transient days
Unless I know false art from true desire.
True is the pitying eye, the pulse of praise,
False is the puppet on ambition's wire.

O live, then, truly. Learn your mummer's part,
Lest, in a patchwork play of joy and pain,
You lose your night-love to a china heart,
Your daybreak-fancy to a sawdust-brain.

Adam

When Adam stood beneath the Knowledge Tree
Naked, and felt the full strength of the sun
Shine on his body, he had mastery
Of every visual form, not yet begun.

When Adam found a leaf, and God called out:
'Who told thee thou wast naked?' he began
To build that heaven from which God cast him out
With all the effort of a conscious man.

He hates the praise his false admirers give,
Who have not suffered. Always his eyes stared,
While these robustly found a way to live,
Into a heaven for which they never cared.

Sonnet

ON THE DEATH OF ALUN LEWIS

He was astonished by the abundance of gold
Light. In the street a beggar stretched her hand,
Dying. Then the shudder ran through him. Once he had planned
To out-distance the sun in a chariot. But how might he hold
That instant, those uncurbed horses, and mix with the mould
Her liquid shadow near the lotus and timeless sand?
A slighter man would have noticed the ripples expand
From the stark, regenerate symbol. But to him that cold

Figure was real. Ah yes, he died in the green
Tree. What was it, then, pierced him, keen as a thorn,

And left him articulate, humble, unable to scorn
A single soul found on Earth? O, had he seen
In a flash, all India laid like Antony's queen,
Or seen the highest, for which alone we are born?

A Dry Prophet

Except for the unreclaimed land
Of wild creatures, birds
And children, he had no planned
Conquest, no territorial dreams.
Cities he did not understand,
Or ways of indulgent thought;
So he picked wry themes,
And finding himself caught
In a cage of fury, he would pluck
The wires, not
For the lyric note struck
But to expose the plot
Of time he tenanted; words were cords
For flagellation, not strings.
How could it be otherwise?
It is in freedom the lark sings.
With his eye for wronged things,
Greed, hypocrisy, lies,
Bitterness fed his words.

Time smouldered in his eyes' furnace
Watching the corruption of days,
A dry prophet, observant –
While the hourglass ran –
Of every false direction
In which life moved.
Say of this man
He was sure in his affection
For the things he loved,
But did not commit his tongue to praise.
Excess of words galled
His instinct. Rather he called
Reticence a truer servant,
More likely to lead to grace.

To judge others
Is to judge ourselves; but he,
Alert to that law
Of merciless scrutiny,
Judged himself first, and saw
Clearly, in a landscape exposed to scorn,
The lines of life on his brothers'
Faces, and his own
Lineaments in theirs, melancholy
Marked there, lines of distress
Leading to judgement slowly,
Traced before he was born.

Butterfly and Man

Courtier, sly satyr falling, this gold season,
Trailing the scholar by his coat laid down,
Diverting, with slant eyes, the eye of reason,
Quaintly attentive, shuttered meadow-brown:

Gently you lean away from all he knows
While he, astonished, waits for you to play.
Behind his coat the tree of knowledge grows.
You know no history earlier than today.

Now that he rises, how can you forget
To keep your distance, both in time and space?
Between you both suspicion casts a net.
How far apart they lie, your kind, his race.

Wakened from history, roused from patterned sleep,
Dreaming those heroes still, as sleepers can,
Faces whose lineaments the leaves still keep,
Roman, Pre-Cambrian, he comes near, as man.

What can you know of him, the tall newcomer,
Trespassing on the crooked ways you go,
Alert, yet languid, in your one-eyed summer?
His threatening shadow is the thing you know.

You shift your ground: he's unconcerned with that.
Far closer to his heart lie distant things.
Twin-eyed upon the petals you lie flat;
Then one eye sees him, as you close your wings.

You quit him, turn, then settle on his book.
There, like a moment tilted on an age,
After engaging him with your first look,
You drop his shadow, like a careless page.

Late

Late in the tower the Western window shines.
There the last light, the gladiator's thrust,
Burns like a star. Yet the grey room enshrines
A butterfly imprisoned, falling on dust.

Intrepid voyager, learn at last to be still.
Autumn has housed, beneath your tattered wings,
A silk-moored boat in the white cocoon of the mill
Guarding the diapered dark of all your Springs.

Logos

Logos, the star-born tongue: how came
So stark a statement from a scroll,
Consumed, as though the dead could tame
All moods by midnight's strict control?

Fire in a moment flies intent
The works of reason to unwind.
How reconcile that element
To the slow writing of mankind?

Who stole the sacred fennel stalk?
The will endures till fetters break.
There the immortal visons walk.
A Titan suffers for your sake.

Come near; crouch low; heap stick on stick.
Throw pine-cones to the Winter's flame.
Gold in the draught, a sudden prick
Tattoos in light a whispered name.

What ransom can the witness give
For prophecy, the loot of thieves?

Future and Past the sparks make live,
Battening like locusts on their sheaves.

In vain you pledge your dearest things
To the rash floor of that dark urn.
Light murders thought, and then gives wings.
No migratory words return.

How fast they vanish: see them die,
The very words you lately breathed.
Lit by a thread, betrayed they lie
Dead in the sunken embers wreathed.

Where whistling, rustling, weaving Fates
Snatch on a gust the shrouds they made
Whose testament a god translates
Where light must learn a dying trade.

The Salmon

Salvation! O the salmon's head, all ages on a stone:
The laddered light is mounting there with angels to the throne.
There the young and old agree, racing from the sea:
Too fast the light is flying for living eyes to see.

Inert against a block of ice, a price is on his head.
Men pass where all the books of time are hanging by a thread.
Streams of light, eternal streams, where do they begin?
The spinners cast him out of time; they sunder what they spin.

Leaping from the Sibyl's pool and swimming through the sky,
All living things are pictures that cross his sage's eye.
A moment taken out of time, a flash along a weir,
The light all men are chasing is lost and living here.

The first is he of all the drops fallen from the sky,
The grain beneath the falling grains as ages fall and die.
The core of every stone he is, the nut of every tree;
The end and the beginning, the source of time is he.

Older than the oldest, yet younger than the young,
He sees the spinners cast him out, their stories are unstrung.
Scales of music's ice and fire, scales that Mozart made,
The certainties ascending, and caught before they fade.

His eyeballs spell a parable: O, the pool of blood!
The whirlpool in the Baptist's eye Salome understood!
Jonah's glittering prophecies take counsel from a fin:
The music of the lost is there, the dead go out and in.

Cry out, though fifty fish-hooks were buried in his scales,
That light would pull an eagle down, and ride upstream to Wales,
Back to Ceridwen's cauldron, where sprang the drops of sight
That lit on Taliesin's tongue, scalding drops and white.

In Elphin's weir the child was caught. All ages then were hung.
The radiant forehead by those drops that lit upon his tongue
Knew all the changes from their birth. His inspiration freed
Souls from the swinish devils that mocked the Saviour's creed.

An Irish tale was told that where the Knowledge Tree took root
A sacred salmon in a pool that fed upon the fruit
Had swallowed everlasting life, and Paradise was shut
To all till one could catch the fish and feed upon the nut.

And waiting for the salmon-flash, to steal immortal life,
An old man crouched beside the pool with net and sharpened knife
Till all his life had ebbed away. He slept and woke in tears,
Knowing he'd missed the little splash that might renew the years.

Before him when he woke stood Finn, who told him he had got
The leaping salmon while he slept, and cooked it in a pot.
His fingers caught three scalding drops, and sucking them, he fed
By luck on Taliesin's tree, rooted in the dead.

To-night for the dark waters, where shivering radiance flies
With scales upon the hunted skin to match the moving skies:
No movement like this movement, that matches ice and flame;
The moment of its vanishing and coming is the same.

Salvation! O the salmon's head red-gilled upon the stone:
The light is married in that head to all the mind has known,
Transfigured by the living flash that runs along the bough,
The light of dawn, the almond-light that fills the ages now.

The Still Garden

Say Earth were sleeping, yet new morning stirs.
How bright the dew after this April frost,

A river, virgin, still by no dead crossed,
Fresh to her trespassing, and yet not hers.
Now, softer than a breath, faith disinters
Neglected lives oblivion overmossed;
She treads the grass and, close above that host,
Her footstep gives the ground the beat of verse.
Still the known shadow makes the known bloom fair.
Still lies in earth that which could tell the air
Each moment of God's breath is brighter than
The brightest and most brilliant hour of man.
She sees that honour save him from despair,
Cast to the shaping dust where he began.

Fragment

I would be flute to that sweet air:
How blasphemous it were
To print her music otherwise
Than in her own true skies.
It were to teach the candle its own flame
Or the deaf grains of sand
Music of rains that wash the christened land
To know, when she looked down, what I became.

Come, come, more Loved

Come, come, more loved than many days,
More dear than many mornings, come.
Without you idle is the praise
Of light on grass or rose in bloom.

Without you empty run the hours.
When you are here they fly too soon.
You pass, and withered are the flowers,
Their sunlight and their nectar gone.

Who would have thought a single step
And voice could widow all the ground
And bring a garland to my sleep
Brighter than all the day had found?

The Many-Peopled Night

Calm of the sea, imagined rest –
Untrue to life, yet true to love.
How secretly, in every breast,
The moonlit waters move.

And who could have foretold this calm
When all was storm and rage before?
That hurricane which felled the palm
Has vanished from the shore.

One silhouette the low sun flings,
Printed against the darkening air:
A hawk, beneath whose quivering wings
The landscape is laid bare.

Now the hawk drops, the moon steals clear,
Brightening the waters far around.
Small fieldmice through the grass in fear
Scurry, exposed, to ground.

Cities and streets the body knows,
Hunter and hunted, hawk and prey.
The limbs interpret in repose
The strength and speed of day.

The athletic body spans the wave,
Braced on firm bones against the storm.
Its runner's mark is in the grave,
And passion gives it form.

Its fingered notes translate the word
The many-peopled night has known,
Low on the breathing waters heard
And locked in every stone.

How dense the inscribed night scroll, yet none
Can sound the fathoms where we lie.
So packed a score must be undone
To make the morning sky.

And dark, where lives and places drift,
Stretches away the midnight sea,
Patterned on lids we dare not lift
For losing what we see.

Fragment from Poems for a Child

Still one, forgotten, awake,
Girl the night gave,
Bright as the rainbow on wave upon wave where they break,
Is there a cave
Under the wings of the sea
Dividing, uniting, dividing, O infinite centuries old,
Where the book that I hold on my knee
Like a bead of the foam may be told,
May be lost in the angelus blinding it, yet on the instant be read?
Shall a voice that I see
Alight on the born and interpret the words of the dead?

Near one, remembered, asleep,
No one will come,
Only the roar of tumultuous waves in their deep
Sea-urchin home.
Rest in the labyrinths there,
In the great blinding dark of our prayer,
In the luck of the ark
That is rocked on the moon-gathered sea, on the night, on the dark
In the crib where great eagles praise Godhead whose wings meet above
The rocks of despair:
You are safe, caught to God, who would perish except for His love.

The Pulse and the Shade

I

How many a man has watched a river flow,
Changing its course through shallow parts or deep,
And where he looked for lightning found it slow,
Then lost his wonder to the speed of sleep.
Conflict remains. The slave of Angelo
Counters with grace the truth he cannot keep,
Embodying by restraint what angels know
Too strong for mortal tears, though mortals weep.

Time has no present till the past is true.
The beating pulse is honoured by its dead.

The centuries are glass, and we look through
The moving river to the river's bed,
And there we lose the dancer overhead
Holding the globe, the drop from which it grew.

2

Declare at last, Master of all our styles:
Is there one soul would have his dead live twice?
Whom death has beggared, him no gift beguiles;
Not all our gifts could reach his ransom price.
He who needs all or nothing truly smiles
In pity at such tender compromise.
What have we here? Inscriptions cut with files
That have no meaning for translated eyes.

We touch closed lids; and instantly the spool
Of sleep unwinds all visions without loss,
Stripped like Diana, naked in her pool.
Does every presence issue from one Cross?
What answer had Saint Hubert when he stood
And saw those antlers in a pagan wood?

3

Mark, above silent strings, the lamp he used,
The trumpet hanging near the bed of wood,
These idle keys by which he was amused
On frost-clear mornings when life tasted good.
Here, like the bustling honours he refused,
Pigeons avoid the hawk of solitude.
Is it neglect of which we stand accused?
I think his ravens brought him the right food.

Porcelain stirs when strangers cross these boards;
The curious read his writings where they lie;
But every relic recollection hoards
Is watched here by a more deliberate eye.
The Shade himself, since he must act as host,
Rewrites those words that use him like a ghost.

4

To-day snow covers all the paths and stiles.
Light through the gateposts, watching the sun rise,
Stealthily brings, on snow's unprinted aisles,

That erect figure, ferried back with sighs.
The chronicle of hours, the map of miles,
Folds to the very door. A ghost is wise
To shake no crystal from the roof of tiles,
Yet animate the room with speaking eyes.

Deep lies the speechless drift; its mound of snow
Conceals a warm, but carries a cold shade.
The leaves bright April made to sing and glow
Now rustle crisp around December's spade.
Time, in its going, dreams that souls will fade.
Soul is immortal: it is time must go.

5

Life and the force of habit bring him back.
A fire is kindled where it last burnt out.
So the husk crumbles that a seed may sprout,
And green will force an exit out of black.
Accept the weight of time, yet know its lack;
Take to the task, make discipline devout,
And, like a ploughman, turn the plough about,
Testing your faith with time's opposing track.

The words of life, whose quickfire candles catch,
Since Jesus walked, are written in the ground.
The true face lights from recognition's match.
The vision only blind men saw is found.
Time's weights are winged. In movement they attach
Witness and cherub to the daily round.

6

His name being said, instantly he appears,
Caught, in a timeless flash, with life's own look
Which none could seize or copy in a book.
I marvel, who had missed that look for years.
Still font of heaven, borne on the moving weirs,
Or christening water in the running brook,
You that restore, by cleansing, what time took:
The man survives; his abstract disappears.

Where is his name's true habitat, so near
In retrospect, and yet so far in state?
An instant's threshold on which angels wait
Still renews time within a timeless year.

Illusions conquered, absent lives are here,
And all is early, though recorded late.

7

I loved this house, Master of all that fades:
From such a house enduring memories rise
Offering their hospitality to Shades
In life, a place of trust for gladdened eyes
Lit by recurring daylight or a lamp,
So dear to thought are these remembered things;
For here affection left so true a stamp
Of joy's integrity, to which all clings.

Yet, while the pulse does honour to my guest
Whose footbeat comes like a response to prayer,
Intuitive lightning which no two can share,
Too brilliant for a Shade, instructs the breast:
'Know that for him, both here and anywhere,
Place has no part in that which makes him blest.'

Elegiac Sonnet

for Dylan Thomas

Over this universal grave the sky
Brings to the grieving earth its great reward,
And it was right to lay ambition by,
The strongest will being deep and the way hard.
This body sleeping where the dead leaves lie
Gives back to trees from colours they discard
The patient light of its own penury
Out of whose silence wakes the living word.
And we who wake, who saw the swallows' wings
Seeking the turning-point of their own cloud,
Draw to one place his love of vanished things.
It is not this that leaves the heart's way ploughed;
It is the shade the sun no longer flings
Of one who touched the humble and the proud.

Dusk Tide

Stilted, stepping curlews prod
With forward beaks the expanse of mud.
Turnstones work like Sisyphus
Lifting their tilted boulders loose.
All the alighted birds are busy
Raiding a luminous waste, the dizzy
Lanes and purlieus of the mud
Left by the receding flood.
That leafy night where herons hide
Being now relinquished by the tide,
Slowly a heron's head inclines
On devious water, through its lines
Finding melodious at his feet
A place where calm and conflict meet.
Wrangling gulls and buzzards rare
Rock the villages of air.
A cormorant, stark from vanishings,
Ecstatic with extended wings,
Dries in the sunlight.
Far and near
The heaven of colour harboured here
Alters its anchorage with each
Bird alighting on the reach.
Down straits a swan and cygnets glide
Awaiting the returning tide.
Only a certain time is given
To each bird, heart of its own heaven,
Before the oblivious tide. Perhaps
The stillness where the curlew steps,
The mirror's face, the watery blaze,
The fiery tail the sun displays,
Is all that may be known of time,
Touched by each walker on the slime,
Until the turn is reached, and then
All is submerged and lost again.
The daylight's ebb is ended. Hark:
The ascending flood invades the dark.

Sly under rock and blackberry hedge,
As from a lock, the water runs.
Lifted on the lapping edge,
Hulls of the sailboats knock the stones.

Creeping and gathering light, the flood
Pushes to every verge the tide.
Birds scatter. Under Autumn's wood
Leaves and petals glide.

What is that fluttering image, white,
Making those other baubles wan?
What feather on a breath of night
Has fallen from the swan?

Night and the Swan

'I am old as night,' sang the wave;
'Soft, in this hunter's cave,
I flood the walls with my tide
Till none of mankind can find,
Not though they grope like the blind,
What creatures lived here and died.'

Then the spray: 'I am cold in air.
Yet, what light can compare
With mine, since the rainbow fell,
Confiding its harmony
Of eternal sky and sea
To the fragile whorls of a shell?'

'I am soul,' sang mortal man;
'Blow me away who can.
I have touched an instant of peace
Beyond time's breakers, more
Than that ocean without a shore
Or its glittering, changing fleece.'

Three voices. Who could forget
Their threefold music, met
In the low sun's level ray?
And there the river ran out
Where passion plucked from thought
What never could pass away.

The sea cried chaos and loss;
But pierced, like an albatross,
Taliesin still sailed on.

What less than death could have given
The music of earth and heaven
To beckon night and the swan?

Sonnet

THE EXPECTATION

Here, Lord, I lie: have mercy on my soul.
My wounds from time were more than time could heal.
Grace had I none, nor health, till I could feel
Those old wounds die, and your wounds mine control.
Then I was fresh and washed, as in a bowl.
I closed my eyes, that you might break the seal,
Then clearly saw the ransom you reveal,
Richer than all the treasures which I stole.

Take from this vault whatever wealth is more
Than just suffices to be blest and bless.
Like the grown child the ungrateful city bore,
Rebuked for faults and clothed in his distress,
If I give all, that gift you can restore,
And I must always grieve if I give less.

Ode on Justice

Sigh without hatred, poet, if you can.
Truth is despised and forgeries are honoured.
Sigh, for the face of justice
Remains, though mocked, the most beautiful known to man.

Let her stay silent while her slanderers speak,
Turbulent guests who delight in broken bridges.
She will translate their language
And trace all streams to the source from which they break.

She is more patient, suffers her neglect
Easily, glad to be assigned the lowest
Place in any surroundings,
Lifting her prayer, the fountain none can reject.

Swift though confusion, though adversity come,
She in her scale will keep the weight of error.
Love shall restore the balance
Through her, of innocent marriage to bride and groom.

Out of materials she constructs a house,
Testing against all winds the joists and timbers.
Light, and the singing river
She clasps and holds in vessels to fit her vows.

Better is love's bed made where she has toiled.
Script, for her music is a part of silence,
Draws from abounding nature
And brings to grace what circumstance might have spoiled.

Joy was once perfect, for in each there hides
That serene one, born of the risen body,
Held for a time in service,
Revealed, through faults, in offspring of grooms and brides.

Has she not freed your soul of error? You
Know, as you raise deception's last defences,
She alone brings forgiveness
And gives the suckling peace, though his tears renew.

Seek, then, her face, by whom the oppressor even
Was once turned servant, Saul of Tarsus blinded,
Struck by her shaft of lightning,
While still there rang in his ears the stones of Stephen.

Rhadamanthus and the Sufferings of Europe

Begin to know me. Sleep's more potent juices
Brought me to Hell, a judge of the oppressed,
Weaned, on their breath, of her the bull seduces,
Who sucked, like my two brothers, at her breast.

Rhadamanthus and the New Soul

Admit the new soul from the tethered boat
Where sorrows fly like seabirds seeking bread.

Men are remembered by the words they wrote.
These, not the printless waters, nurse their dread.

'Is it not true, the dead forget their pains?
The pains of others, then, outlast our own.
Too much is gone, too little now remains.
Weep, and efface the writing on the stone.'

In crafts of evil who compares with man?
How many in the death-cells learnt his ways.
What victims could not overcome, I can.
Speak low, for where you walk, another prays.

'I saw too much, and did not wish to live.
My pity ran too deep for time to kill.
Read in my eyes their sorrow, and forgive
Those others who obeyed a tyrant's will.'

Death cannot heal the dead of all their pains.
Life is a tree that blossoms in the stone.
Its root is sacred; every hour it gains
Until at last it masters all that's known.

'Stern judge, you understand us more than I.
Mercy there was, and kindness, in the stream.
I prayed for death, and still I could not die.
My dream still holds me. Wake me from my dream.'

Cast off the tethered boat, while overhead
The starving seabirds cry and veer away.
He is of those whose fingers crushed the bread,
And who can perish, born on Judgment Day?

The Ballad of the Outer Dark

INTRODUCTION

The Prologue* to *The Ballad of the Outer Dark* came to me when my earlier Ballad, *The Ballad of the Mari Lwyd,* was produced in Swansea by Elizabeth Iorwerth Jones at the beginning of 1948, but it was not until the middle of the fifties that the new Ballad began to take shape. Like *The Ballad of the Mari Lwyd,* it is concerned with the tension between Figures in a firelit room on the last night of the year who are identified with the Living, and Voices outside the door, in the Outer Dark, who may be drunkards, but who hint at holiness, identified with the Dead. The outsiders are carrying the Mari Lwyd – the Grey Mari or Grey Mare – which is a horse's skull. This was, in an old Welsh tradition, carried from house to house on the night of New Year's Eve by a party of singers and impromptu poets, who challenged the inmates of the house to a rhyming contest and if they won, gained entry and the right to demand food and drink. If they lost, they had to go away.

The party of impromptu rhymers carrying the skull has already been driven away after the rhyming contest when *The Ballad of the Outer Dark* begins. Midnight has already struck, and the firelit room is bolted again. All is security and peace. But all is not quite still. The circumscribed firelit room is there, with its familiar objects; and the clock keeps living time. The enemy, the unknown, the force of violence and upheaval, has been expelled into the Outer Dark. But there is still the fear that it may return and take possession. Judgment hangs in the balance, just after midnight, between the Old Year and the New.

Vernon Watkins
October, 1966

Clock striking midnight

VOICE *inside*

Come to me, Mother of God, come down as the Old Year ends,
Frost-Mother, Mother of the stars and of the white, wave-beaten sands.
I hear the seawave fall like a knife, dividing exiles and friends.

NARRATOR

Stay in your lighted windows. Your terrified eyes accost
The colossal skull of the Outer Dark, the ribboned Mare of all men lost,
That blind, hilarious image has frozen you stiff with frost.

**In the final version there was no Prologue, the original Prologue forming the first lines of text.*

VOICE

Yet fear itself returns, and speaks, while we hold our breath;
While the door is shut and the embers fall from the snowflakes' hissing
shibboleth,
I hear the beat of sleet on the pane, like feet of remorseful death.

NARRATOR

The wood of the fire and the wood of the door can resist what ghosts go by;
But with rattling jaws the bony Judge, like the broken seawave's sigh,
Returns to be your Assessor, in the twinkling of an eye.

VOICE

Who knows, as we shut the door, as we stack the fire inside,
What spectres spurned will have gathered strength, what legion of shadows
pride,
To trample this house to ruin, where forgiveness was denied.

NARRATOR

The sigh of the year is not their sigh: it was you yourselves who sighed.

NARRATOR

So quick a thing, so lost a thing
And cast beyond recall:
Night on a frosted window
And snowflakes on the wall.
The drunkards all are gone to bed.
There's silence in the hall.

Tic toc
Tic toc
The room in the house is dumb.
The beer is sunk, the dregs are drunk,
And dry the brandy and rum.
Earth has burdens enough to bear,
But what of the spirits out in the air?
No footstep comes to shake the clock,
But wait: you will hear the fall
Of flake upon flake in a crusted block
On gable, window and wall.
As the weight of the lead in the pendulum's knock
Goes forward and then flies back,
The clock saves up
For the drinking cup
The treasure hid in the sack.
It is hard for the dead beneath that lead
To stay in the grave at all;

It is hard for the dead to stay in bed,
And yet it is hard to come.
The frost is bitter, the road is rough.
For certain dead it is easy enough:
It is hardest of all for some.

Pendulum, pendulum, slow, slack,
Nobody dead will ever come back.
All is trickery, all untrue
Of the Mari Lwyd's drunken crew.
What of those white, pretentious claims
Brought by singers with muffled names?
Nothing the dead can tell
After the midnight bell;
Yet if they will, they will.
There are some who will not lie still.
Stilled though the beating of the blood,
There are some who will not lie still.

With a thirst for time when time has fled
The legions of night have left the lead;
The future hangs on a chain.
The dead may know or they may not know
Where they are going or where these go,
But all is tangled in such a knot,
No mortal fingers can know the plot:
To work at the threads were vain.
That bitter thirst should be left behind,
But comfort nowhere can they find,
For the vessels of thirst remain.

Whatever the hour the clock intones,
And it moves from twelve to one,
When you hear the knock of the knuckle-bones
And you feel you ought to run,
You will know by the tread and wicked knock
Of the fingering dead who pick the lock
That the voice you hear was dumb;
And just as you thought it was too late,
Be certain of this, that while you wait
The returning host will come.

FIRST FIGURE
Why argue about what cannot be?
You know they are nothing to you and me.

When the grey mare ploughing the field dropped dead,
Somebody buried her old head,
Then dug it up, four years having gone,
And found a number of hangers-on
To dress the skull in ribbons, and so
Begging from house to house they go.

SECOND FIGURE

They work the jawbones with a string
Using the head to rhyme and sing,
And claiming everywhere for a wager
In a battle of wits it will prove the sager.

THIRD FIGURE

I think I hear them coming now.

FIRST FIGURE

Your hand still follows a ghostly plough.
Today we live and they do not.
We eat our victuals while they rot.
Today decides what we pay tomorrow.
Why keep your mind on yesterday's furrow?

SECOND FIGURE

One life is enough for honest traders;
But all is confused when masqueraders
Come, like foxes on a farm,
Leaving a trail of theft and harm.
To make a skull blaspheme in drink
Is about as low as a man can sink.

FIRST FIGURE

We've had enough, but our strong liquor
Makes no pretence to a holy figure.
We need no blessing of nun or monk
To tell us plainly that we're drunk.
There's no hypocrisy among us,
But they would see haloes in deadly fungus.

THIRD FIGURE

Hark, a dog's barking out in the yard.
The night is black, and the frost is hard.
Whether you like it or not, I know
The snow outside is not just snow.
The scuffle of feet is coming again.
Bend your ear, and you'll hear it plain.

The river of fire, the blackened Styx,
For every second the old clock ticks
Brings them a little nearer the walls
Under and over the snow that falls,
Under the sands in the glass of time
Hands of discord, comfort's bane,
Hands that knock on the frosted pane,
Steps that stop in the crisp white rime,
Pulled like criminals back to the crime.

FIRST FIGURE
Not one drunkard
Shall touch my tankard.

SECOND FIGURE
And I'll not foster
One impostor
With liquor or meat –

THIRD FIGURE
The feet, the feet!

Distant voices are heard:

FIRST VOICE
From Hebron to Harlech

SECOND VOICE
From Dan to Machynlleth

THIRD VOICE
The birds of Rhiannon

FOURTH VOICE
The dead sons of Llywarch

FIFTH VOICE
Hail, and the raven

SIXTH VOICE
Of grief at the windows,

FIRST VOICE
White drops from the cauldron

SECOND VOICE
Brewed by Ceridwen,

THIRD VOICE
Stones that remember

FOURTH VOICE

A tongue to set free,

FIFTH VOICE

Bring Taliesin
The child of the ages.

SIXTH VOICE

Bring Taliesin,
The child of the sea.

FOURTH FIGURE

My God, it is true:
We were quiet, and yet
That insolent crew
Still owed us a debt.
Already against us their faces were set.

Hard as the hail,
Deadly and pale,
Darker than pain,
Freezing the rain,
Hark at the lead on the pendulum's chain!

Footsteps approaching: they halt

FIRST VOICE

Lay down that weight you carry,
Lay the long burden down.
There's many a midnight Mari
From here to Fishguard town.
There's many a vengeance flying
From hell to this door's crack.
No use in your replying,
'Leave us alone, go back!'

SECOND VOICE

Observe this Head. We offer
A scapegoat for your sin.
Her term of penance over,
She bids you take us in.
Her eyes are torches burning;
She wagers wit for stout.
She knows the end of learning:
You cannot keep her out.

FIRST FIGURE

What raving lunatic is come
Of all that star-struck host?
What hundred-year-old brandy
Could entertain that ghost?
Who are you, Doctor of the Law,
And who that mounted Head,
Whose insolence with wagging jaw
Beckons the countless dead?

FIRST VOICE

Draw back, and let the Mari speak:
She bids us jerk the thread.

THIRD VOICE

Two hundred years ago tonight
That girl became my own.
The shots they fired in Dowlais
Have only just come down.
Yours was the house she lived in.
This road was then a track
No use to shield and hide her.
I come to fetch her back.

SECOND FIGURE

How many ghosts? What number
Are massed against our door,
With eyes on rape and plunder
And who knows what things more?
Not till the light of morning
Shall drop or dreg be found.
We'll quench your thirst for learning,
However great the round.

FIRST VOICE

First count the fingers of your hand
Then see them multiplied
By all the yellow grains of sand
That fall beneath the tide.
After so long and strict a fast
We come to claim our right.
Do not pretend your flagons last
Longer than New Year's Night.

FIRST FIGURE

How many are you? Tell me,

For I'll not be denied.
Those ribbons now compel me
To test the wits they hide.
Who are you, Doctor of the Law,
And who are these who bring
The Day of Judgment to a jaw
Worked by a wagging string?

FIRST VOICE

I am but one of many
And Spokesman for the rest,
But you'll not know our number
Till I become your guest.
Another's claim by right of fame
Might make you turn the key,
But I'll not give a man my name
Who shuts the door on me.

SECOND FIGURE

Then who is that beside you?
Grey Mari, who are you?
Why let those villains hide you
And mock the frozen dew?
Had they not done enough of harm
Wherever their feet trod,
That they must hoist you from the farm
Against the will of God?

FIRST FIGURE

And who are you who pluck those reins
And work what's cold and dull,
Bent, where no breath of life remains,
To train a talking skull?
Have you no better trade than this,
To prop a stiffened Head
And set what was against what is,
Painting with life what's dead?

FOURTH VOICE

I am come back and almost in
Whom least you long to see.
My trade is barter, skin for skin.
The fire has set me free.
The leaping shades upon your wall
Sprung from the poker's thrust

Are always at my beck and call.
I barter them for dust.

Yet, till you tip the hogshead up
To slake the thirst it gave,
How can you quench with any cup
The dry mouth of the grave?
Do this, we'll teach you how to eat
The marrow of each day
And taste the substance of its meat
Though all be torn away.

SECOND FIGURE

How plausibly you put the case.
Do you, indeed, declare
That flesh and blood are properties
Less true than bone and air?
The circling moths are lunatic,
And you, as life burns on,
Assault the flame with wings that flick
And into dust are gone.

Whether we suffer or rejoice
Like singing birds in leaves,
You dead despise the living voice
Like bats beneath the eaves.
Your fungus crowning trunk and well
Poisons the very tomb.
Go back, and mix your brew in hell,
But do not taint our room.

SECOND VOICE

Think of the firstborn laid in earth
Under the sprouting year,
The frost set hard against their birth,
Each icicle a spear.
The flush of life is on your skin
Like snow on midnight's black,
But we complete what you begin,
We hold the truth you lack.

FIRST FIGURE

How cunningly you gnaw the cords
To gain forbidden food
And set your teeth against our boards

As though to test the wood.
What though we lack what you possess,
What forfeit lies in that?
Unless disease and plague can bless,
Who bargains with a rat?

THIRD FIGURE

Yet we were warned, a ghost might come
After the midnight chime.
'Be quick and lock', so ticked the clock,
'The shutters in with time!'
If we should stop the pendulum
That first set time to go
And let that wicked spirit come,
What might the room not know?

SECOND VOICE

You hesitate, you hesitate:
I hear a plummet fall.
The shipwrecked embers in the grate
Go down beneath the wall.
The darkness vomits like a whale
His Jonahs, one by one.
If I could reach that cask of ale
I'd drink to every son.

SECOND FIGURE

I've heard it said, the faithful dead
Stay in their graves quite still,
That only traitors leave that bed,
Plotting to thieve and kill.
But you the leprous night has cursed
And hunted from your graves.
Where did you get that head of thirst,
That foaming head of waves?

THIRD VOICE

We seek no harder thing than food,
No softer thing than wine.
The fire that glitters in your blood,
Born of a fast, is mine.
These walls are empty, and you say
The kegs are empty, too.
Is this the end for which men pray?
What eunuch friends are you?

SECOND FIGURE

Be honest, be honest: between us a fool sets a glass.
He calls you the drunken, the lost, the deceived and the dead.
The mare that you carry was good when she went out to grass,
But if her old skull is the totem round which the years pass,
The wits that might save you are sunk in the socketed Head.

FIFTH VOICE

He is mocking our Spirit –

FOURTH VOICE

Mocking his own.

FIFTH VOICE

He laughs at our Mari.

FOURTH VOICE

Soon he shall groan,
All his fine arguments
Withered to bone.

SECOND FIGURE

I challenge your right to come near to our feasting at all.
Snuff out this lamp, and the shadows fade from the wall.
The wax of the candles in darkness inviting a rat
To scrape at the barrels, the brandy, the cheese and the fat,
Has brought you, and all your temptation is centred in that.

FIFTH VOICE

I that am bone,
Let me remember
Centuries gone
This December,
A circle smaller
Lit by flame,
Known to the caller
Each by name;
Climbing the turret
In deathlike weather,
I, a spirit,
Hold them together,
Embers falling
As now they fall,
All I remember,
All, all.

VOICES

All we remember,
All, all.

SIXTH VOICE

Harlech was ours,
The sea at dawn,
Stone walls, towers,
Barrels of wine,
Cellars, boards
Trundling it home.
Come, come and feed us,
In pity, come.

Narrow the bridge,
Naked the hill.
After the siege
All lay still.
Out they drove us
Seeking a home.
Come, come and feed us,
In pity, come.

Crazy for sleep
In body and head,
Aching deep
And without a bed,
Driven we were
Like blinding foam:
Come, come and feed us,
In pity, come.

SECOND FIGURE

If you are truly down on your luck
And came here before when midnight struck
Pummelled the door, then went again,
Tell what your Mari is. Explain
Why the confusion of this hour
Makes the historical put on power.
I would have had you sleep as sound
As the dead knight lying above his hound.
Why this wicked will to cross
The quilt of snow that covers the fosse?
Why the Mari, why the Mare?
What can you hope to gain but air?

FOURTH VOICE

Our Mari is come from the hood of the wave
To demand of you comfort and light.
If once we could lose the remorse of the grave,
To think of the bed and comfort it gave
We would take our revenge in a night.

A shadow, a shadow the pendulum flings
As the clock gathers strength for the chime.
Our Mari is timeless, to nothing she clings,
And your wit cannot counter the curses she flings
As they come at you, one at a time.

We are outside the shadow, its strength we can mock
When the night of companionship ends.
We can tighten her rein like the chain of the clock
And her wit will come down like a knife on the block
Dividing the traitors and friends.

THIRD VOICE

The beat that you dread which the pendulum gave
Is the beat of your heart in its side.
A wise man respects the demands of the grave,
But if you deny us the crumb that we crave
Your greed will be doubly denied.

SECOND FIGURE

You mock-holy shape,
Who helped you escape
Jail or the gallows, for thieving and rape?

You hater of order,
Go back to your border.
Every inch that you gain is an inch towards murder.

THIRD VOICE

But if we leave without a drop
Nothing we'll make or mar.
It was your window lighted up
That led us like a star.
Dead, we remembered in the grave
The mite we had not given;
That pitched us forward like a wave
To give, and be forgiven.

THIRD FIGURE

Vileness, be gone: grimace at our window no longer
And do not disguise with a halo your hate and your hunger.
Death is your horse, your leprous light is the foam's,
Your breath a poison infecting innocent homes.
Learn from the saints and martyrs to leave us in peace.
The good acquiesce when a candle compels them to cease.
Your spur of unrest is the hater of firelight and love;
The gloom you bring is the gloom of the criminal's glove.
Though you covet the food and drink we store in our room,
The peace of our cellar is one thing, the peace of the tomb
Another: the two are distinct, for gladness of heart
Depends for its life on the pleasures where death has no part.
But you who are out of our life and the swing of the slow
Pendulum, have you not learnt from the lightning to go
Where verses are honoured? There's none here to pull at your bridle.
To stay under Philistines' windows is foolish and idle.

SECOND VOICE

Say we are drunkards if you will
But give our Mare respect.
There's none beneath this window-sill
To match her intellect.
Know, if you drive our Head away
And mock the life of verse,
The curse that on your threshold lay
Will breed a darker curse.

Her verse is summoned by the chill
Where all your gains are lost,
This frost is not forever still;
It's but one winter's frost.
Your barrels are all locked and safe,
Your larder stocked with cheese.
The famished Mari from the grave
Shall never taste of these.

FIRST FIGURE

So thick a Head would not go through
Unless we opened wide,
And how could such a Head speak true
When all her bearers lied?
You pitch your poet's game so high
That Snowdon seems a speck,

And yet, to drain one barrel dry,
You'll risk your Head, and neck.

FIRST VOICE

Are we such monsters that you guard
Your firkins with such care?
Would we were fire-lit, drinking hard,
And you, fine bones in air;
And yet, although you spurn us now,
One night it shall be so,
And you beneath the starry Plough
Sharing the cakes of snow.

You then shall hear a miser's chime
Ring in a time of dearth,
A clapper dealing death to time
That brings your wits to birth.
Into the dark at which you stared
You shall yourselves be thrown:
The dead can keep the cup they shared,
They cannot keep their own.

SECOND VOICE

But how prevent that evil night
And how blot out that sin?
Muster the flagons, bring a light,
Unbolt, and let us in!
Our ribboned Doctor here, she knows
What evil comes of fear.
A moment's guilt, and endless goes
Your penance, hard and drear.

THIRD VOICE

She has been with the drowned in the sea, with the dead in repose
She galloped where all was forgotten, and halted where goes
The stream with the ferry that hurries beneath the blind snows.
How can you, unless you admit us, be taught what she knows?
Draw back now, in fear of the fire, for the crossing of Styx
Will find you in need of her caul and her nosebag of tricks.

THIRD FIGURE

The dead and the living are too much together.
There's a blight on all spirits that walk in this weather.
Give me one or the other, a goblet that clinks,
But a curse on all spirits that mix up the drinks.

I was born in the Rhondda, and even from birth
That smell of the charnel-house tainted the earth;
And gay though the girls were we walked with as boys
An odour of death always hindered our joys.

The running, I reckon, is not worth the race,
Unless we can challenge the shade to its face.
The nightmare you carry I know to the bone,
But how can her sorrow be strong as my own?

FOURTH VOICE

If but a hand would stop the clock,
Then soon you'd hear the beat
None with an honest mind can mock:
It comes from pilgrim feet.
A wall of crystal round you thrown
Shall hide the mountain pass.
The feet you hear shall be your own
Upon that sheet of glass.

SECOND FIGURE

If you deserved our charity
We should not hold it back;
But through the window who can see
Until the room is black?
Snuff out the light and stop the clock.
Now all is black, you dare not mock.
The devil howls to have his due
And the old nag her trough.
The fires you left are calling you;
Now look for them. Be off!

FIRST VOICE

Hold back, hold back the tether.
She strains to leap inside.
Her night would bring together
Whom daylight hours divide.
But we who know their going,
Midnight is at our back.
She hides from you our knowing:
We know the thing you lack.
Your windows all are fastened
And bolted hard your door.
By thirst our tongues are chastened
And the long fast we bore.

You dread the thing we carry,
The wit to light your rooms, –

THIRD FIGURE
Take back, take back your Mari.
How could the quick love tombs?

SECOND VOICE
Dear darkness, are these human
Who keep us still at bay,
While we as man or woman
Would give so much away?
Run round the house and enter
By any lucky breach.
Let time run down, their centre,
Then claim the heart in each.

FIRST VOICE
Stay by the door. No other
Shall be our right of way.
Why should confusion smother
The words our Head would say?
Surely our claim is better
Than felons' to their wealth.
No strict and honest debtor
Should force a pane by stealth.

THIRD FIGURE
On with the light!

FOURTH FIGURE
It will not go on.

FIFTH FIGURE
In with the key!

FOURTH FIGURE
The key has gone.

FIFTH FIGURE
While he was talking we were distracted.

FOURTH FIGURE
One with a skeleton key has acted.

FIRST FIGURE
Castles of sand
How can they stand?

SECOND FIGURE
As the door creaks
What horror speaks?

THIRD FIGURE
As the wood splinters
What guest enters?

FOURTH FIGURE
They who astound us
Are all round us.

FIFTH FIGURE
The skull's a candle.
Hark at the handle!

FIRST FIGURE
Look at the shadow
Where it climbs,
Queen of wit
And mother of rhymes,

SECOND FIGURE
Upward thrown
By the candle's cone:

THIRD FIGURE
Like a wave stealing
From floor to ceiling,

FOURTH FIGURE
In origin small,
Huge on the wall,

FIFTH FIGURE
Possessing the room,
Black as the tomb.

NARRATOR
The outer dark, the outer dark
Has let the deluge in.
The snowflake hisses on the spark
Of them who crouch within.
The light is gone that kept the door
Between the quick and dead
And shining there above the floor
I see the Mari's head.

FIRST VOICE

Truth is the great unmasker.
For us you waited long.
Now show us something better
Than argument or song.
A hogshead will give pleasure
And two may satisfy.
None estimates your treasure
Like us whose throats are dry.

Then offer her, the lightning's ghost,
The best of all your fare.
She has an eye for a good host
And hates the mean who spare.
First bring your noblest gift, and then
Multiply that by nine.
The sea would not exhaust my men
Though all its waves were wine.

FIRST FIGURE

For vacant pounders of the sand
How could a cask have worth?
A holy saint makes no demands,
A drunkard asks the Earth.
Or how can victuals match your taste?
What vessel but a sieve
Can break so terrible a fast
And teach a ghost to live?

FIRST VOICE

She stares at you, and lets her stare
Transfix your flesh and blood.
There's nothing spoken to the Mare
She has not understood.
Your cellar goads affection on,
So fetch us more and more,
And she'll protect you when you're gone;
But never bolt your door.

SECOND VOICE

Bring mugs of ale to toast the dead;
Bring bread, and cut the cheese.
Too long I waited in my bed
For nourishment like these.

FIRST VOICE

And did you not lie buried
Where faithless ones were ferried?

SECOND VOICE

The Mari's head, the Mari's head
Is nodding, and agrees.

SECOND FIGURE

Though I should live a hundred years
I'll not believe my eyes
That these are spirits a man fears,
Not drunkards in disguise.
But tell us first who picked the lock:
We may absolve the crime.
Of all the jackdaws in your flock
How many have done time?

SECOND VOICE

Still do you think of justices,
A Judge with book and seal?
It's no good now invoking
That old Court of Appeal.
The miser's mildew and the spot
Corrupt the very leaf.
To steal dishonesty from thought
Is honour to the thief.

THIRD VOICE

But where is she who knew this house
And left it in the fall?
I call upon the Mari,
And on her friends I call:
Bring darkness down upon these heads
That robbed me of my right.
When is the night of marriage-beds
If this is not that night?

You waited here, and all went well
Until the midnight chime.
Your bolt and firelight could repel
And keep us out of time.
But love and hatred would not mix
After the chime had struck.
For souls that cross the blackened Styx
There's no such thing as luck.

You live as long as fate permits,
But always live in fear.
You dread the force of keener wits
That come to beg your beer.
But you defile ancestral things,
Leaving no lovely trace.
Now bless the Mari's head that brings
Reprisal to this place.

FIRST FIGURE

Never was a ghost so evil
As those blaspheming jaws.
I hate your bony Devil
And hate her with good cause.
But though like robbers you are come
Using the mask of night,
There's not a flagon in this home
You'll take without a fight.

Bring all your ravening, wolflike host
And flay us if you can.
Your Skull has yet to prove a ghost
Can match a living man.
Though you have learnt from blind despair
A secret no man knows
Which gives your tongue that haughty air,
It cannot speak like blows.

FIRST VOICE

We come to make that sacred
Your presence would profane.
Now you yourselves shall be as moths
Against the window-pane,
And drift away like flakes of snow
That wander, seeking rest.
The anguish of the dead you'll know
Whom none will take for guest.

SECOND VOICE

Listen. The ashes fall.
Ill-use us if you dare.
You strike, but strike a wall
Of insubstantial air.
To try your souls we came,
The balance being in doubt.

Now you shall do the same,
In banishment cast out.

FIRST VOICE

You cannot live the middle
Between divine extremes.
The Mari sets the riddle
Of which the body dreams.
But now like snowflakes you are sent
To beat on windows thin.
You are yourselves the argument
Of us who drink within.

SECOND FIGURE

You'd have us now change places
To expiate your crime,
And use a skull's grimaces
To mock the midnight chime?

SECOND VOICE

The firelight of your living
Has fallen through the grate.
There can be no forgiving
For them who give too late.

FIRST FIGURE

I'll never want your pardon –

FIRST VOICE

Therefore a wall of snow
Shall hide this house and garden
As out of life you go.
Your bones must now return here
Because your flesh and blood
Denied the right we earn here
To courtesy and food.

SECOND FIGURE

'Lay down that weight you carry':
I recollect those words,
But then we crouched and listened
Who now are wild as birds.
We've nothing but the Mari's head
In all the empty night,
No fire, no clock, no house, no bed,
Only a distant light.

FIRST FIGURE

Hell burn that whited window!
A curse upon those eaves!
The fire we loved, the hours we lived
Are snatched away by thieves.
What is there left in all this frost
To guide us to mankind?
The Buried Skull must lead us
Because her eyes are blind.

THIRD FIGURE

A hush has fallen through the night.
We cannot hear the clock.
We are ourselves the shafts of white
Those men of firelight mock.
And we must drift like flakes of snow
That know not where to rest,
So soft upon the night they go
Whom none will take for guest.

FIRST FIGURE

The death's-head moth, the beating moth,
The lighted window-pane,
The little flame how sacred,
The shadows how profane!
But help me now to carry
The bony Skull inside:
Who bears the midnight Mari
Has Poverty for Bride.

The Breaking of the Wave 1979

Affirmation

Out, sceptic, betrayed by your own style:
No faith and loose measures go hand in hand.
Call grandeur untrue, but truth is grand,
And truth no man can alter, no, nor defile.
Sprung from infinite sorrow breaks the smile
Of grace, altering the path ambition planned,
Whose joy, given, must unforgettably stand,
Relaxed order, charm, for none to revile.

Learn then of love, shine from the truth men shun.
Build, soul, your city, honour the state
Innocence gave to wisdom, there made one.
Joy singing governs all we create
As weir waters, feeling the Earth rotate,
Amass, falling, a music always begun.

Tempters

Tempters longer than my arm,
Voices in the flood,
Try to entice, to charm
With time's recurring shadow
My pulse, whose beats repel
The chain and flight of fame,
The figured oracle,
The bird-winged pendulum.

How like a plummet is
This ancient, long-willed
Groper of the seas.
I am no more than a child
Of the dead, whom time
Forgets, adorning the winds
With turncoats flying upon the chime
Of counties and kinds.

Soft, with a leaden knock,
Appear those treacheries
Tricked out by the clock,
Prompted by those degrees,

By every story gone,
To make the mind conform
To the known carrion
They take by storm.

Months, hireling seasons come
Dissembling their voices,
Frail Spring, blind Winter numb.
Confronted with time's choices,
I, who am their marked man,
Sink the pulse they mock
Deeper and darker than
The figures of the clock.

I have a bond with dust
To resist their summons,
A thread of music to trust
In the sea of omens,
Here to enact for all
Blood, and for no time,
What is not theatrical,
What outlives mime.

O plummet intent
To repel that sea,
To outlast by a moment
The figured treachery,
O sound, light's burials
Touch, in the blacked-out room,
When I have waited for time's falls,
Let nothing come.

Let the years retreating
Know themselves powerless
Hearing the beating
Heart beneath Earth's dress,
And let time's paragon
Fear love, that is
More terrible than the moon
To the pulled seas.

Let nothing be planned
Further than a stone.
Giant age of the sand,
Cromlech and throne,

Must certainly redound
To the pulse-beat at last
From which all signs rebound,
One fathom cast.

Corrupt Birth

Sighs have engendered sighs.
The bones take shape.
Faint grows the hammer of the striking man
Swung to corruption, and the sun's escape.

That sound on silence dies.
Light is let loose.
The dark wave mounts as when the world began,
Mounts to possess the bride, and find a sluice.

That tide disturbs the grains.
The blinded kiss
Builds in revolt a ponderous image formed
From wet bonds and the lover's avarice.

Force of rebellious reins
Pulls nape and neck
Stiff as a mast, by naked sirens stormed,
Straight, where dark currents plot the leaning wreck.

Rope-wrung, the fingers feel.
The unshed tears
Are salt in air; a storm above the mast
Of unrepentant grief the dumb loin bears.

Then sinks the sliding keel
Through bone-ribbed sides.
The quickened hope alters, that once was fast,
And pulls heaven down, plunging to tread old tides.

I Have No Name

I have no name. Where strange lips meet
And strenuous reins are locked, I climb

Beyond the extremes of natural heat,
To the dumb pivot of known time.

They climbed this burning height through snow;
Now they are still as mountain stones.
This is a land they do not know,
Their river and their tower of bones.

Heaven itself changes. Fire must fall.
So these two spirits dive to find
First print of loveliness, they stall
Like birds, against the unknown wind;

Then fly to locked, green branches, sprung
In the first field from which they came,
Rooted in round limbs of the young
Sun-dazzled tree which has no name.

Next, in the firm bark bound, the shell
Windy and brittle, fingers find
Sweet daylight in the seed of hell,
In the shut branch the pattern shrined.

Still the light changes, and these know,
Where delight deepens, sweet distress;
That dayspring which their love made grow
Now makes a million days grow less.

I see in mist their mountain graves
Over whose dark the starlight swarms.
Still, under wind, a mute voice raves:
'Heaven is not wider than these arms.'

The Field

There is a goldcup-field upon the hill;
—Say nothing, nothing—
Dance, early wind, across those dazzling cups,
Across the frail gold cups to that round hill
That stares astounded by the dumb June day
Wide-eyed yet sleeping, stupefied by light,
Where all the may has opened in a night.

Unbroken lies the dew. A rabbit-hole
Or emerald darkness of the burrowing mole,

So velvet and so thieflike, deepening now
Under the sleeping, starless, upturned plough,
Mock the blunt shares, of motive dispossessed,
A wheel whose fingers under earth have rest.

Then, if we touch the fronds, if we peer close,
—O faint the breathing—
How grips earth's green arm the dilated sense
With patterns intricate where ants run out;
How scented springs the breast on which we lean.
If we look up from that green arm that clings,
The light will meet us, black as a rook's wings.

Light has so touched us that our lips are sealed;
Then rustling sound the steps on Enna's field
Of that white girl, by Pluto's hand delayed,
Caught in a shaft of noon that flings no shade,
Plunged from that mother calling her sad name
While her he crowns with subterranean flame.

Over their bridal sleep the grass uncurls.
The goldcup wreathing
Its candelabra can make bright our hands
With its bent lamp. Black light assails our eyelids.
The jealous sun would buy us with black pearls.
Black now is radiant, and the glowworm's belly
Draws the heavens down to dreaming Botticelli.

Press down your eyes. Blind gold the petals break.
Pure darkness, green-shot, glorious as a drake
Caught in the blaze of love's abounding stream,
Purging of every stain the fixed eye-beam,
Reveals those two banks love's own light makes fairer,
Dipinte di mirabil primavera.

A Point of Light

Certain motion in the sun
Rainbows from a navel spun
Light and frail as thistledown
Draw my life as I lie down.
Patterns of leaf, sky and ground
Like a plate are spun around

Round this centre where I lie:
Sleep is like a butterfly.
Wide the settled wings are spread,
Great shut glittering eyes have read
All the scheming of the clouds.
The tired pillow's fold enshrouds
What tormented planets taught.
Monstrous sums are set at nought,
Shattered darkness will run out
Into every crack of thought.
At last, where steep-urned water runs,
Light is balanced in two stones.
Earth is hand-held where I lie,
The slowing foot begins to fly;
Uncertain motion which begins
Far behind the moving suns
Snaps the encircling, measured thread
Joining life to lives long dead.
A point of light has scattered there
All the stars that wheel in air
Or in those thinner elements
Oracular, stony sleep invents;
How reconcile that swiftness to
This breath, the fingers breaking through
The spinning and the slowing plate
The distance that was dancing late
Blurred to sleep, where that sly track
Summons cold creation back.
The comet guides the tortoise-shell,
Lightning strikes the moving snail,
How shape that music for the Earth,
While the thrushes sing my birth?

The Second Fire

A second fire in ashes glows,
That phoenix of my theme.
Reality must fly from those
Who lack the power to dream;
Its carapace forgotten,
The mayfly leaves the stream.

The second creature cannot raise
The weight it leaves behind,
The burden of laborious days,
The groping of the mind.
It neither knows its essence
Nor how it was designed.

Where solitude compels a crowd
The crowd brings loneliness.
When all is won to make it proud
The heart is comfortless;
True joy knows only of the place
Which love has come to bless.

Man's spirit sighs for vision
That once in Eden sighed.
It thirsts for definition
And will not be denied.
What is it kindles him to life?
The rib from his own side.

The Path of Light

Light comes from stillness, and the leaves are made
Where a beam kills time's origin and scheme,
Leaving pure terror, till they wind and gleam,
Twice-born, of marvel, sleeping in light's shade.
Then to the fair, bright, gentle, savage head
Delight coils upward, bursting from the stem.
Men see not this, for light is blinding them,
Which flies, outrunning time, yet has not fled.

Whether leaves move in wind or, windless, stay,
Light's ancient path revives them. Let the flight
Of birds make one leaf fall, the others play.
That leaf which flourished and was graced with light
Changes no atom, and through senseless night
Moves, in its burial, on the selfsame way.

The Dove

Look in these eyes, my first and only love.
Substance is cloyed. Men have great themes in mind,
Dig for lost treasure, measure, gauge the wind;
Even now some men are loosening ships to move
Out to strange harbours. None your youth should bind.
Or think: birds quit those branches linked above,
Fly in the Fall to a new land, new kind:
Look in these eyes, my first and only love.

Infinite particles wise men will find,
And scribes will prophesy what histories prove,
Argue, distil, look forward or behind,
Chase thoughts, wide nature, not this lonely dove
That broods above one stream, one head declined:
Look in these eyes, my first and only love.

The Silence of Love

Love, that in silence writes upon these eyes
The script of that sweet music her eyes bear,
Whose light was born not, changes not, nor dies,
But makes the living dumb, the dead aware,
Pronouncing great philosophers unwise,
Her truth being breathed upon the impassioned air
So secretly that thought, remembering, cries:
'Tell me, my God: was she not always there?'
Love, that in silence writes, makes youth and age
Divide her light, light that is swift and slow,
The living light, and light from the dead page
That sees her newly, and says long ago:
'In her all myths have found their period,
Being herself the handiwork of God.'

May You Love Leaves

May you love leaves, complete yet unfulfilled,
Dancing in the light, in the shade where light is stilled.
May the wild woodpecker, knocking on the hollow

Treetrunk remind you, and the voice of the late swallow
That distance is mortal. May you then run complete
Into that circle created by your feet
And may you be astounded, when the rest are gone,
By the chill water splashing on the stone.
Wait, then, for patience is the friend of love,
Wait, on the last breath, last echo where you move,
Then it shall come, the miracle you sought,
Not in the leaves, nor in your own thought,
Joy will surround you, which you thought had fled,
In safety, in silence, in the steps of the dead.

For a First Birthday

Lay, gentle Christ, Your hands upon this child,
And let her stature, this first year fulfilled,
Spring from the font made pure by darkest tears,
Since the deep love the woman bears
Quickens her life already, gives her grace
As if all light were born again
And the first love the Virgin bore to men
Entered her eyes and streamed forth from her face.

I cannot doubt that infants are with God.
The wonder of their inarticulate word
Is naked greenness while the old trees' leaves
Rustling with Winter sweep the graves.
In them the distant territory of song
Is growing fibre; yet I pray
That though her words are washed with light, words may
Protect her constantly and make her strong.

How can I teach her, before time surprise
Defenceless youth and truth antagonize,
That simplest art is like a running stream?
Clouded indeed are eyes that dream
Our souls have not been purchased by His love.
Their speculation is all vain
Who think to live life once, but not again;
Eternal life is promised by the dove.

To-morrow, then, may nothing be disturbed
Of that first piety. Great impulse curbed

Excels in glory strong desire released.
Her Saviour in the East
Rises eternally and will not set,
So may she shine from this first day
By this true cup and in the fountain play
With whose fair testament our lips are wet.

Child of the Fountain

Child of the fountain falling late
From spent October through the gust
And frosty spears of Herod's hate,
Protected by the turtle's wing,
Balanced on the plume of Spring
And longed for by these lips of dust:
All that's lost is gathered up,
Caught by a fine, a slender chain
In a stone cup, a ringing cup,
To prove that all things known are vain
Save that strength which You ordain
From a child's mouth, a suckling's mouth;
Isaiah cursed his country's drouth
And Jeremiah cursed the state
Withered by polluting wars.
O, how sweet upon our lips
Fall these drops, in time's eclipse,
Child of the fountain falling late
And image of the moving stars.

I Do Not Ask a Gentle Way

I do not ask a gentle way.
Let the road be hard.
Drag or muster all you may
To hinder or retard.
Making opposition strong,
Fit me for the task of song.

No milder teacher than the worst
The athletic body knows.

However hated, harassed, cursed,
Its balance is repose.
Wrinkled though the outer skin,
A perfect body lies within.

Since the letters first were cut
Moss and grass have grown,
Yet what tenderness is shut
Under every stone.
I proclaim in all I sing
Tenderness the hardest thing.

Why, Then, Complain

Why, then, complain of evil days
If days you knew before were good?
That is a shallow kind of praise
Which cannot thrive on bitter food.

I know too great a recompense
For any tempest to destroy.
When joy has lost its last defence,
Then is the time to learn of joy.

Let discord beat about my ears,
I know too well what time may bring,
Nor can it touch the truest tears,
Such is the secret of their spring.

That I May Love You Right

That I may love you right, teach me the pains of winter,
Drive against all my bonds, after the cold tribunal
Judging my many wrongs, freeze me with perfect manners,
Number my exile.

Then, as the night runs on, I shall correct my compass,
See the processions pass, make of a stone my pillow,
Hearing ungrateful words beat in my head like hailstones,
Warring companions.

Take to the unshared bed wisdom, for separation
Opens as many doors as there are lives about us;
Yet of all these one stays; after the snow this violet
Breaks more divinely.

Villanelle

Time will come round again,
Our lightest joys be just,
If constancy remain.

Though we encounter pain
And winter's ice and frost,
Time will come round again.

The bow that breaks through rain
Will never quite be lost
If constancy remain.

Light has so spun the skein
Of ecstasy and dust,
Time will come round again.

Why should my heart complain
Of distance or distrust
If constancy remain?

Love's voice will not refrain
But tells me, as it must:
Time will come round again
If constancy remain.

Separations

Who knows how near they are
Who are lost today to human fellowship,
How near to their known star,
Being of that dust created?
In ancient time when dust was consecrated
There always was a voyage and a ship.
Dumb lyre and burial jar,
Wine, scroll and music kept the dead elated.

Why are we struck when rings
Or images are lifted from the ground?
Their contemplation brings
Light to extinguished eyes.
To stillness made with hands, stillness replies.
Lifted stone-still, the identity comes round
Of time's lost bird, whose wings
Close on each contour as the relics rise.

My words are forced from me
By separations and by souls unborn.
Who knows how distantly
These present words are sent
That one may place this antique ornament
Close to the heart, where gold is sometimes worn,
And hear how timelessly
Hearts beat, being nourished by what is not spent?

To these that now are near
I say that wit transfigures all that is,
Making it doubly dear.
The true thing that we say
Shall remain true when time is far away.
The present voice, enriched by absences,
Can check in full career
The flight of ages, and make moments pray.

Were it established ever
That two could walk, as here they did, attuned
To that harmonious river
Long after death, and speak
In the known tongue, and feel that force unique
Linking their lives in union, though impugned
By doubt, nothing could sever
The inviolate bond whose pattern here I seek.

The Muse of Homer

There burned Achilles' anger unsubdued,
Fanned by the battle where Patroclus died.
Axe and spear flashed, where darkness sought to hide
The ships of Agamemnon and their feud.

Four walls of blindness and of solitude
Fashioned that room, where every door I tried
Opened on treasure when I pushed it wide,
The brightening spoil a demigod pursued.
But most upon one vase I fixed my eyes.
This, the most ancient witness on that board,
Seemed poised to speak, yet looked where language dies.
I said: 'This cannot capture, nor record
Our life, nor share our suffering.' Scarce the word
Had left my lips, it was paid back with sighs.

Though to Please Man

Though to please man I might
Affect a scornful air
Setting against the night
Strong emblems of despair,
I am too much in debt
To that strong love which cried:
Lay your life down, and set
No store by scorn or pride.
For what were all men's praise
Or worldly recompense
If in the coming days
A dropped voice, more intense
Than any other, said:
I too had solitude
And felt, being clothed and fed,
Nothing but gratitude?
How can I fail to see
That living fountain spill
In equal harmony
Over Assissi's hill
And here, wherever feet
Walk with considerate pace,
No intellect complete
Lacking the hand of grace?

The Choice

'Kneel, and I'll cut your life-thread with my shears.
No great philosopher shall wake so wise.
Vision will issue from those jails of eyes
And the stars' music fall about your ears.
Then you shall hear that song no mortal hears,
No, not the mightiest man, until he dies;
Not even the martyr, who saw Paradise,
Could wrest that music from the moving spheres.'

But the sick answers: 'Cut, or do not cut.
Not for your spacious heaven would I succumb.
Deaf to that music, blind to light, and dumb,
Life in me suffers, quickens in my gut.
Because my fingers choose the book you shut,
Then, when you summon me, I shall not come.'

Prometheus

How could Prometheus, chained, and from the first
Bound to the sufferer, aiding man with art,
Loosening his children, learn a change of heart
Where, in the Tyrant's eye, he stands accursed?
By little footsteps, so mankind was nursed
To live the eternal in a narrow part
Of time, and rubbing sticks together, start
The fire he stole, who gluts an eagle's thirst.

Who sees him sees his valour and must mourn.
Yet, if he take his confidence for pride,
He cannot know true gold when it is tried,
Nor read that compass holding time in scorn
Which makes all terrors, if a god decide,
To die upon the instant they are born.

Samson

Old years must mourn him; yet the moment saves him.
Cords will not bind him. See him, darkly yearning,

Draw the long light when evening takes the water,
Lion from Gaza.

Swerves round the sealed eyes deep and deeper azure,
Veers, grows vivid in the flash of sunlight.
Rise there the quired scents, softly there the rosebush
Teems with fresh blossom.

Sheathed in the slow stem lies the lily's dagger,
Pale by the tree's root hangs the limpid primrose.
Earth in the quick Spring listening for the footfall
Throbs, and is silent.

Grave years, architects, lead him to his long grave
Haunted with echoes, chain him to the temple.
Dark in the pillars groans the bitter shadow:
'Time has assailed me'.

See him the conquered, breath still is near him,
Shorn of his greatness, praying in the pure light.
'Strength for this moment!' Samson pulls the columns.
Sky is renewed there.

The Death Mask

I stop because a footfall with no sound
Passes. The laurel is too young as yet
To feed with berries him it has not crowned;
Nor would he now regret
More tender fingers: praise is not enough,
And though the Sibyl in her rock repeat:
'No, none shall draw his likeness, even in rough',
The death-mask does not cheat.

The Last Poems of Yeats

These verses written so near his death
Show the man stopped in his path.

Look, the slow words beat back dawn.
O the clamour of that swan!

Love and hatred pull light down.
Loyalty to a fallen town

Picks at last particular friends,
Naming a man at light's last ends.

Child and fossil, youth and age,
A white girl springing from a sage,

Wisdom hidden in a tome
Then the divine light born of foam

Show, where astonished servants kneel,
Grief has kissed a dancer's heel.

Under those last words cut in lime
Drums the pulse: 'I carry time.'

And where the water runs four ways
Staying he flies, and flying stays.

What great arguments have gone
To cut that simple burial-stone.

Out of the peopled sky he dives
And moves inside the ploughman's knives,

Pitched, as he says, by the diggers' grind,
Back into the human mind.

Who shall unravel his winding-sheet?
A peasant woman with bare feet.

From the quenched candle cries aloud
The stifled breath no hand could shroud;

And none shall see the forms run back
To birth's bare Winter, rough and black.

A young man challenges an old.
A fierce man praises a moon that's cold.

An old man and a young man fight
And each puts out the other's light.

Then that iron, bitter tongue
Praises the fury of the young.

This last verse written so near his death
Holds my eye, and breath on breath

Even as I read those letters there
Two white swans are meeting in air;

Two white swans are beating their wings.
Terrified, lost in light, he sings.

One Theme

Why should you wander in the clouds
If art has but one theme?
Did not those transfigured shrouds
Shake you from your dream?

What lightning crowned the Sibyl's head
Till blindness made her fair?
What spirit came to Job in bed
And crossed the upright hair?

Fine is the needle. Trace below
The thread where you began.
One who was wronged should make you know
You cannot outrun man.

The Cave

I seek a cave where fall the unending weirs
Through distances no mortal understands,
Holding that vision the mind's eye demands
To match the immediate miracle to seers
Who guard, like shells, that music in their ears
Of ancient oars and waves that beat the sands,
Yet reveal nothing in the grasp of hands
Until that secret echo disappears.
What exiles found it first, whose lips of stone
Recall lost music, though the limbs are still?
I heard my footsteps hollow on the hill
Beneath whose crooked path their ghosts had gone
Who in the blood of sunlight made me start,
And here console them for their lack of heart.

The Breaking of the Wave

The seawave breaks, breaks, and remakes the year.
See how the sea casts out the shapes it bore,
Each tide forgetting what was here before,
Seeking oblivion's pure and perfect sphere.
That ringing music lingers in the ear,
Falling through shells and sleeping in their core,
Music of waves that beat the level shore
Where footprints come, then pause, then disappear.

Yet by a pledge stronger than waves' wide span
Night can reclaim what nature overthrew.
The exalted vision Donne or Dante drew
Is lightning guarded in the mind of man.
Let the sea take what smouldering spoil it can,
Still to that fire the suffering heart is true.

Index of First Lines

The Still Garden p. 428

Taliesin & the Stones of Vision p. 224